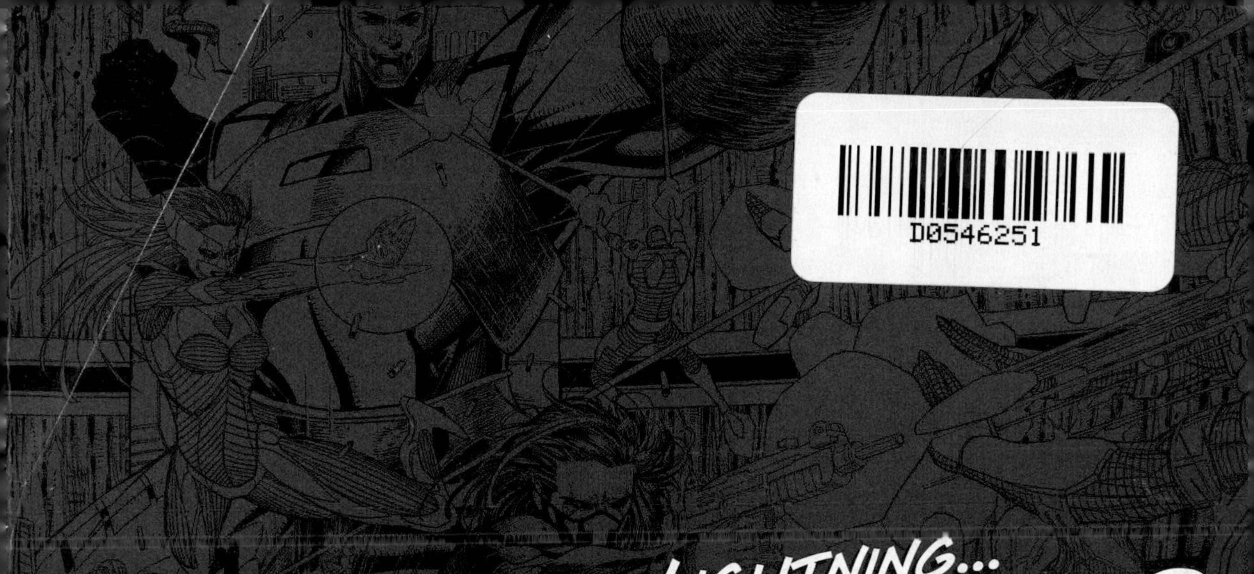

JUSTICE, LIKE LIGHTNING...

THUNDERBOLTS

THERE IS NO HIGH ROAD

JIM ZUB
WRITER

JON MALIN (#1-5) & **SEAN IZAAKSE** (#6)
ARTISTS

MATT YACKEY
COLOR ARTIST

VC's JOE SABINO
LETTERER

JON MALIN & **MATT YACKEY**
COVER ARTISTS

TOM BREVOORT & **ALANNA SMITH**
EDITORS

COLLECTION EDITOR: **MARK D. BEAZLEY**
ASSOCIATE MANAGING EDITOR: **KATERI WOODY**
ASSOCIATE EDITOR: **SARAH BRUNSTAD**
SENIOR EDITOR, SPECIAL PROJECTS: **JENNIFER GRÜNWALD**

VP PRODUCTION & SPECIAL PROJECTS: **JEFF YOUNGQUIST**
SVP PRINT, SALES & MARKETING: **DAVID GABRIEL**
BOOK DESIGNER: **ADAM DEL RE** WITH **CARLOS LAO**

EDITOR IN CHIEF: **AXEL ALONSO**
CHIEF CREATIVE OFFICER: **JOE QUESADA**
PUBLISHER: **DAN BUCKLEY**
EXECUTIVE PRODUCER: **ALAN FINE**

THUNDERBOLTS VOL. 1: THERE IS NO HIGH ROAD. Contains material originally published in magazine form as THUNDERBOLTS #1-6. First printing 2016. ISBN# 978-0-7851-9668-6. Published by MARVEL WORLDWIDE, INC., a subsidiary of MARVEL ENTERTAINMENT, LLC. OFFICE OF PUBLICATION: 135 West 50th Street, New York, NY 10020. **Printed in the U.S.A.** ALAN FINE, President, Marvel Entertainment; DAN BUCKLEY, President, TV, Publishing & Brand Management; JOE QUESADA, Chief Creative Officer; TOM BREVOORT, SVP of Publishing; DAVID BOGART, SVP of Business Affairs & Operations, Publishing & Partnership; C.B. CEBULSKI, VP of Brand Management & Development, Asia; DAVID GABRIEL, SVP of Sales & Marketing, Publishing; JEFF YOUNGQUIST, VP of Production & Special Projects; DAN CARR, Executive Director of Publishing Technology; ALEX MORALES, Director of Publishing Operations; SUSAN CRESPI, Production Manager; STAN LEE, Chairman Emeritus. For information regarding advertising in Marvel Comics or on Marvel.com, please contact Vit DeBellis, Integrated Sales Manager, at vdebellis@marvel.com. For Marvel subscription inquiries, please call 888-511-5480. **Manufactured between 11/4/2016 and 12/12/2016 by QUAD/GRAPHICS WASECA, WASECA, MN, USA.**

10 9 8 7 6 5 4 3 2 1

BUCKY BARNES WAS CAPTAIN AMERICA'S SIDEKICK IN WORLD WAR II...UNTIL HE GOT BLOWN UP, CAPTURED BY THE SOVIETS AND TURNED INTO THE DEADLY WINTER SOLDIER. NOW HE HAS NICK FURY'S OLD JOB AS THE MAN ON THE WALL, PROTECTING EARTH FROM UNSEEN THREATS.

THE **THUNDERBOLTS** WERE BAD GUYS PRETENDING TO BE GOOD GUYS...UNTIL SOME OF THEM REALIZED THAT BEING GOOD GUYS WAS ACTUALLY KIND OF NICE. BUT THEIR CHECKERED PASTS LANDED THEM IN PLEASANT HILL, S.H.I.E.L.D.'S SUPER-PRISON RUN BY A SENTIENT COSMIC CUBE.

BUCKY BROKE THEM OUT, AND NOW HE FIGURES THEY OWE HIM...

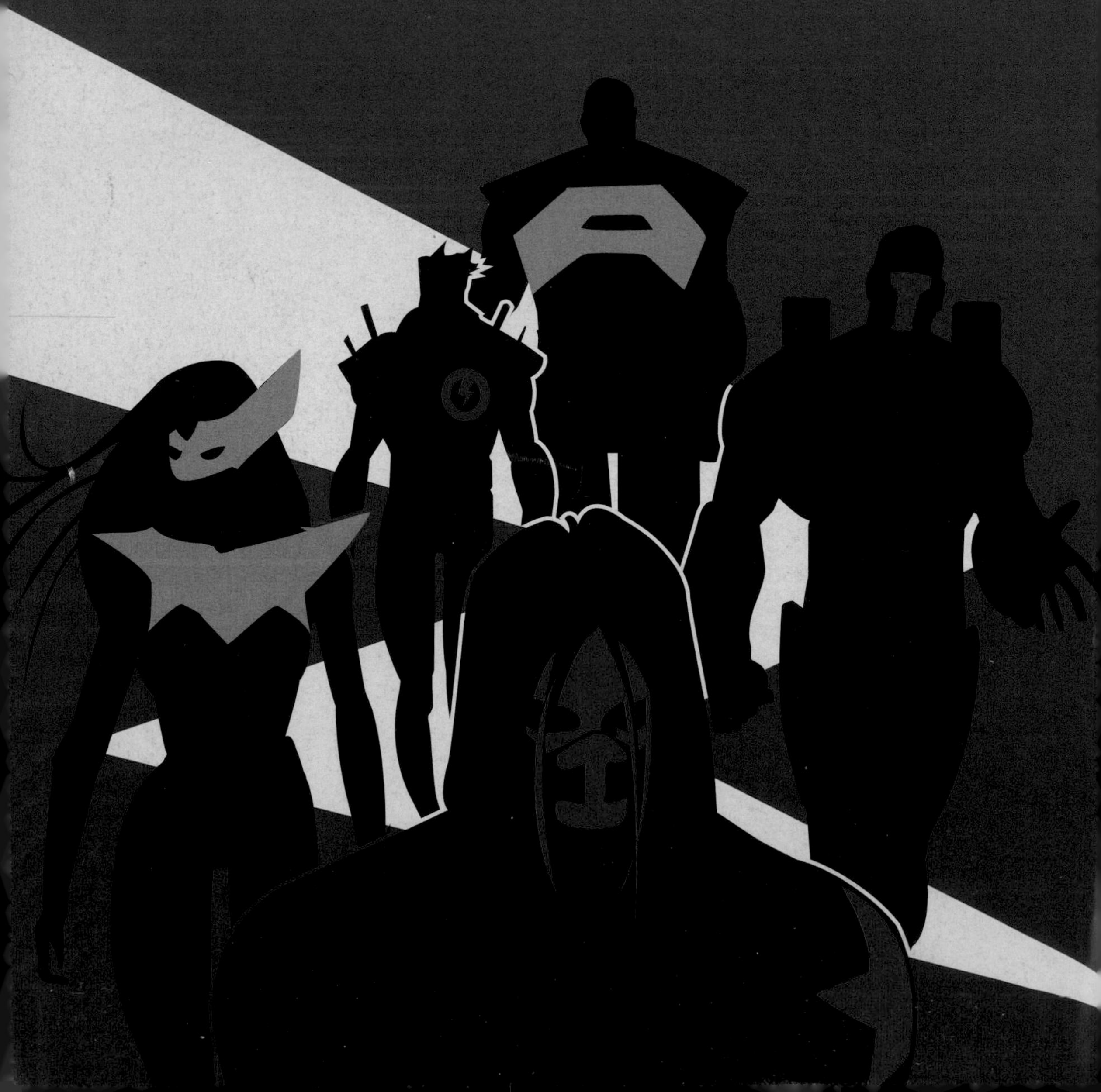

THE WINTER SOLDIER

James "Bucky" Barnes was Captain America's fighting partner and best friend during World War II. He was presumed dead after the drone plane explosion that caused Captain America to be frozen in ice, but he'd actually been captured by the Soviets, who fitted him with a cybernetic arm and brainwashed him into becoming an assassin. Eventually, he regained his memories and even took up the shield as Captain America before replacing Nick Fury Sr. as the Man on the Wall, secretly protecting Earth from external threats.

KOBIK

Kobik was created when several fragmented Cosmic Cubes accidentally combined in a S.H.I.E.L.D. laboratory and gained sentience. Even though Kobik was immensely powerful and could bend reality to her will, her newfound conscious-ness left her confused and frightened, so she took on the form of a small child. S.H.I.E.L.D. used her to create the small-town super-prison known as Pleasant Hill, and Bucky rescued her when the prisoners rebelled.

MOONSTONE

Dr. Karla Sofen is a highly intelligent psychiatrist who trained under the notorious villain Dr. Faustus. The original Moonstone was one of her patients. She manipulated him into rejecting the alien gem that gave him his powers and took it all for herself. The power of the moonstone provides her with superhuman strength and durability, and also allows her to fly and emit energy blasts.

MACH-X

Bored at his job as a mechanical engineer, Abner "Abe" Jenkins invented a suit of power armor that he used to become the career criminal known as the Beetle. When Baron Zemo recruited him for the original Thunderbolts, he took on the identity of MACH-1. With a new set of armor created by the Fixer, Abe became a human fighter jet with high maneuverability and powerful aerial weaponry. Later, Abe went straight and was actually working at Pleasant Hill as a civilian contractor when the operation fell apart.

FIXER

P. Norbert Ebersol was a child prodigy whose talent for engineering got him jobs as fast as his arrogance lost them. For a while, he turned to crime, and even provided his original Thunderbolts teammates with the disguises that would fool the world into thinking they were heroes. But now he mostly works for whoever cuts his check. He can reconfigure his mentally-controlled tech-pac at will to create whatever equipment and weaponry he needs.

ATLAS

Erik Josten worked for Heinrich Zemo as a smuggler and mercenary, but exposure to various devices and experiments gave him enhanced strength and durability as well as the ability to increase his size dramatically. Atlas enjoyed pretending to be a hero so much that he stuck with the Thunderbolts when Hawkeye took over as leader, but his own self-doubts and emotional instability would hinder him throughout his super hero career.

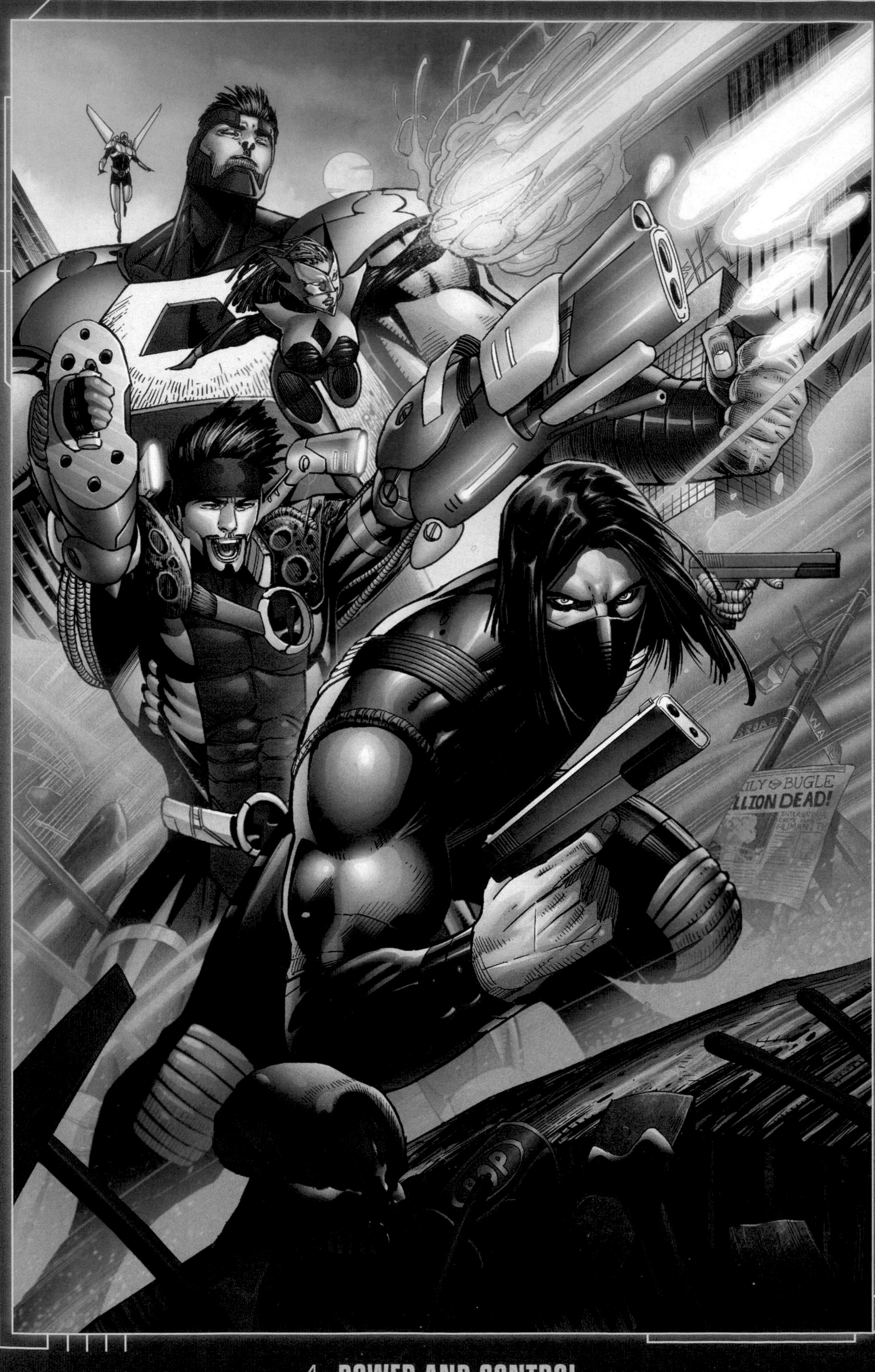

1: POWER AND CONTROL

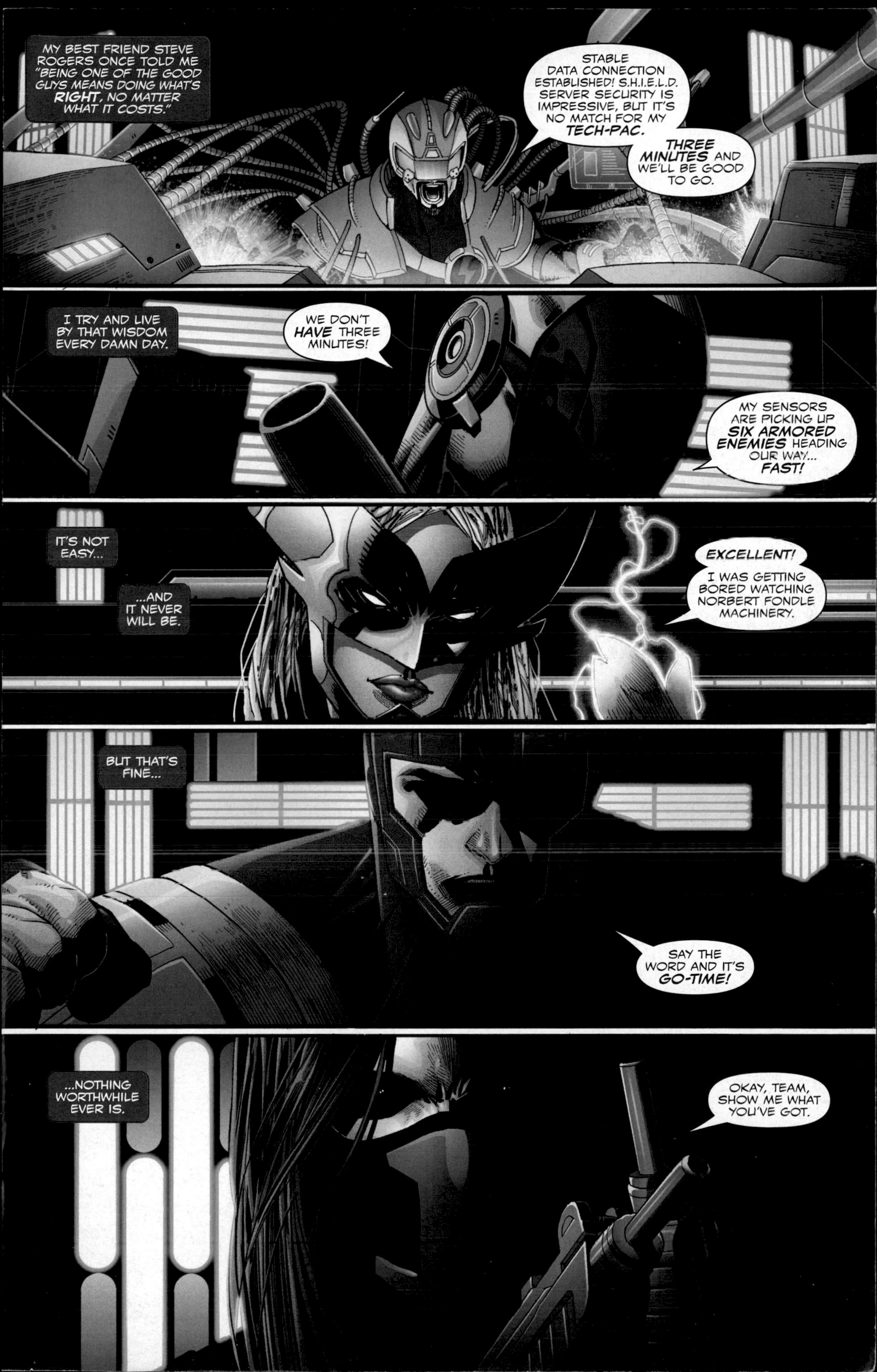
MY BEST FRIEND STEVE ROGERS ONCE TOLD ME "BEING ONE OF THE GOOD GUYS MEANS DOING WHAT'S RIGHT, NO MATTER WHAT IT COSTS."
STABLE DATA CONNECTION ESTABLISHED! S.H.I.E.L.D. SERVER SECURITY IS IMPRESSIVE, BUT IT'S NO MATCH FOR MY TECH-PAC.
THREE MINUTES AND WE'LL BE GOOD TO GO.
I TRY AND LIVE BY THAT WISDOM EVERY DAMN DAY.
WE DON'T HAVE THREE MINUTES!
MY SENSORS ARE PICKING UP SIX ARMORED ENEMIES HEADING OUR WAY... FAST!
IT'S NOT EASY...
...AND IT NEVER WILL BE.
EXCELLENT!
I WAS GETTING BORED WATCHING NORBERT FONDLE MACHINERY.
BUT THAT'S FINE...
SAY THE WORD AND IT'S GO-TIME!
...NOTHING WORTHWHILE EVER IS.
OKAY, TEAM, SHOW ME WHAT YOU'VE GOT.

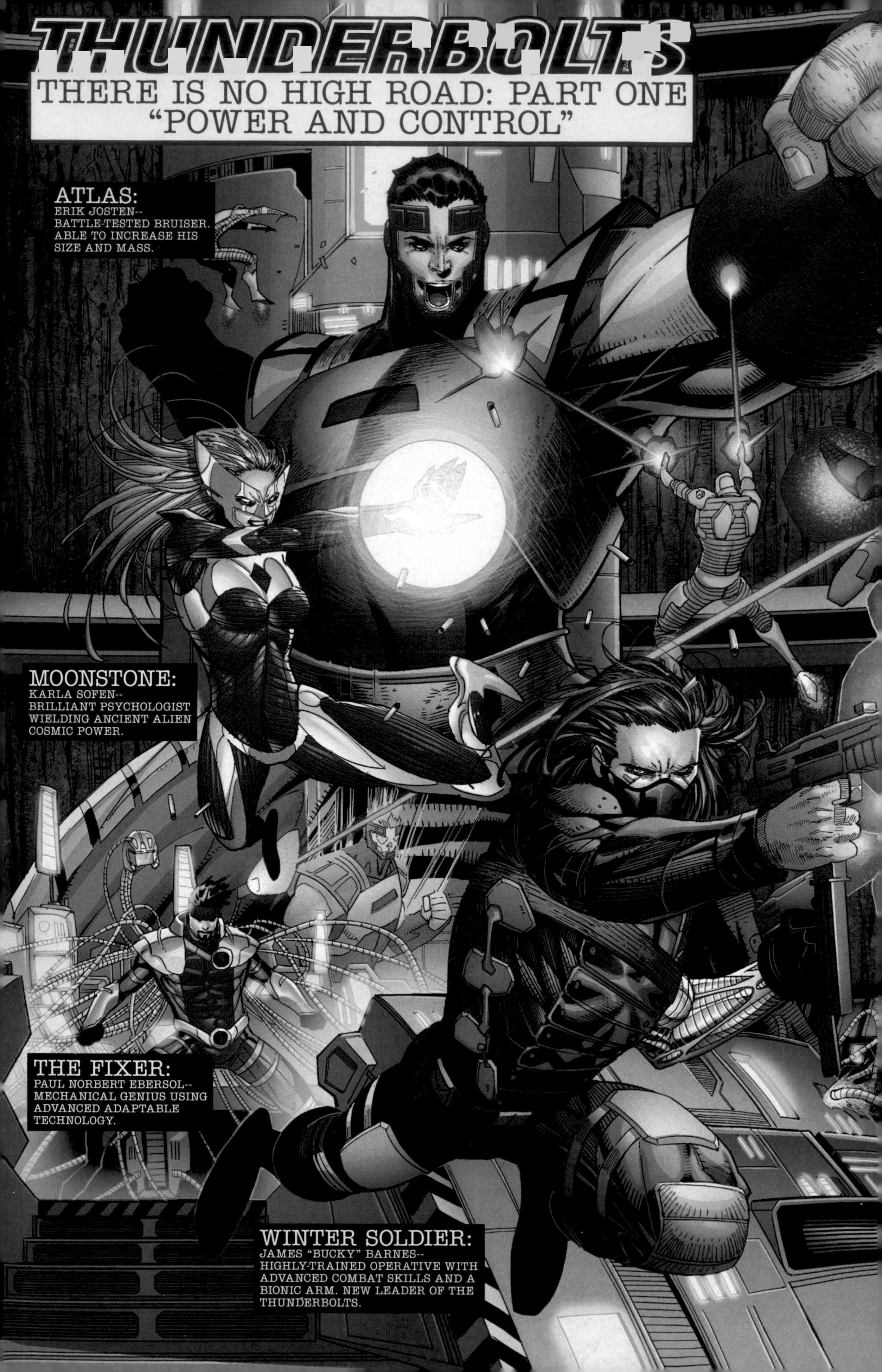
THUNDERBOLTS
THERE IS NO HIGH ROAD: PART ONE
"POWER AND CONTROL"
ATLAS:
ERIK JOSTEN--
BATTLE-TESTED BRUISER.
ABLE TO INCREASE HIS
SIZE AND MASS.
MOONSTONE:
KARLA SOFEN--
BRILLIANT PSYCHOLOGIST
WIELDING ANCIENT ALIEN
COSMIC POWER.
THE FIXER:
PAUL NORBERT EBERSOL--
MECHANICAL GENIUS USING
ADVANCED ADAPTABLE
TECHNOLOGY.
WINTER SOLDIER:
JAMES "BUCKY" BARNES--
HIGHLY-TRAINED OPERATIVE WITH
ADVANCED COMBAT SKILLS AND A
BIONIC ARM. NEW LEADER OF THE
THUNDERBOLTS.

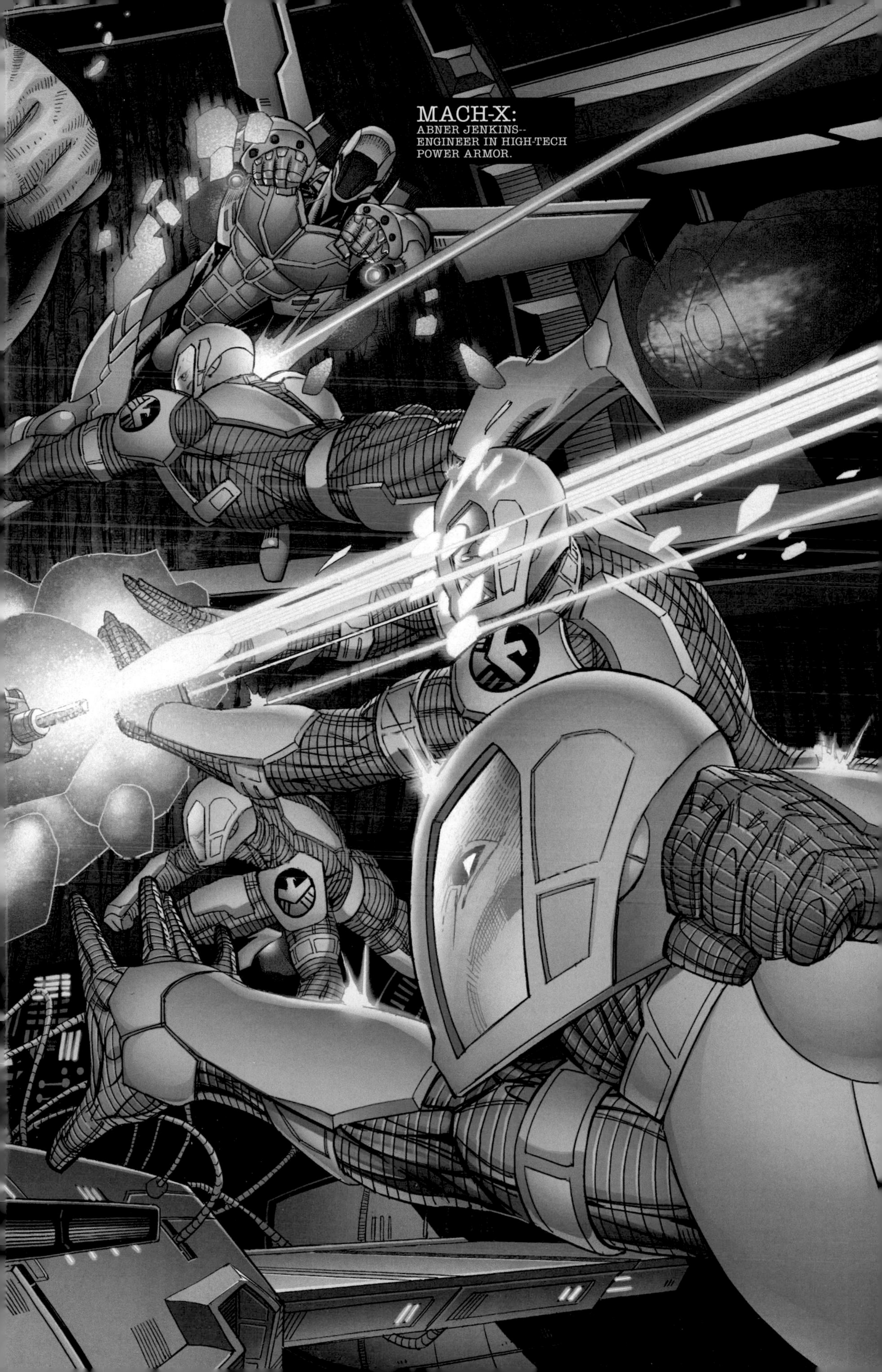
MACH-X:
ABNER JENKINS--
ENGINEER IN HIGH-TECH
POWER ARMOR.

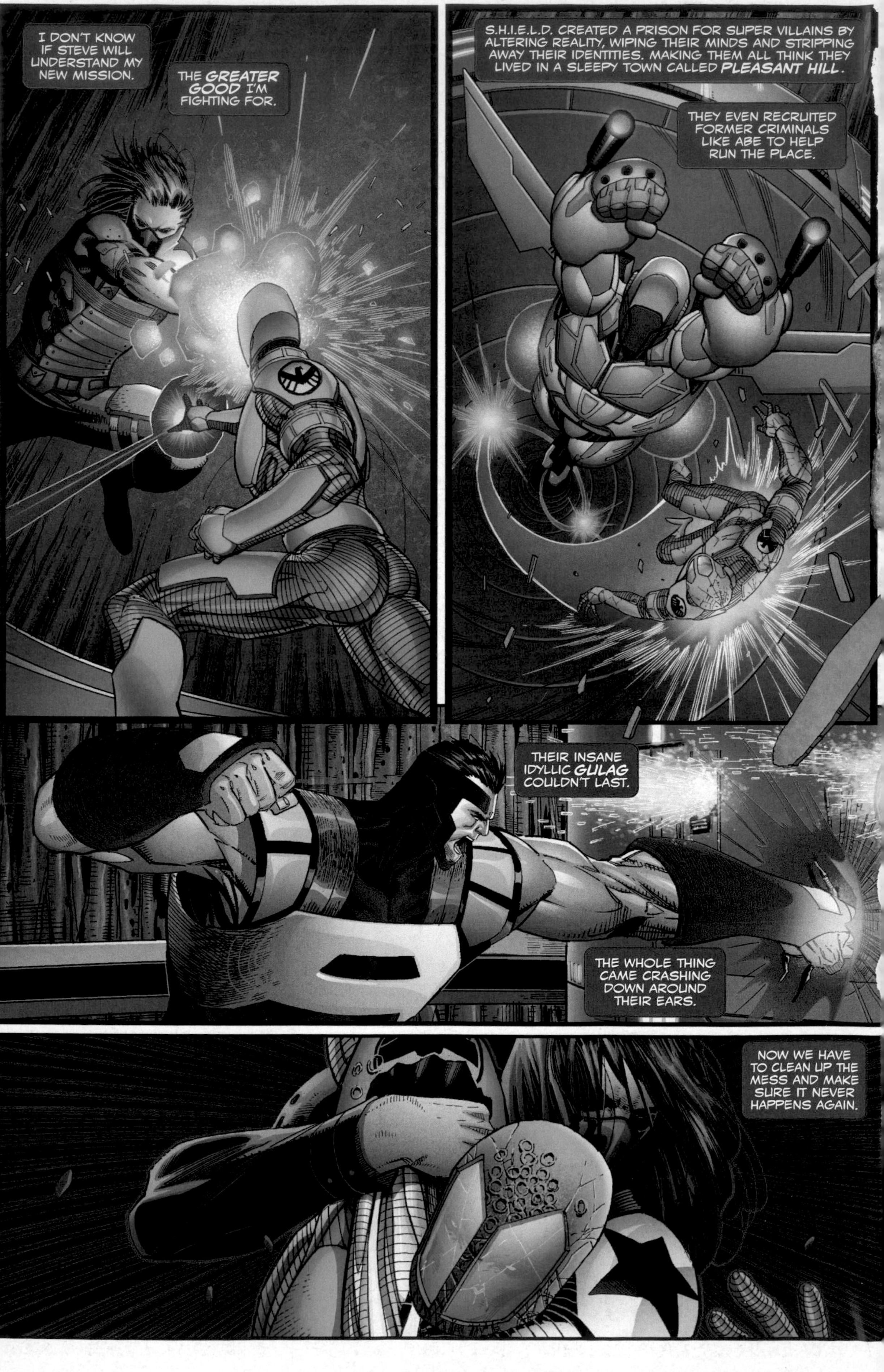
I DON'T KNOW IF STEVE WILL UNDERSTAND MY NEW MISSION.
THE GREATER GOOD I'M FIGHTING FOR.
S.H.I.E.L.D. CREATED A PRISON FOR SUPER VILLAINS BY ALTERING REALITY, WIPING THEIR MINDS AND STRIPPING AWAY THEIR IDENTITIES. MAKING THEM ALL THINK THEY LIVED IN A SLEEPY TOWN CALLED PLEASANT HILL.
THEY EVEN RECRUITED FORMER CRIMINALS LIKE ABE TO HELP RUN THE PLACE.
THEIR INSANE IDYLLIC GULAG COULDN'T LAST.
THE WHOLE THING CAME CRASHING DOWN AROUND THEIR EARS.
NOW WE HAVE TO CLEAN UP THE MESS AND MAKE SURE IT NEVER HAPPENS AGAIN.

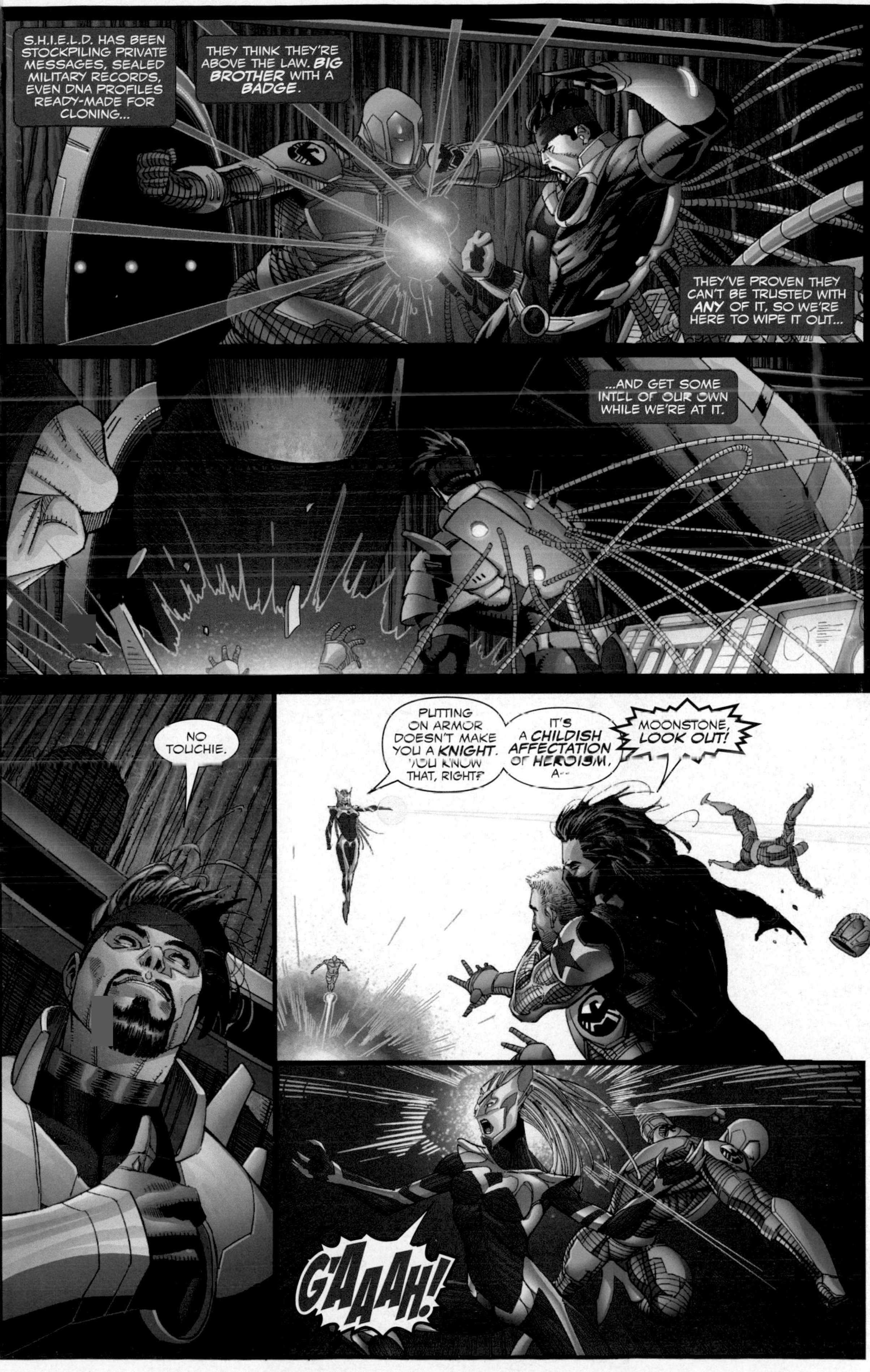
S.H.I.E.L.D. HAS BEEN STOCKPILING PRIVATE MESSAGES, SEALED MILITARY RECORDS, EVEN DNA PROFILES READY-MADE FOR CLONING...
THEY THINK THEY'RE ABOVE THE LAW. BIG BROTHER WITH A BADGE.
THEY'VE PROVEN THEY CAN'T BE TRUSTED WITH ANY OF IT, SO WE'RE HERE TO WIPE IT OUT...
...AND GET SOME INTEL OF OUR OWN WHILE WE'RE AT IT.
NO TOUCHIE.
PUTTING ON ARMOR DOESN'T MAKE YOU A KNIGHT. YOU KNOW THAT, RIGHT?
IT'S A CHILDISH AFFECTATION OF HEROISM, A--
MOONSTONE, LOOK OUT!
GAAAH!

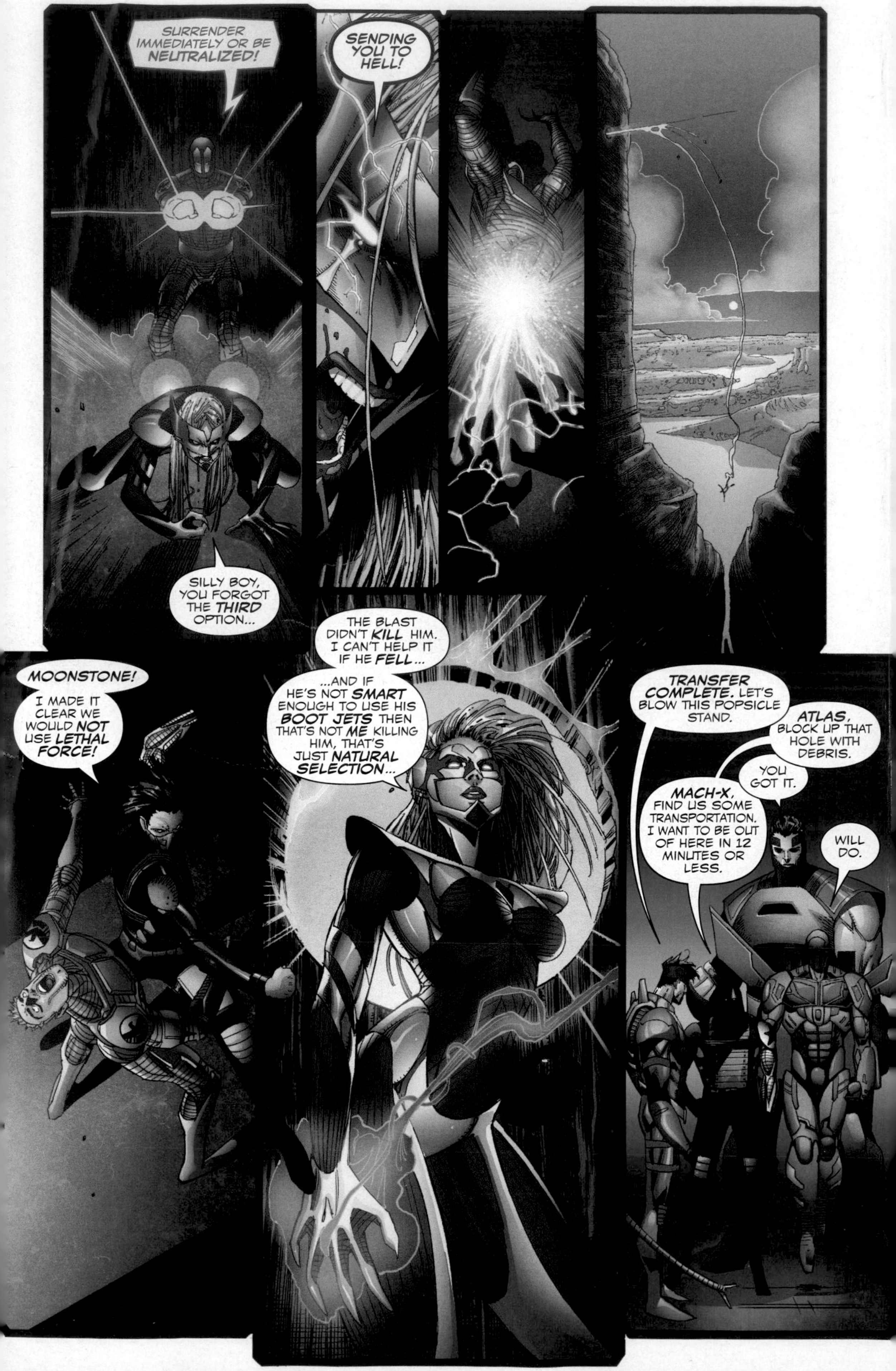
SURRENDER IMMEDIATELY OR BE NEUTRALIZED!
SILLY BOY, YOU FORGOT THE THIRD OPTION...
SENDING YOU TO HELL!
MOONSTONE!
I MADE IT CLEAR WE WOULD NOT USE LETHAL FORCE!
THE BLAST DIDN'T KILL HIM. I CAN'T HELP IT IF HE FELL...
...AND IF HE'S NOT SMART ENOUGH TO USE HIS BOOT JETS THEN THAT'S NOT ME KILLING HIM, THAT'S JUST NATURAL SELECTION...
TRANSFER COMPLETE. LET'S BLOW THIS POPSICLE STAND.
ATLAS, BLOCK UP THAT HOLE WITH DEBRIS.
YOU GOT IT.
MACH-X, FIND US SOME TRANSPORTATION. I WANT TO BE OUT OF HERE IN 12 MINUTES OR LESS.
WILL DO.

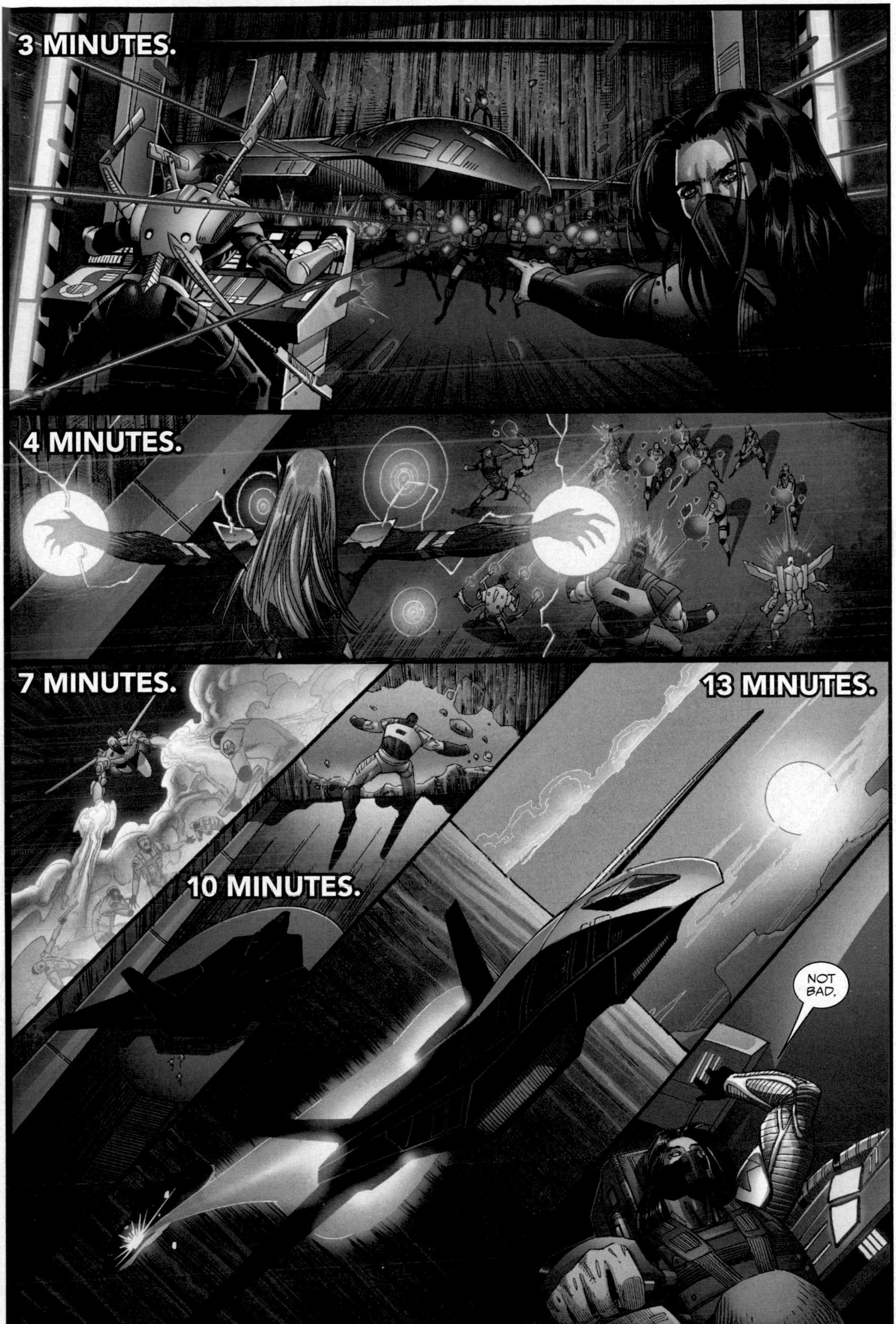
3 MINUTES.
4 MINUTES.
7 MINUTES.
10 MINUTES.
13 MINUTES.
NOT BAD.

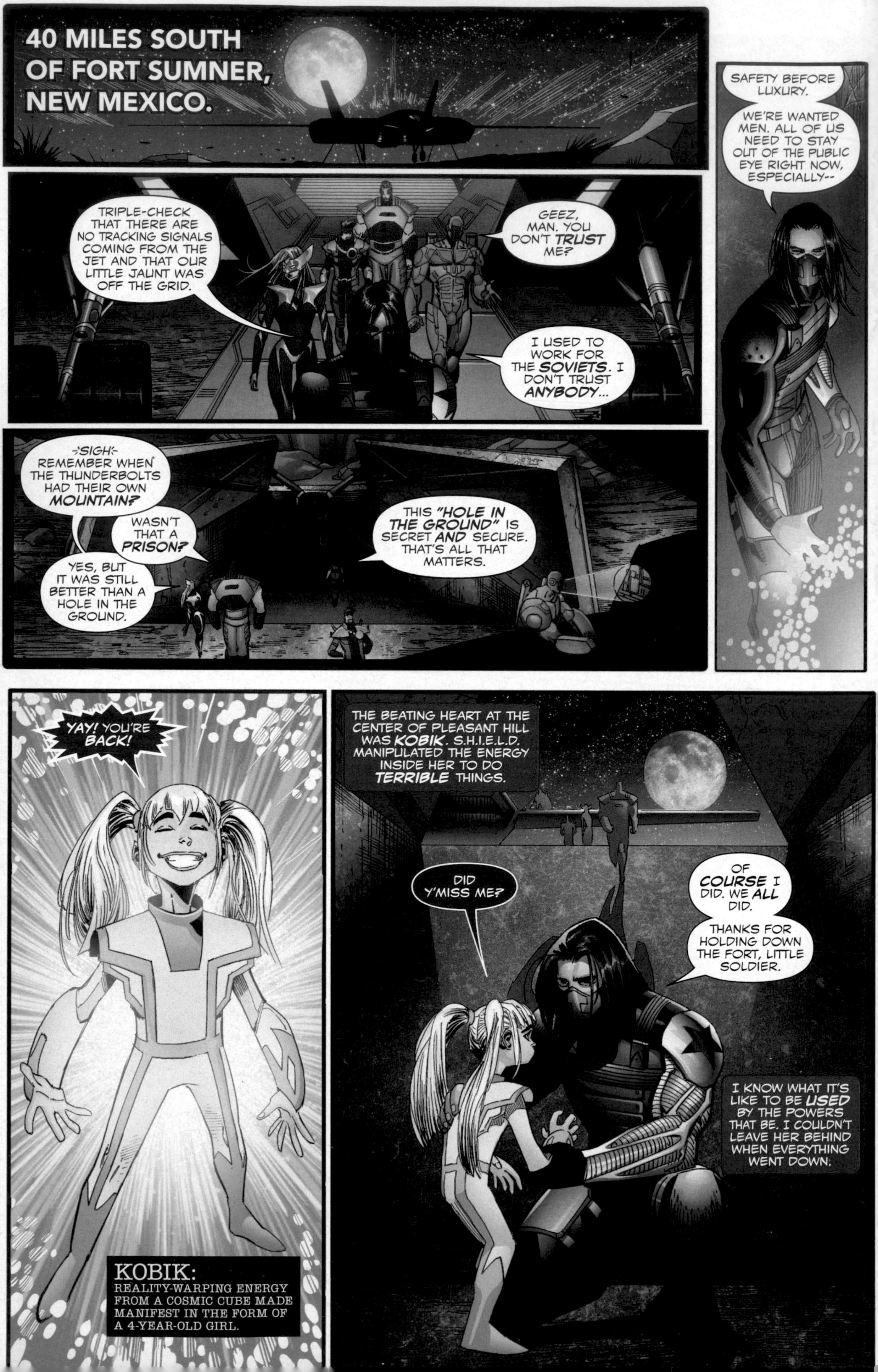
40 MILES SOUTH OF FORT SUMNER, NEW MEXICO.
TRIPLE-CHECK THAT THERE ARE NO TRACKING SIGNALS COMING FROM THE JET AND THAT OUR LITTLE JAUNT WAS OFF THE GRID.
GEEZ, MAN. YOU DON'T TRUST ME?
I USED TO WORK FOR THE SOVIETS. I DON'T TRUST ANYBODY...
SAFETY BEFORE LUXURY.
WE'RE WANTED MEN. ALL OF US NEED TO STAY OUT OF THE PUBLIC EYE RIGHT NOW, ESPECIALLY--
-SIGH- REMEMBER WHEN THE THUNDERBOLTS HAD THEIR OWN MOUNTAIN?
WASN'T THAT A PRISON?
YES, BUT IT WAS STILL BETTER THAN A HOLE IN THE GROUND.
THIS "HOLE IN THE GROUND" IS SECRET AND SECURE. THAT'S ALL THAT MATTERS.
YAY! YOU'RE BACK!
KOBIK: REALITY-WARPING ENERGY FROM A COSMIC CUBE MADE MANIFEST IN THE FORM OF A 4-YEAR-OLD GIRL.
THE BEATING HEART AT THE CENTER OF PLEASANT HILL WAS KOBIK. S.H.I.E.L.D. MANIPULATED THE ENERGY INSIDE HER TO DO TERRIBLE THINGS.
DID Y'MISS ME?
OF COURSE I DID. WE ALL DID.
THANKS FOR HOLDING DOWN THE FORT, LITTLE SOLDIER.
I KNOW WHAT IT'S LIKE TO BE USED BY THE POWERS THAT BE. I COULDN'T LEAVE HER BEHIND WHEN EVERYTHING WENT DOWN.

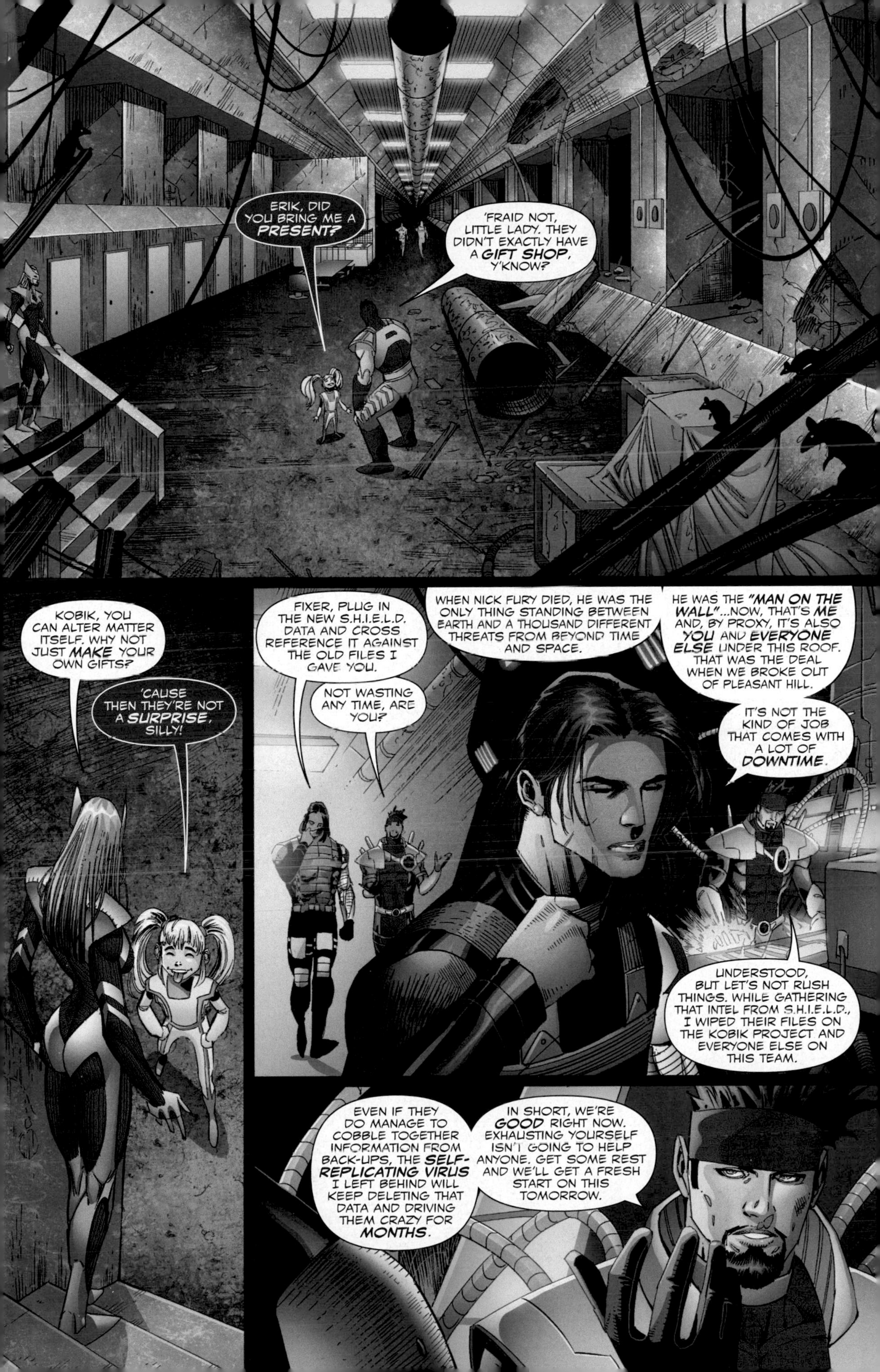
ERIK, DID YOU BRING ME A PRESENT?
'FRAID NOT, LITTLE LADY. THEY DIDN'T EXACTLY HAVE A GIFT SHOP, Y'KNOW?
KOBIK, YOU CAN ALTER MATTER ITSELF. WHY NOT JUST MAKE YOUR OWN GIFTS?
'CAUSE THEN THEY'RE NOT A SURPRISE, SILLY!
FIXER, PLUG IN THE NEW S.H.I.E.L.D. DATA AND CROSS REFERENCE IT AGAINST THE OLD FILES I GAVE YOU.
NOT WASTING ANY TIME, ARE YOU?
WHEN NICK FURY DIED, HE WAS THE ONLY THING STANDING BETWEEN EARTH AND A THOUSAND DIFFERENT THREATS FROM BEYOND TIME AND SPACE.
HE WAS THE "MAN ON THE WALL"...NOW, THAT'S ME AND, BY PROXY, IT'S ALSO YOU AND EVERYONE ELSE UNDER THIS ROOF. THAT WAS THE DEAL WHEN WE BROKE OUT OF PLEASANT HILL.
IT'S NOT THE KIND OF JOB THAT COMES WITH A LOT OF DOWNTIME.
UNDERSTOOD, BUT LET'S NOT RUSH THINGS. WHILE GATHERING THAT INTEL FROM S.H.I.E.L.D., I WIPED THEIR FILES ON THE KOBIK PROJECT AND EVERYONE ELSE ON THIS TEAM.
EVEN IF THEY DO MANAGE TO COBBLE TOGETHER INFORMATION FROM BACK-UPS, THE SELF-REPLICATING VIRUS I LEFT BEHIND WILL KEEP DELETING THAT DATA AND DRIVING THEM CRAZY FOR MONTHS.
IN SHORT, WE'RE GOOD RIGHT NOW. EXHAUSTING YOURSELF ISN'T GOING TO HELP ANYONE. GET SOME REST AND WE'LL GET A FRESH START ON THIS TOMORROW.

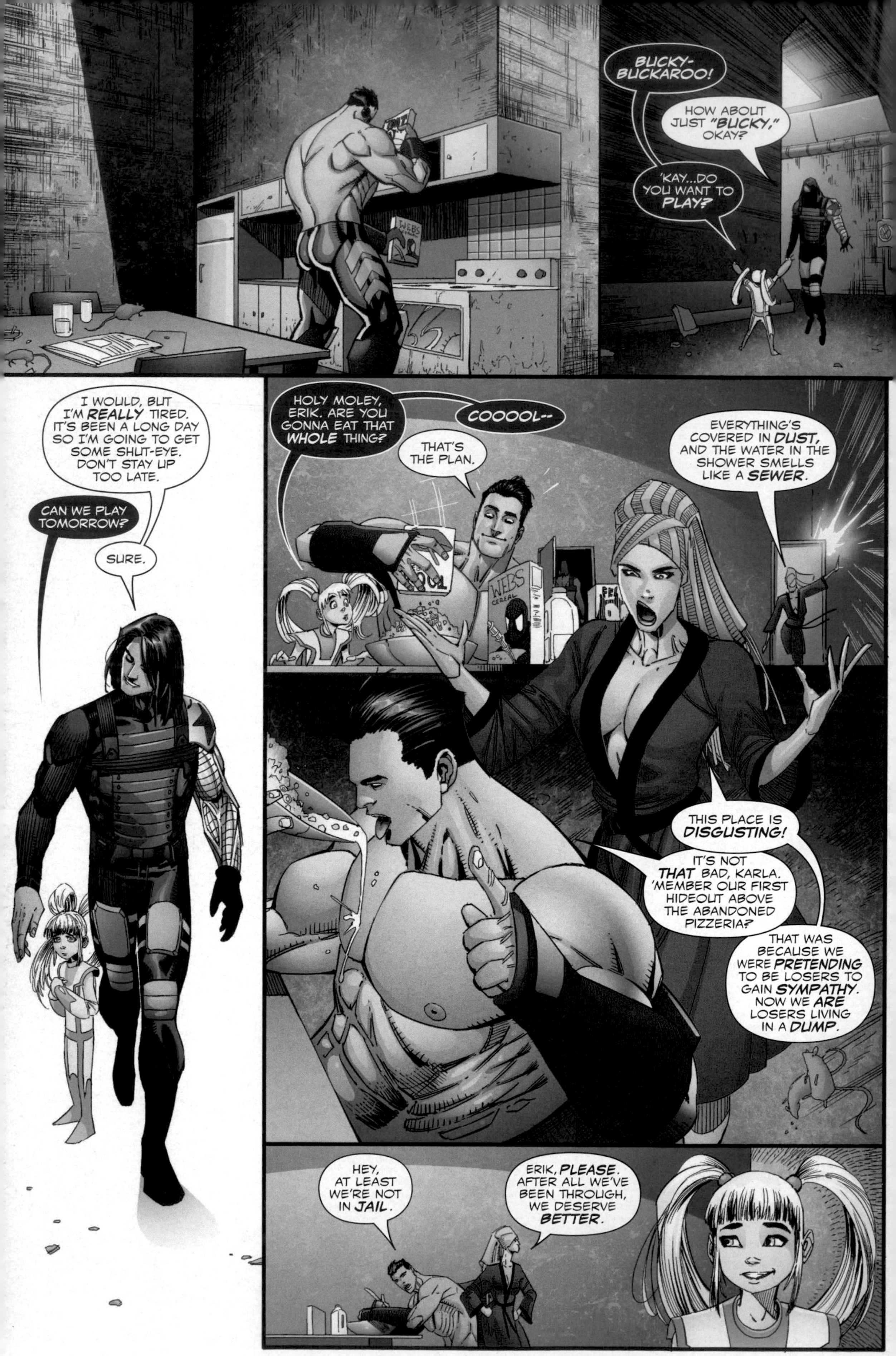

BUCKY-BUCKAROO!
HOW ABOUT JUST "BUCKY," OKAY?
'KAY...DO YOU WANT TO PLAY?
I WOULD, BUT I'M REALLY TIRED. IT'S BEEN A LONG DAY SO I'M GOING TO GET SOME SHUT-EYE. DON'T STAY UP TOO LATE.
CAN WE PLAY TOMORROW?
SURE.
HOLY MOLEY, ERIK. ARE YOU GONNA EAT THAT WHOLE THING?
COOOOL--
THAT'S THE PLAN.
WEBS CEREAL
EVERYTHING'S COVERED IN DUST, AND THE WATER IN THE SHOWER SMELLS LIKE A SEWER.
THIS PLACE IS DISGUSTING!
IT'S NOT THAT BAD, KARLA. 'MEMBER OUR FIRST HIDEOUT ABOVE THE ABANDONED PIZZERIA?
THAT WAS BECAUSE WE WERE PRETENDING TO BE LOSERS TO GAIN SYMPATHY. NOW WE ARE LOSERS LIVING IN A DUMP.
HEY, AT LEAST WE'RE NOT IN JAIL.
ERIK, PLEASE. AFTER ALL WE'VE BEEN THROUGH, WE DESERVE BETTER.

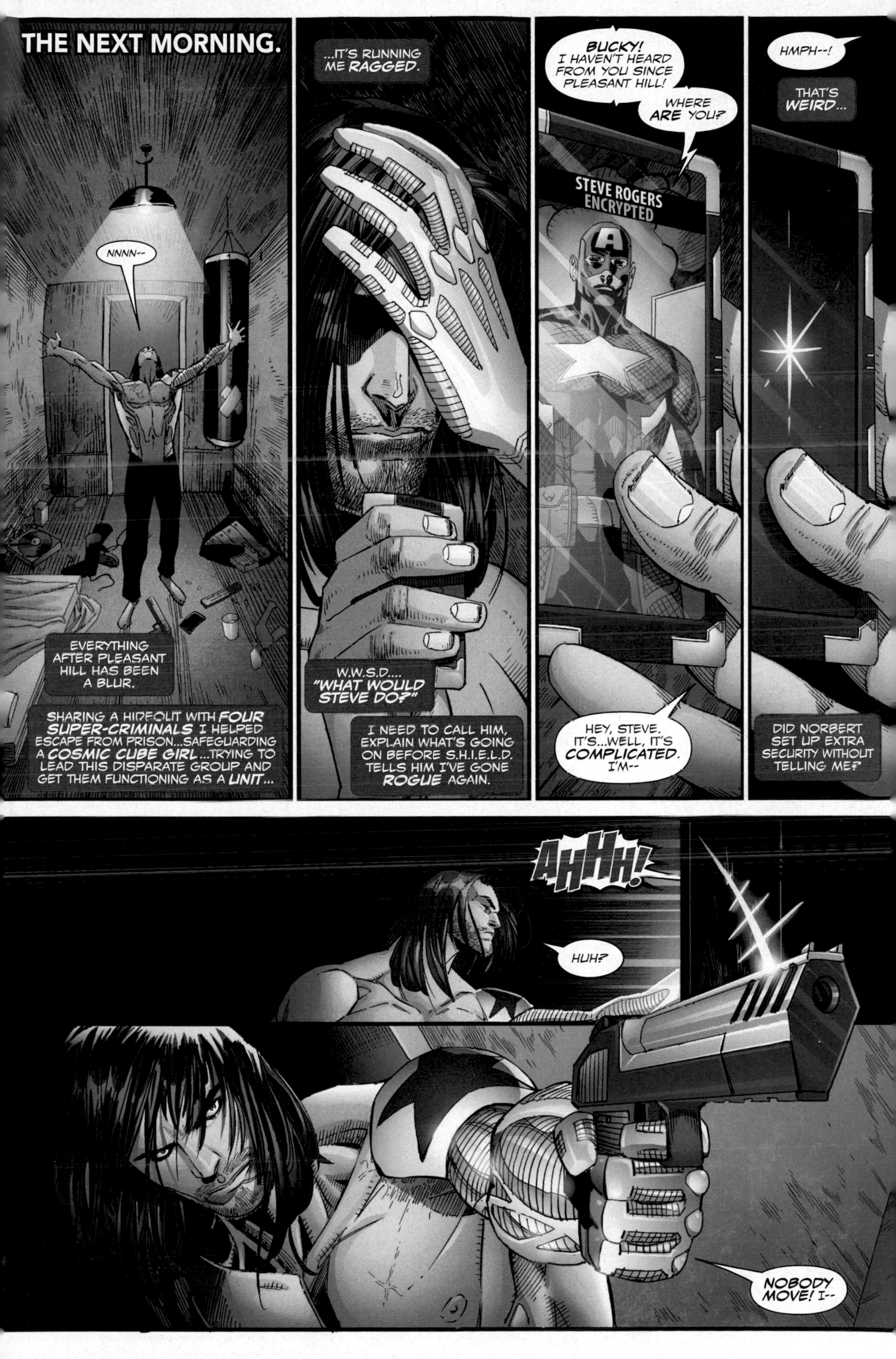
THE NEXT MORNING.
NNNN--
EVERYTHING AFTER PLEASANT HILL HAS BEEN A BLUR.
SHARING A HIDEOUT WITH FOUR SUPER-CRIMINALS I HELPED ESCAPE FROM PRISON...SAFEGUARDING A COSMIC CUBE GIRL...TRYING TO LEAD THIS DISPARATE GROUP AND GET THEM FUNCTIONING AS A UNIT...
...IT'S RUNNING ME RAGGED.
W.W.S.D.... "WHAT WOULD STEVE DO?"
I NEED TO CALL HIM, EXPLAIN WHAT'S GOING ON BEFORE S.H.I.E.L.D. TELLS HIM I'VE GONE ROGUE AGAIN.
BUCKY! I HAVEN'T HEARD FROM YOU SINCE PLEASANT HILL!
WHERE ARE YOU?
STEVE ROGERS
ENCRYPTED
HEY, STEVE. IT'S...WELL, IT'S COMPLICATED. I'M--
HMPH--!
THAT'S WEIRD...
DID NORBERT SET UP EXTRA SECURITY WITHOUT TELLING ME?
AHHH!
HUH?
NOBODY MOVE! I--

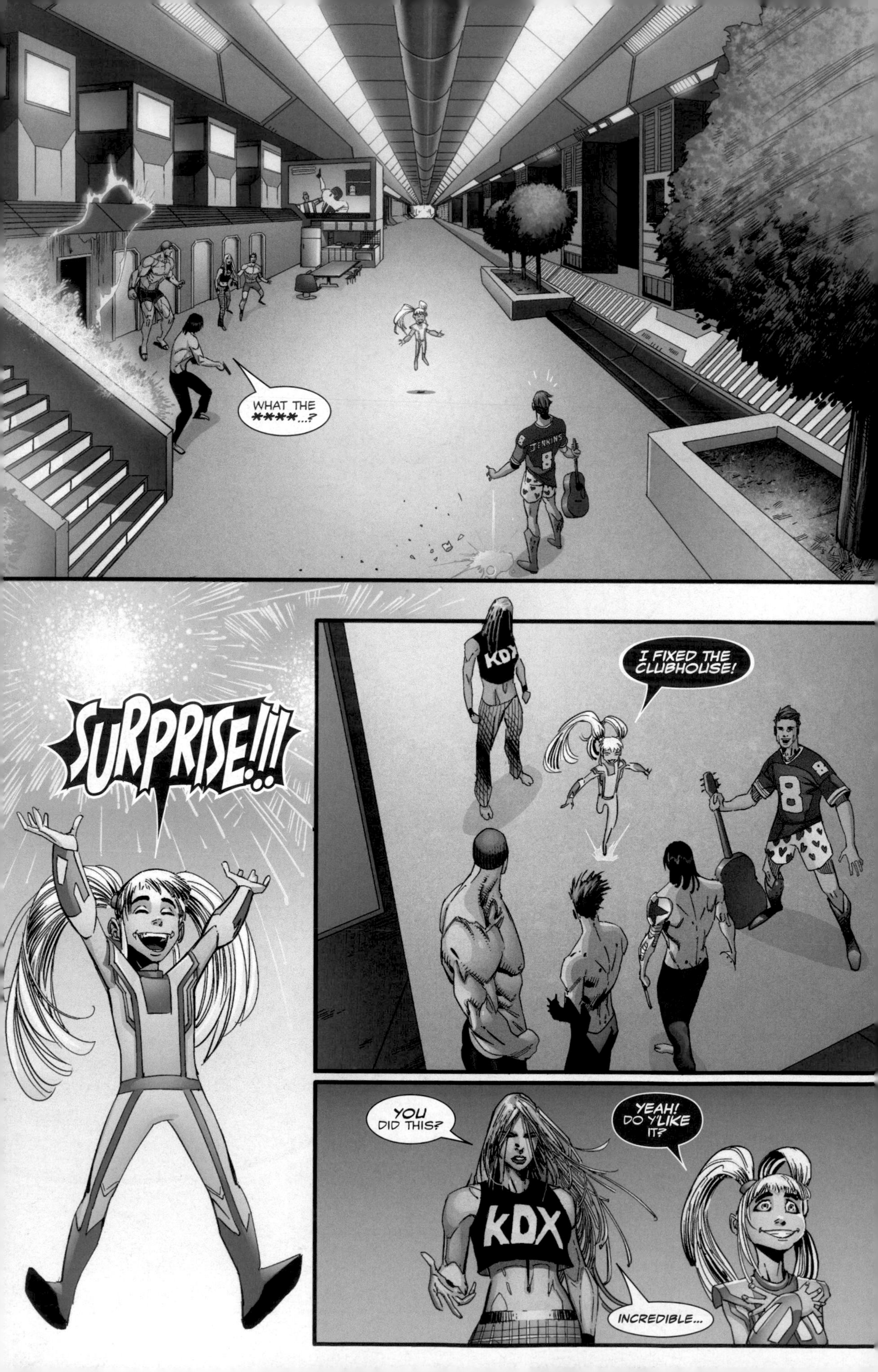
WHAT THE ****...?
SURPRISE!!!
I FIXED THE CLUBHOUSE!
YOU DID THIS?
YEAH! DO Y'LIKE IT?
INCREDIBLE...

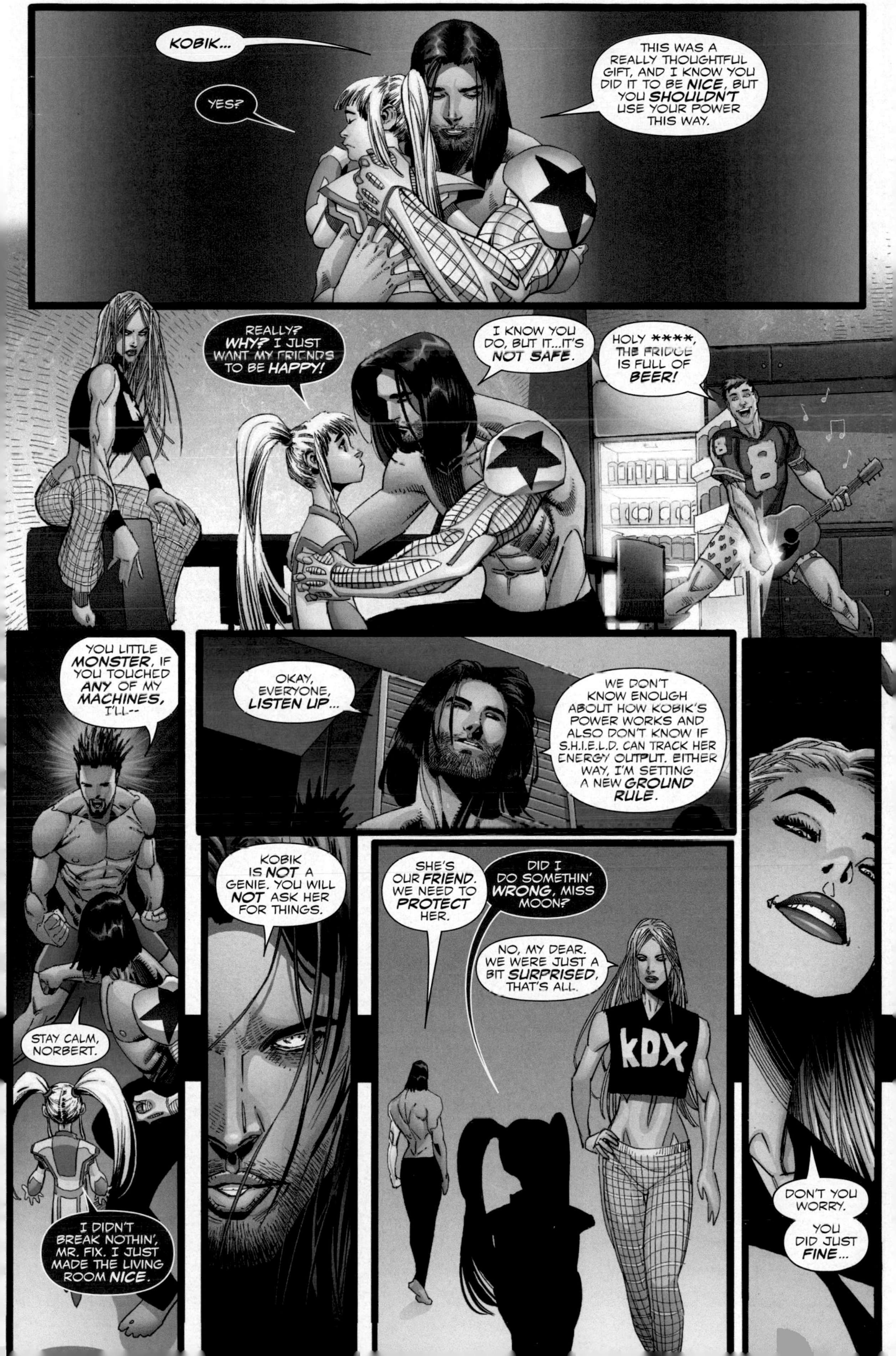
KOBIK...
YES?
THIS WAS A REALLY THOUGHTFUL GIFT, AND I KNOW YOU DID IT TO BE NICE, BUT YOU SHOULDN'T USE YOUR POWER THIS WAY.
REALLY? WHY? I JUST WANT MY FRIENDS TO BE HAPPY!
I KNOW YOU DO, BUT IT...IT'S NOT SAFE.
HOLY ****, THE FRIDGE IS FULL OF BEER!
YOU LITTLE MONSTER, IF YOU TOUCHED ANY OF MY MACHINES, I'LL--
STAY CALM, NORBERT.
I DIDN'T BREAK NOTHIN', MR. FIX. I JUST MADE THE LIVING ROOM NICE.
OKAY, EVERYONE, LISTEN UP...
WE DON'T KNOW ENOUGH ABOUT HOW KOBIK'S POWER WORKS AND ALSO DON'T KNOW IF S.H.I.E.L.D. CAN TRACK HER ENERGY OUTPUT. EITHER WAY, I'M SETTING A NEW GROUND RULE.
KOBIK IS NOT A GENIE. YOU WILL NOT ASK HER FOR THINGS.
SHE'S OUR FRIEND. WE NEED TO PROTECT HER.
DID I DO SOMETHIN' WRONG, MISS MOON?
NO, MY DEAR. WE WERE JUST A BIT SURPRISED, THAT'S ALL.
KDX
DON'T YOU WORRY.
YOU DID JUST FINE...

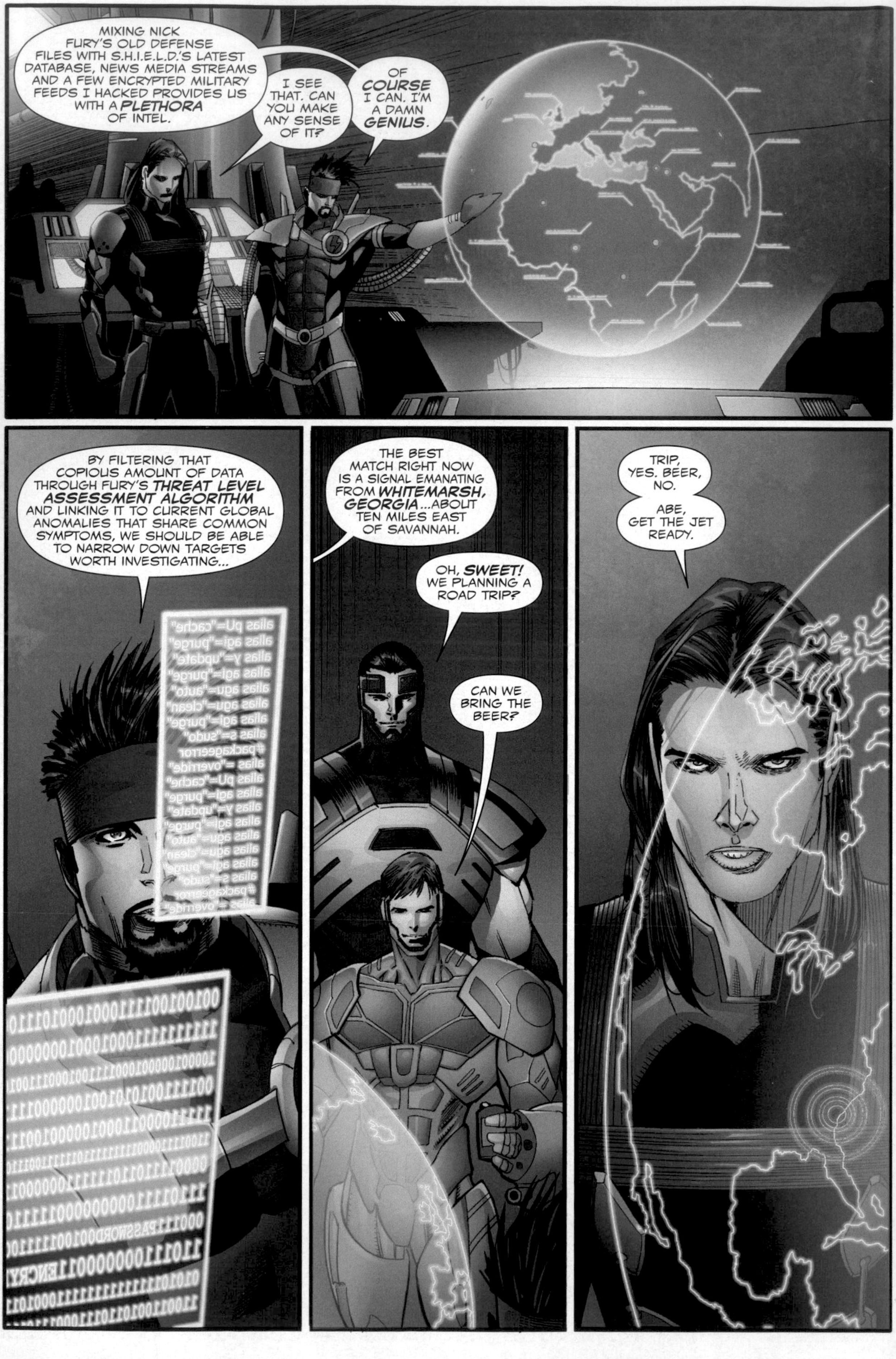
MIXING NICK FURY'S OLD DEFENSE FILES WITH S.H.I.E.L.D.'S LATEST DATABASE, NEWS MEDIA STREAMS AND A FEW ENCRYPTED MILITARY FEEDS I HACKED PROVIDES US WITH A PLETHORA OF INTEL.
I SEE THAT. CAN YOU MAKE ANY SENSE OF IT?
OF COURSE I CAN. I'M A DAMN GENIUS.
BY FILTERING THAT COPIOUS AMOUNT OF DATA THROUGH FURY'S THREAT LEVEL ASSESSMENT ALGORITHM AND LINKING IT TO CURRENT GLOBAL ANOMALIES THAT SHARE COMMON SYMPTOMS, WE SHOULD BE ABLE TO NARROW DOWN TARGETS WORTH INVESTIGATING...
THE BEST MATCH RIGHT NOW IS A SIGNAL EMANATING FROM WHITEMARSH, GEORGIA...ABOUT TEN MILES EAST OF SAVANNAH.
OH, SWEET! WE PLANNING A ROAD TRIP?
CAN WE BRING THE BEER?
TRIP, YES. BEER, NO.
ABE, GET THE JET READY.

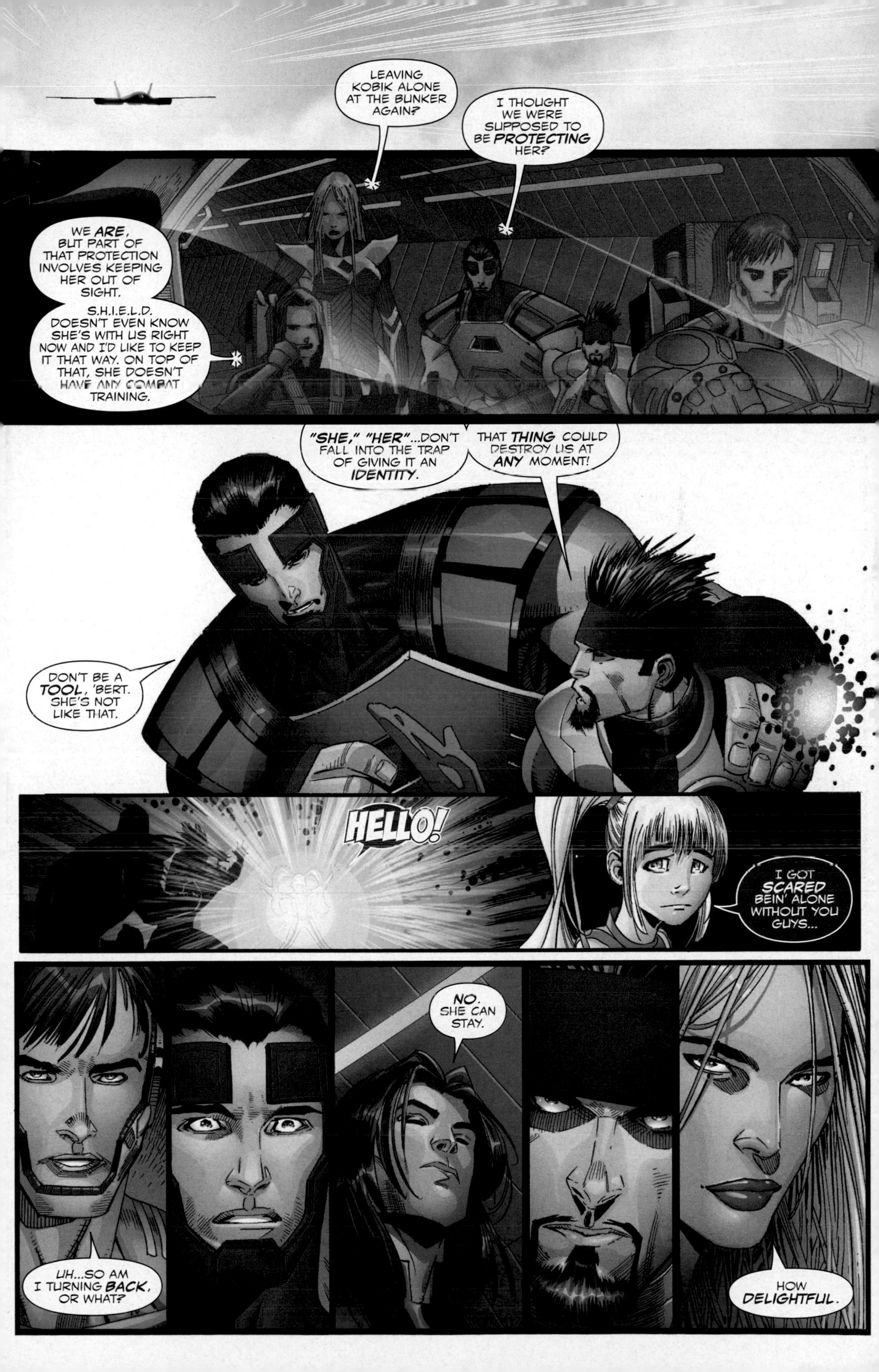
LEAVING KOBIK ALONE AT THE BUNKER AGAIN?
I THOUGHT WE WERE SUPPOSED TO BE PROTECTING HER?
WE ARE, BUT PART OF THAT PROTECTION INVOLVES KEEPING HER OUT OF SIGHT.
S.H.I.E.L.D. DOESN'T EVEN KNOW SHE'S WITH US RIGHT NOW AND I'D LIKE TO KEEP IT THAT WAY. ON TOP OF THAT, SHE DOESN'T HAVE ANY COMBAT TRAINING.
"SHE," "HER"...DON'T FALL INTO THE TRAP OF GIVING IT AN IDENTITY.
THAT THING COULD DESTROY US AT ANY MOMENT!
DON'T BE A TOOL, 'BERT. SHE'S NOT LIKE THAT.
HELLO!
I GOT SCARED BEIN' ALONE WITHOUT YOU GUYS...
NO. SHE CAN STAY.
UH...SO AM I TURNING BACK, OR WHAT?
HOW DELIGHTFUL.

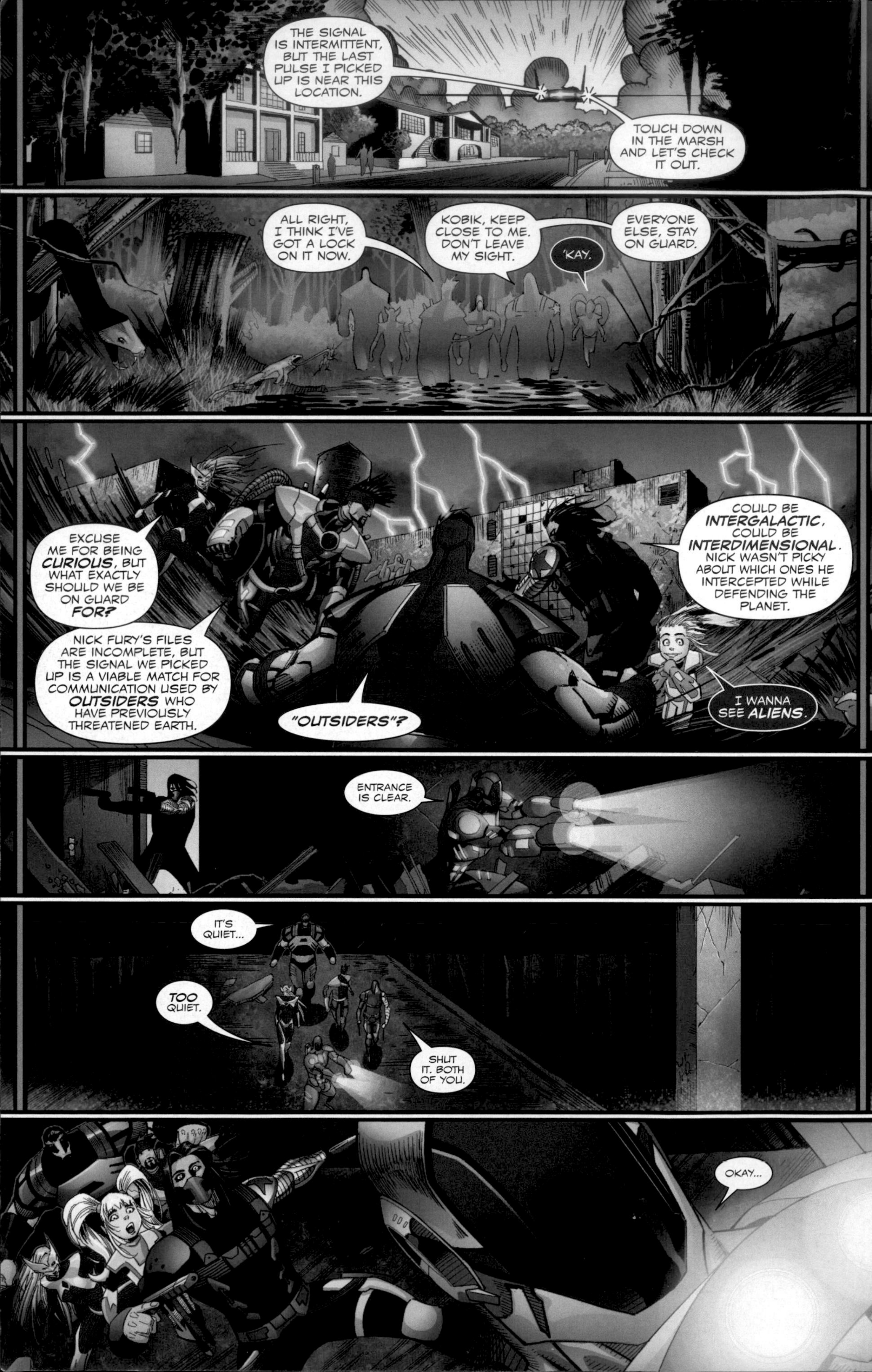
THE SIGNAL IS INTERMITTENT, BUT THE LAST PULSE I PICKED UP IS NEAR THIS LOCATION.
TOUCH DOWN IN THE MARSH AND LET'S CHECK IT OUT.
ALL RIGHT, I THINK I'VE GOT A LOCK ON IT NOW.
KOBIK, KEEP CLOSE TO ME. DON'T LEAVE MY SIGHT.
EVERYONE ELSE, STAY ON GUARD.
'KAY.
EXCUSE ME FOR BEING CURIOUS, BUT WHAT EXACTLY SHOULD WE BE ON GUARD FOR?
NICK FURY'S FILES ARE INCOMPLETE, BUT THE SIGNAL WE PICKED UP IS A VIABLE MATCH FOR COMMUNICATION USED BY OUTSIDERS WHO HAVE PREVIOUSLY THREATENED EARTH.
"OUTSIDERS"?
COULD BE INTERGALACTIC, COULD BE INTERDIMENSIONAL. NICK WASN'T PICKY ABOUT WHICH ONES HE INTERCEPTED WHILE DEFENDING THE PLANET.
I WANNA SEE ALIENS.
ENTRANCE IS CLEAR.
IT'S QUIET...
TOO QUIET.
SHUT IT. BOTH OF YOU.
OKAY...

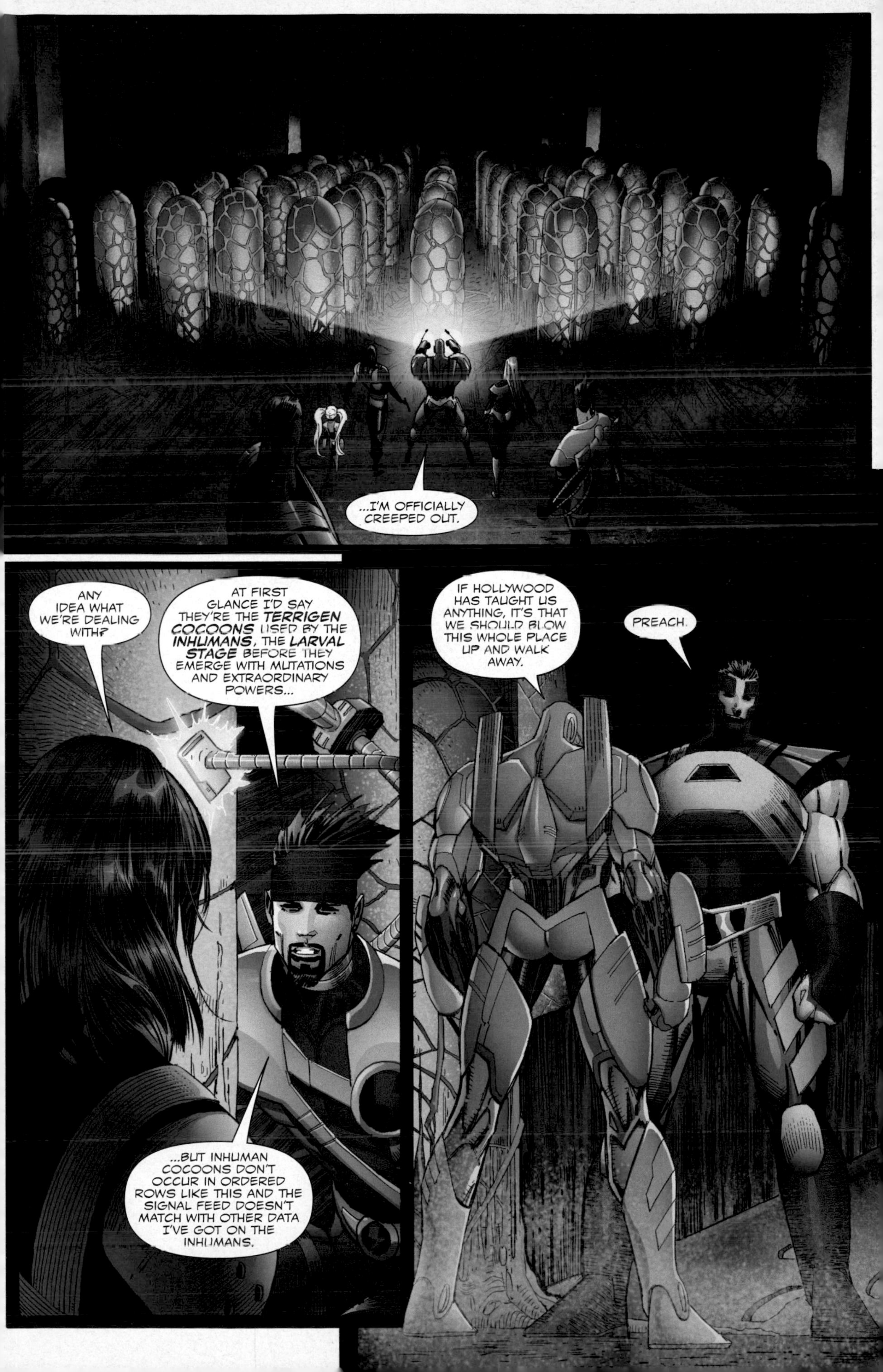
...I'M OFFICIALLY CREEPED OUT.
ANY IDEA WHAT WE'RE DEALING WITH?
AT FIRST GLANCE I'D SAY THEY'RE THE TERRIGEN COCOONS USED BY THE INHUMANS, THE LARVAL STAGE BEFORE THEY EMERGE WITH MUTATIONS AND EXTRAORDINARY POWERS...
...BUT INHUMAN COCOONS DON'T OCCUR IN ORDERED ROWS LIKE THIS AND THE SIGNAL FEED DOESN'T MATCH WITH OTHER DATA I'VE GOT ON THE INHUMANS.
IF HOLLYWOOD HAS TAUGHT US ANYTHING, IT'S THAT WE SHOULD BLOW THIS WHOLE PLACE UP AND WALK AWAY.
PREACH.

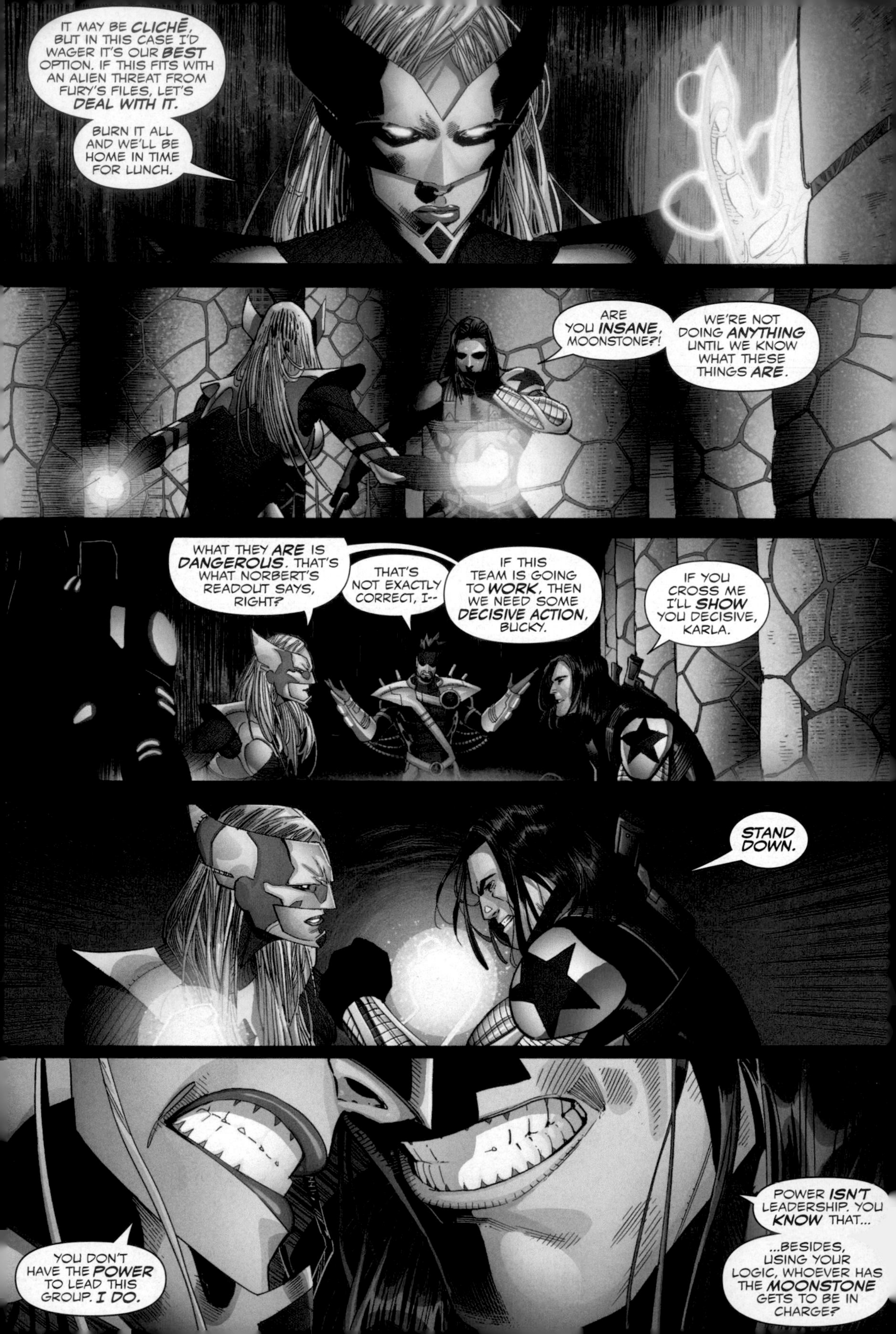
IT MAY BE CLICHÉ, BUT IN THIS CASE I'D WAGER IT'S OUR BEST OPTION. IF THIS FITS WITH AN ALIEN THREAT FROM FURY'S FILES, LET'S DEAL WITH IT.
BURN IT ALL AND WE'LL BE HOME IN TIME FOR LUNCH.
ARE YOU INSANE, MOONSTONE?!
WE'RE NOT DOING ANYTHING UNTIL WE KNOW WHAT THESE THINGS ARE.
WHAT THEY ARE IS DANGEROUS. THAT'S WHAT NORBERT'S READOUT SAYS, RIGHT?
THAT'S NOT EXACTLY CORRECT, I--
IF THIS TEAM IS GOING TO WORK, THEN WE NEED SOME DECISIVE ACTION, BUCKY.
IF YOU CROSS ME I'LL SHOW YOU DECISIVE, KARLA.
STAND DOWN.
YOU DON'T HAVE THE POWER TO LEAD THIS GROUP. I DO.
POWER ISN'T LEADERSHIP. YOU KNOW THAT...
...BESIDES, USING YOUR LOGIC, WHOEVER HAS THE MOONSTONE GETS TO BE IN CHARGE?

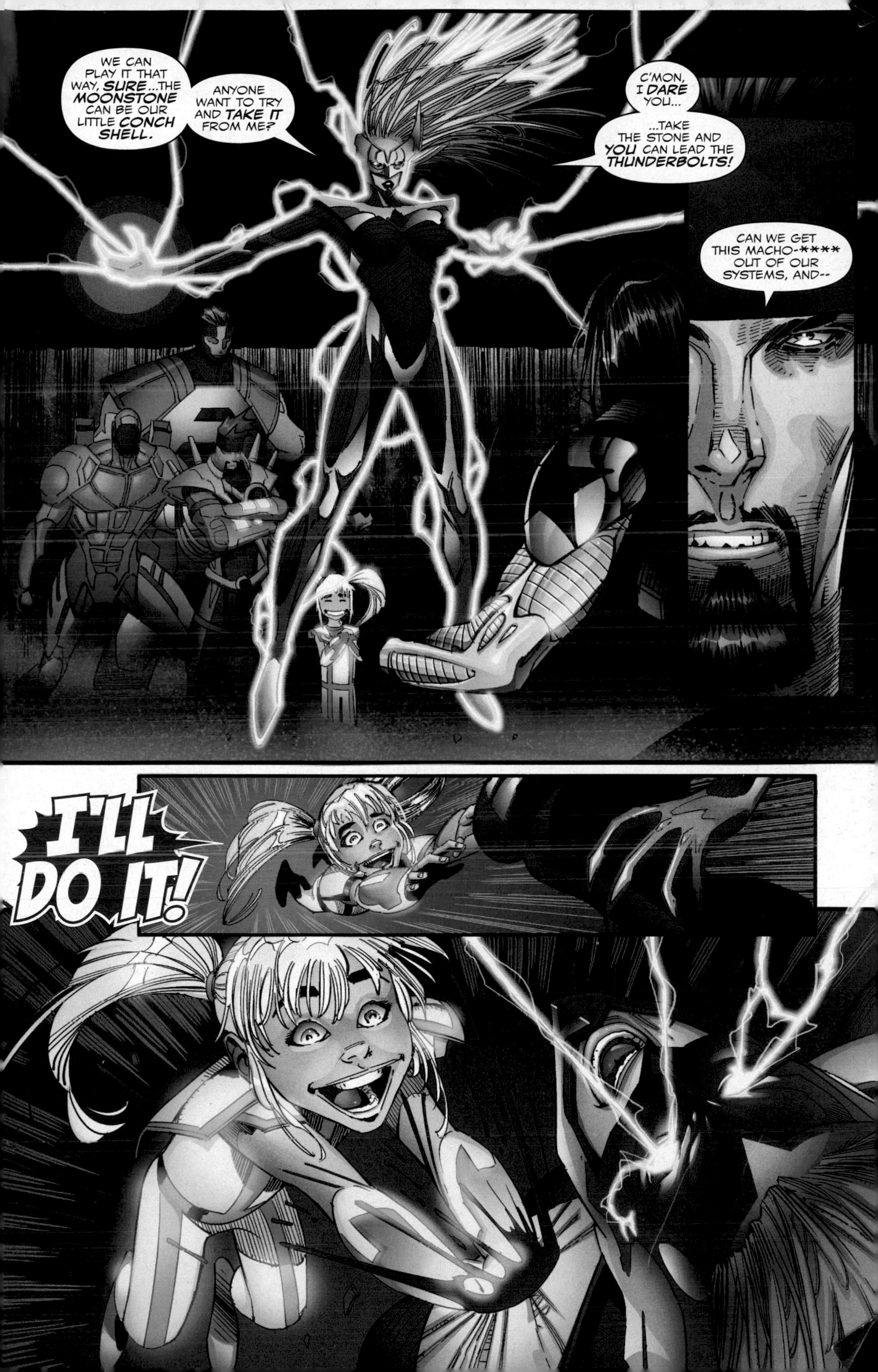
WE CAN PLAY IT THAT WAY, SURE...THE MOONSTONE CAN BE OUR LITTLE CONCH SHELL.
ANYONE WANT TO TRY AND TAKE IT FROM ME?
C'MON, I DARE YOU...
...TAKE THE STONE AND YOU CAN LEAD THE THUNDERBOLTS!
CAN WE GET THIS MACHO-**** OUT OF OUR SYSTEMS, AND--
I'LL DO IT!

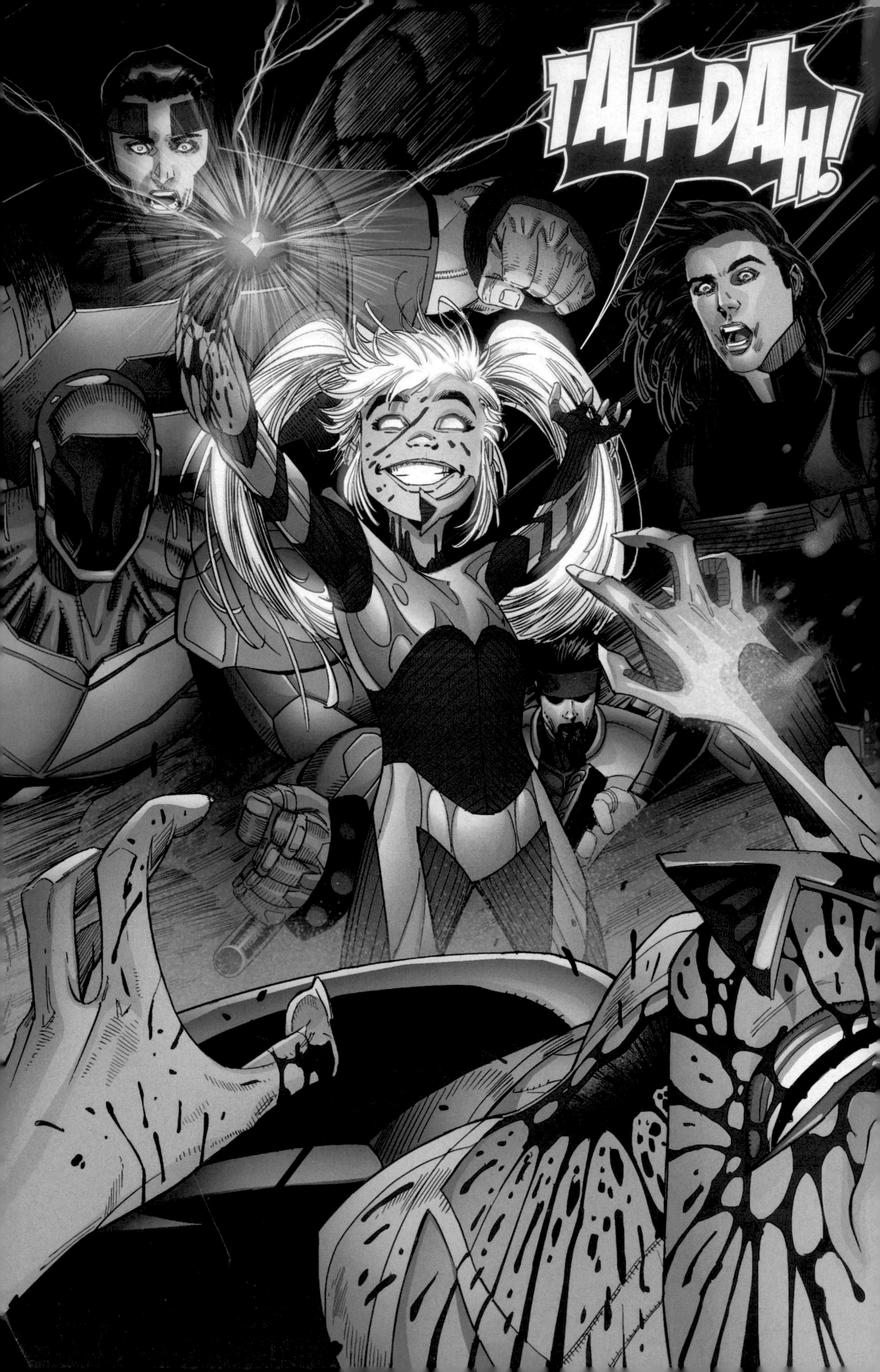
TAH-DAH!

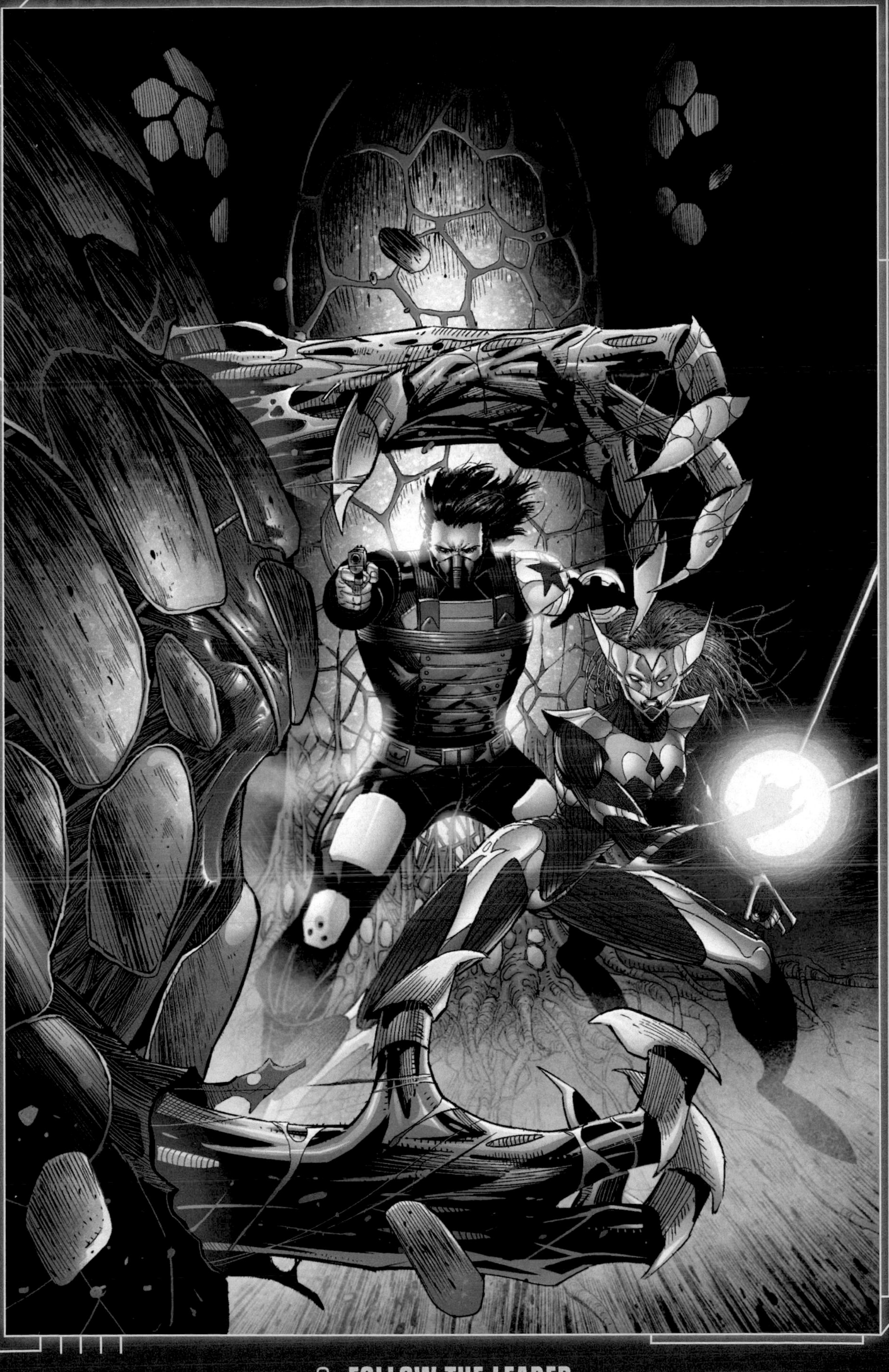

2: FOLLOW THE LEADER

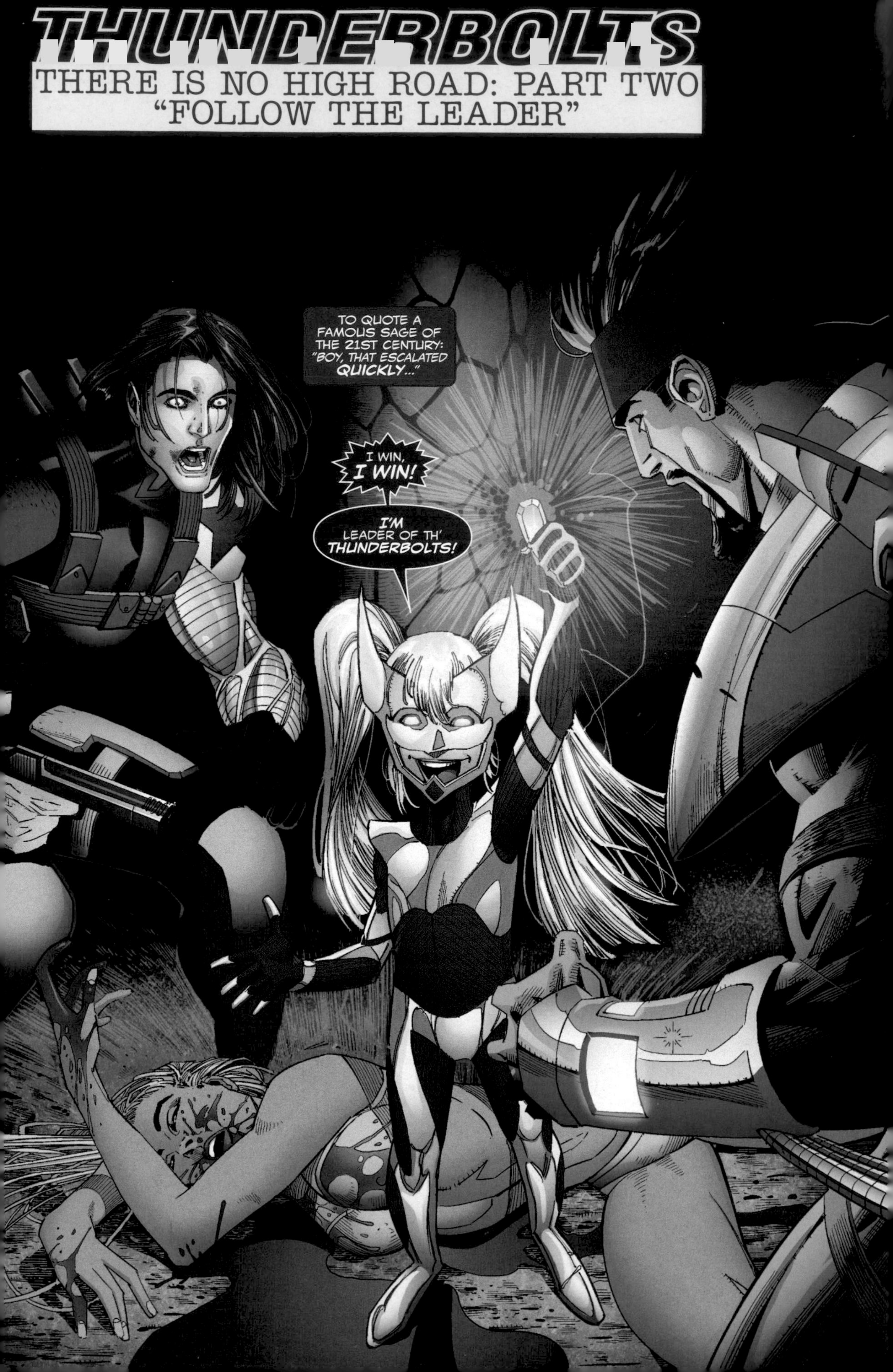
THUNDERBOLTS
THERE IS NO HIGH ROAD: PART TWO
"FOLLOW THE LEADER"
TO QUOTE A FAMOUS SAGE OF THE 21ST CENTURY: "BOY, THAT ESCALATED QUICKLY..."
I WIN, I WIN!
I'M LEADER OF TH' THUNDERBOLTS!

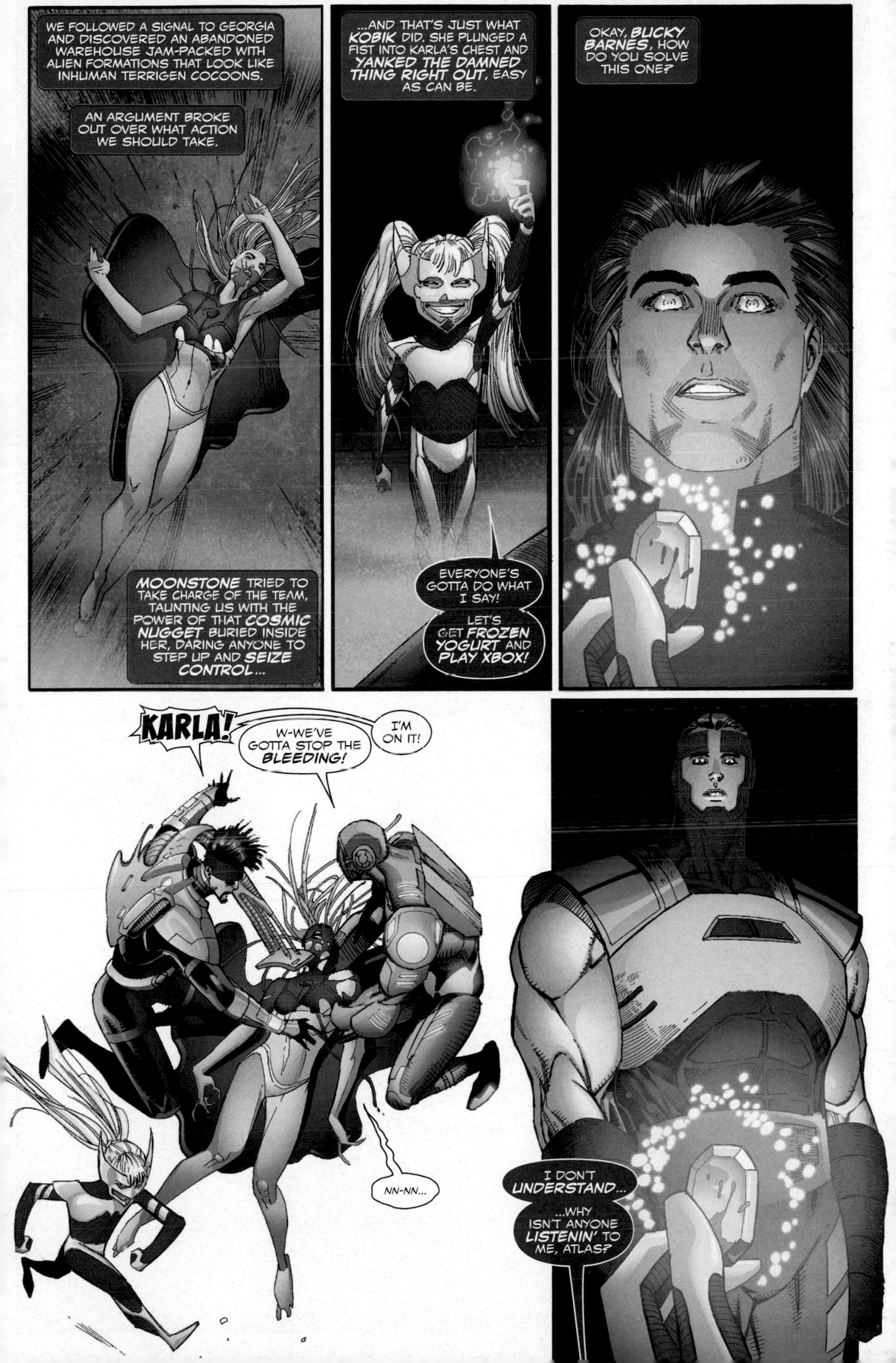
WE FOLLOWED A SIGNAL TO GEORGIA AND DISCOVERED AN ABANDONED WAREHOUSE JAM-PACKED WITH ALIEN FORMATIONS THAT LOOK LIKE INHUMAN TERRIGEN COCOONS.
AN ARGUMENT BROKE OUT OVER WHAT ACTION WE SHOULD TAKE.
MOONSTONE TRIED TO TAKE CHARGE OF THE TEAM, TAUNTING US WITH THE POWER OF THAT COSMIC NUGGET BURIED INSIDE HER, DARING ANYONE TO STEP UP AND SEIZE CONTROL...
...AND THAT'S JUST WHAT KOBIK DID. SHE PLUNGED A FIST INTO KARLA'S CHEST AND YANKED THE DAMNED THING RIGHT OUT, EASY AS CAN BE.
EVERYONE'S GOTTA DO WHAT I SAY!
LET'S GET FROZEN YOGURT AND PLAY XBOX!
OKAY, BUCKY BARNES, HOW DO YOU SOLVE THIS ONE?
KARLA!
W-WE'VE GOTTA STOP THE BLEEDING!
I'M ON IT!
NN-NN...
I DON'T UNDERSTAND...
...WHY ISN'T ANYONE LISTENIN' TO ME, ATLAS?

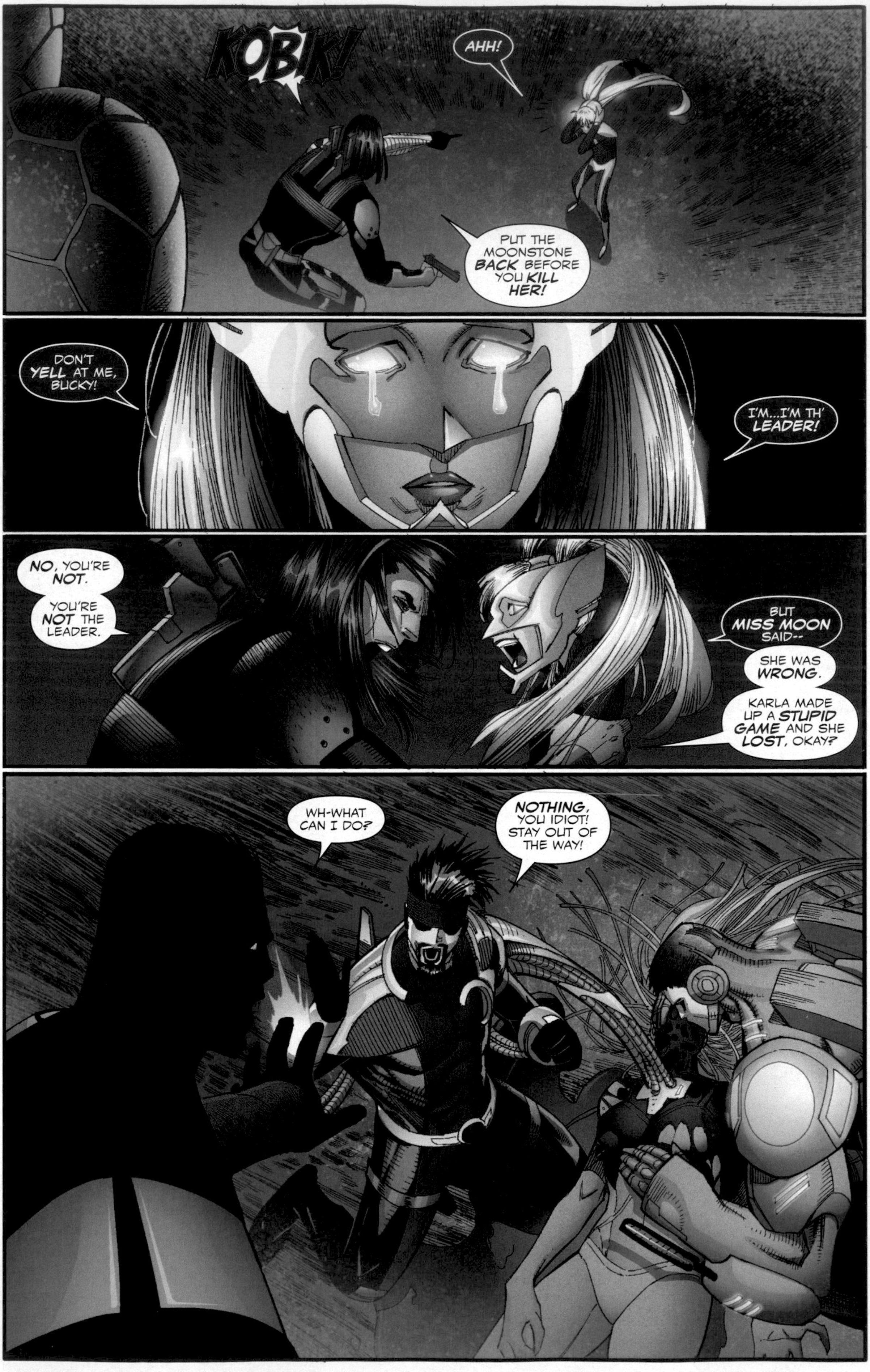
KOBIK!
AHH!
PUT THE MOONSTONE BACK BEFORE YOU KILL HER!
DON'T YELL AT ME, BUCKY!
I'M...I'M TH' LEADER!
NO, YOU'RE NOT.
YOU'RE NOT THE LEADER.
BUT MISS MOON SAID--
SHE WAS WRONG.
KARLA MADE UP A STUPID GAME AND SHE LOST, OKAY?
WH-WHAT CAN I DO?
NOTHING, YOU IDIOT! STAY OUT OF THE WAY!

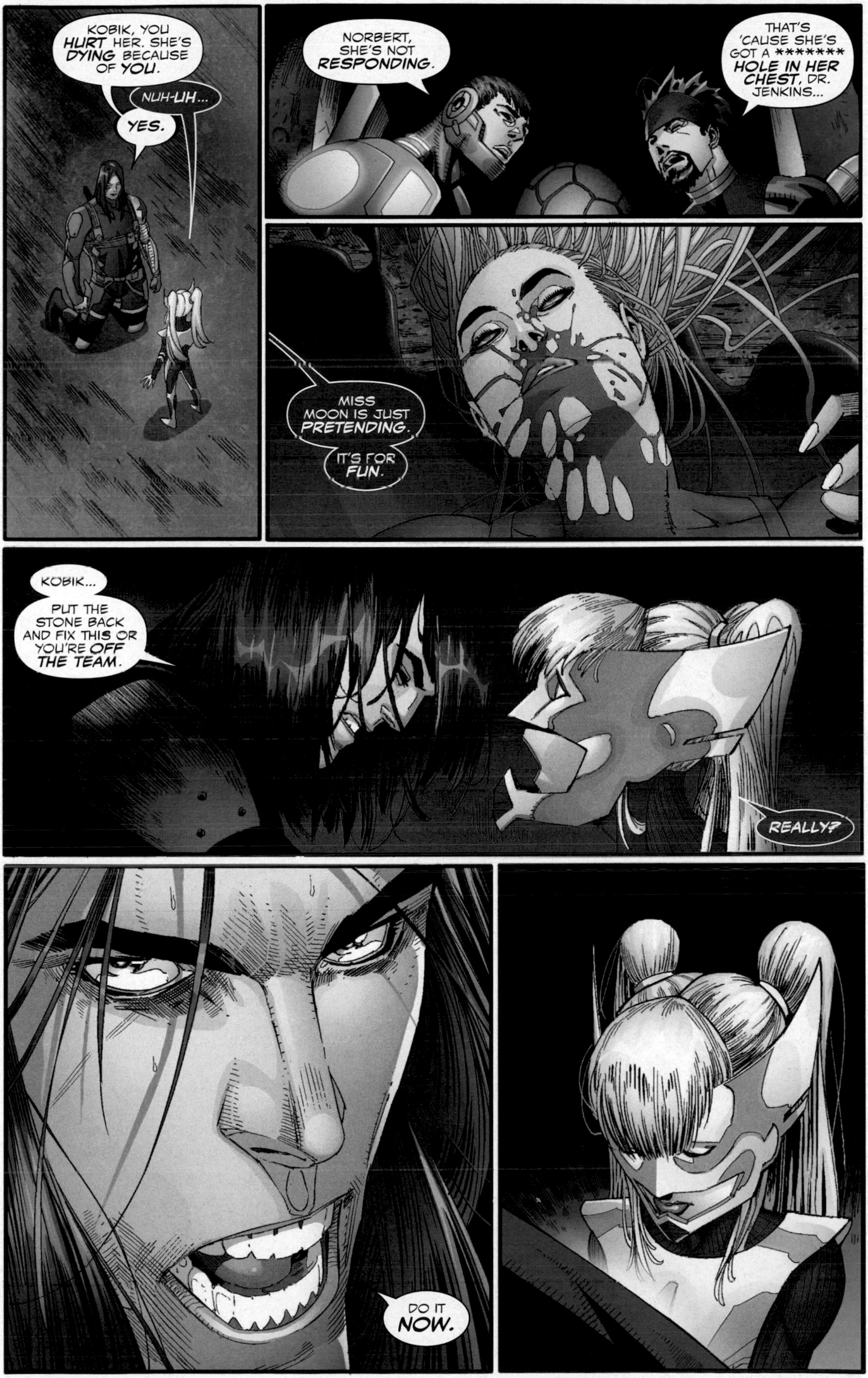
KOBIK, YOU HURT HER. SHE'S DYING BECAUSE OF YOU.
NUH-UH...
YES.
NORBERT, SHE'S NOT RESPONDING.
THAT'S 'CAUSE SHE'S GOT A ******* HOLE IN HER CHEST, DR. JENKINS...
MISS MOON IS JUST PRETENDING.
IT'S FOR FUN.
KOBIK...
PUT THE STONE BACK AND FIX THIS OR YOU'RE OFF THE TEAM.
REALLY?
DO IT NOW.

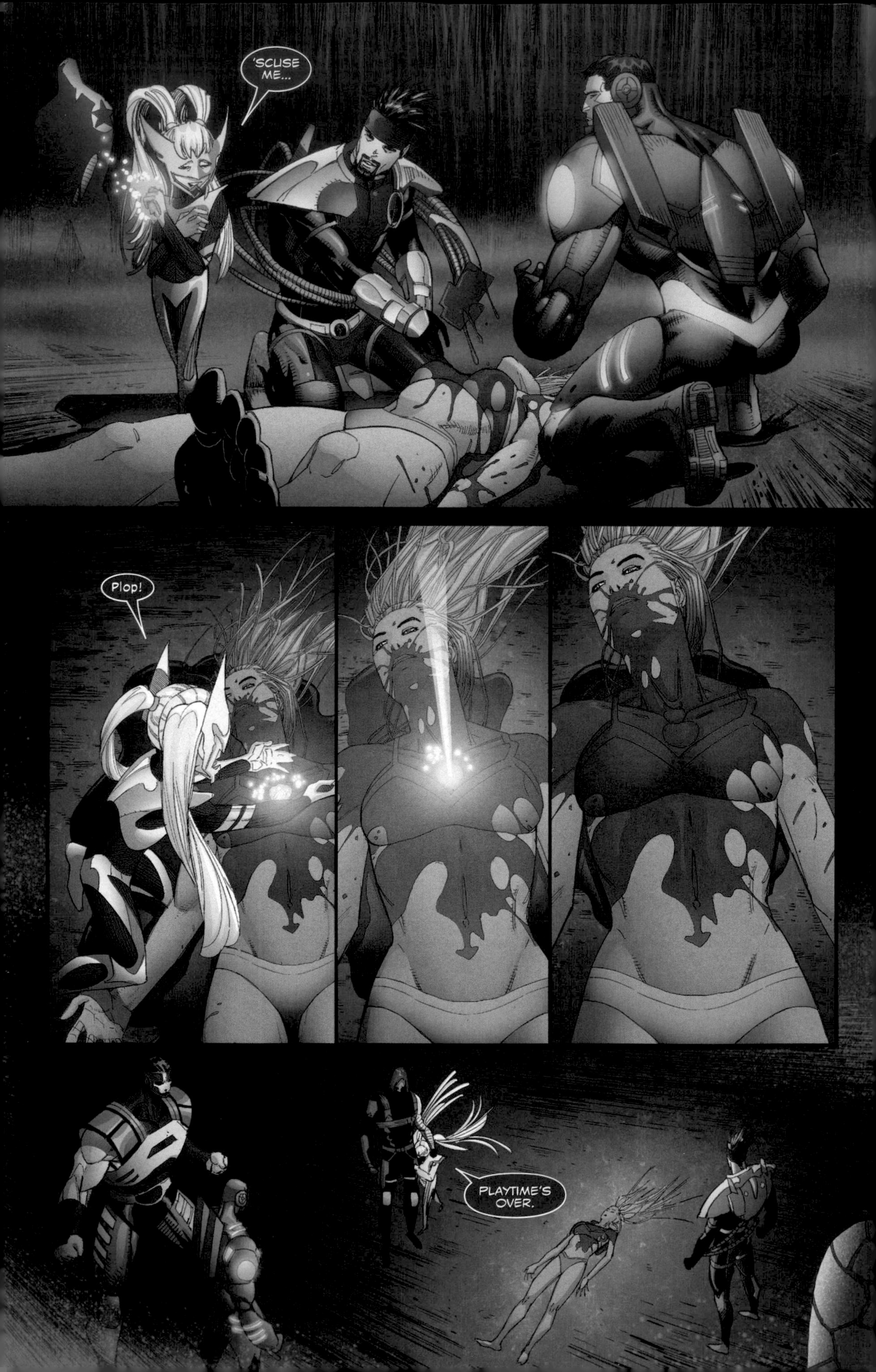
'SCUSE ME...
Plop!
PLAYTIME'S OVER.

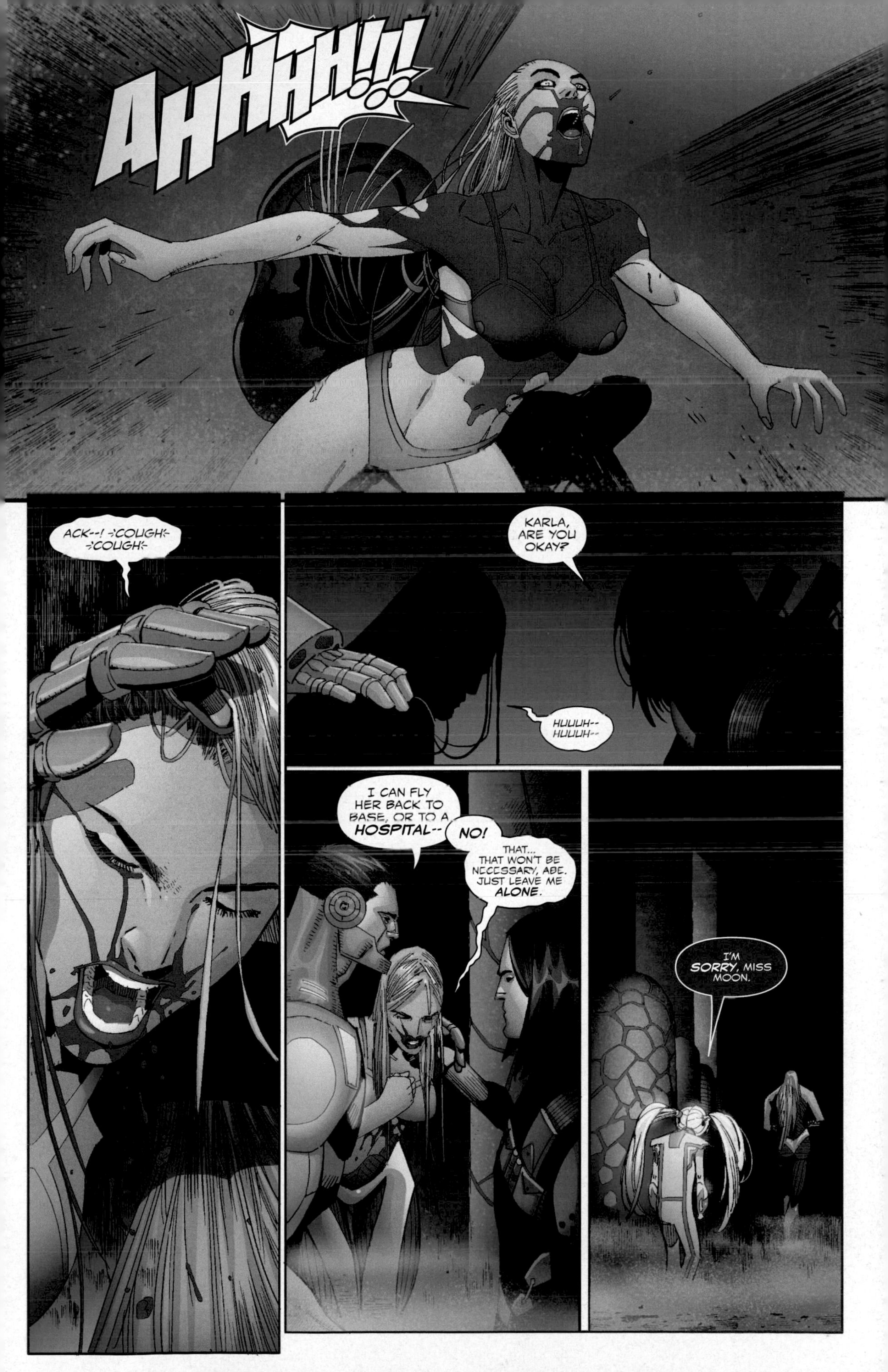
AHHHH!!!
ACK--! -COUGH- -COUGH-
KARLA, ARE YOU OKAY?
HUUUH-- HUUUH--
I CAN FLY HER BACK TO BASE, OR TO A HOSPITAL--
NO!
THAT... THAT WON'T BE NECESSARY, ABE. JUST LEAVE ME ALONE.
I'M SORRY, MISS MOON.

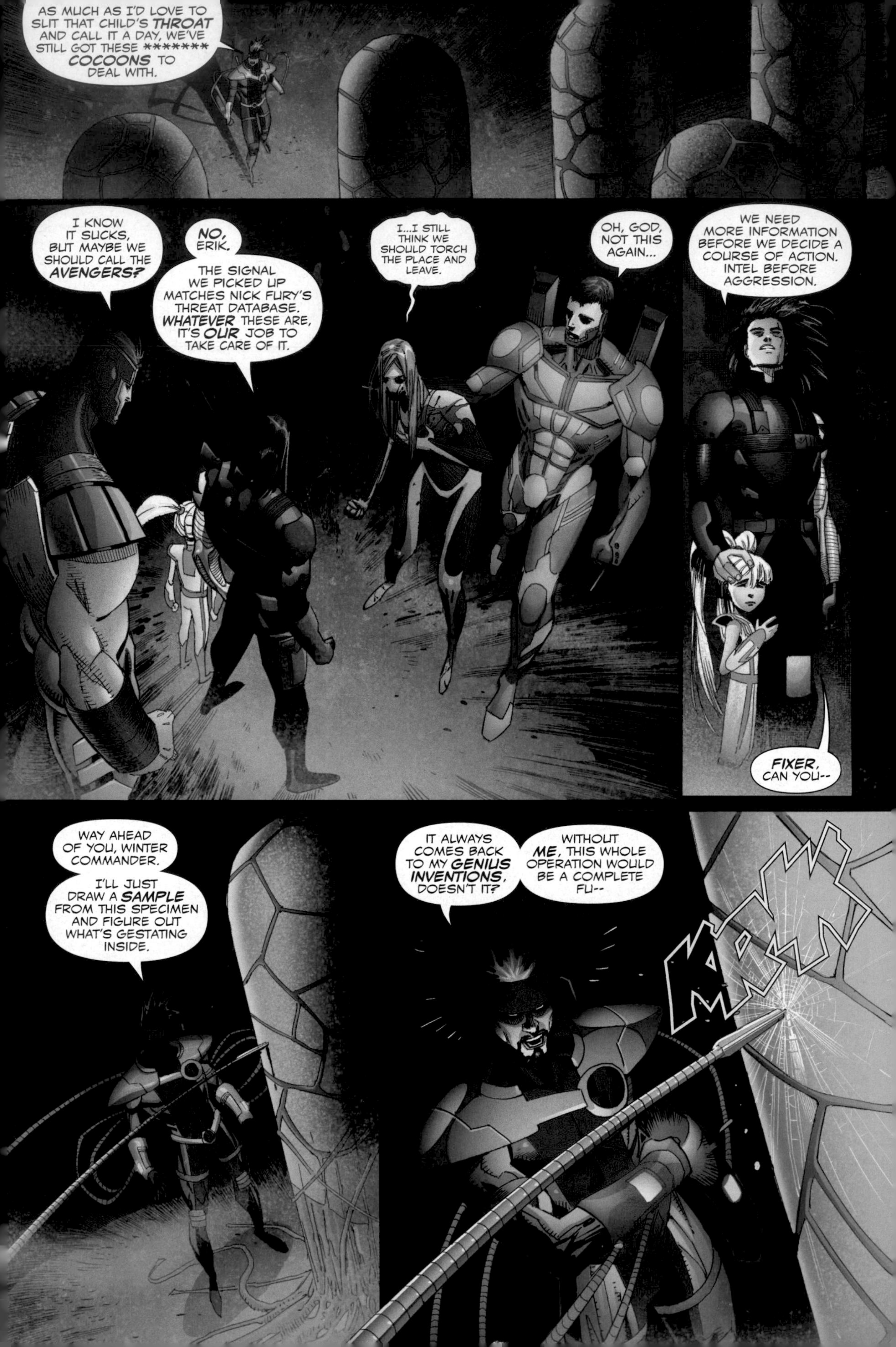
AS MUCH AS I'D LOVE TO SLIT THAT CHILD'S THROAT AND CALL IT A DAY, WE'VE STILL GOT THESE ******* COCOONS TO DEAL WITH.
I KNOW IT SUCKS, BUT MAYBE WE SHOULD CALL THE AVENGERS?
NO, ERIK.
THE SIGNAL WE PICKED UP MATCHES NICK FURY'S THREAT DATABASE. WHATEVER THESE ARE, IT'S OUR JOB TO TAKE CARE OF IT.
I...I STILL THINK WE SHOULD TORCH THE PLACE AND LEAVE.
OH, GOD, NOT THIS AGAIN...
WE NEED MORE INFORMATION BEFORE WE DECIDE A COURSE OF ACTION. INTEL BEFORE AGGRESSION.
FIXER, CAN YOU--
WAY AHEAD OF YOU, WINTER COMMANDER.
I'LL JUST DRAW A SAMPLE FROM THIS SPECIMEN AND FIGURE OUT WHAT'S GESTATING INSIDE.
IT ALWAYS COMES BACK TO MY GENIUS INVENTIONS, DOESN'T IT?
WITHOUT ME, THIS WHOLE OPERATION WOULD BE A COMPLETE FU--

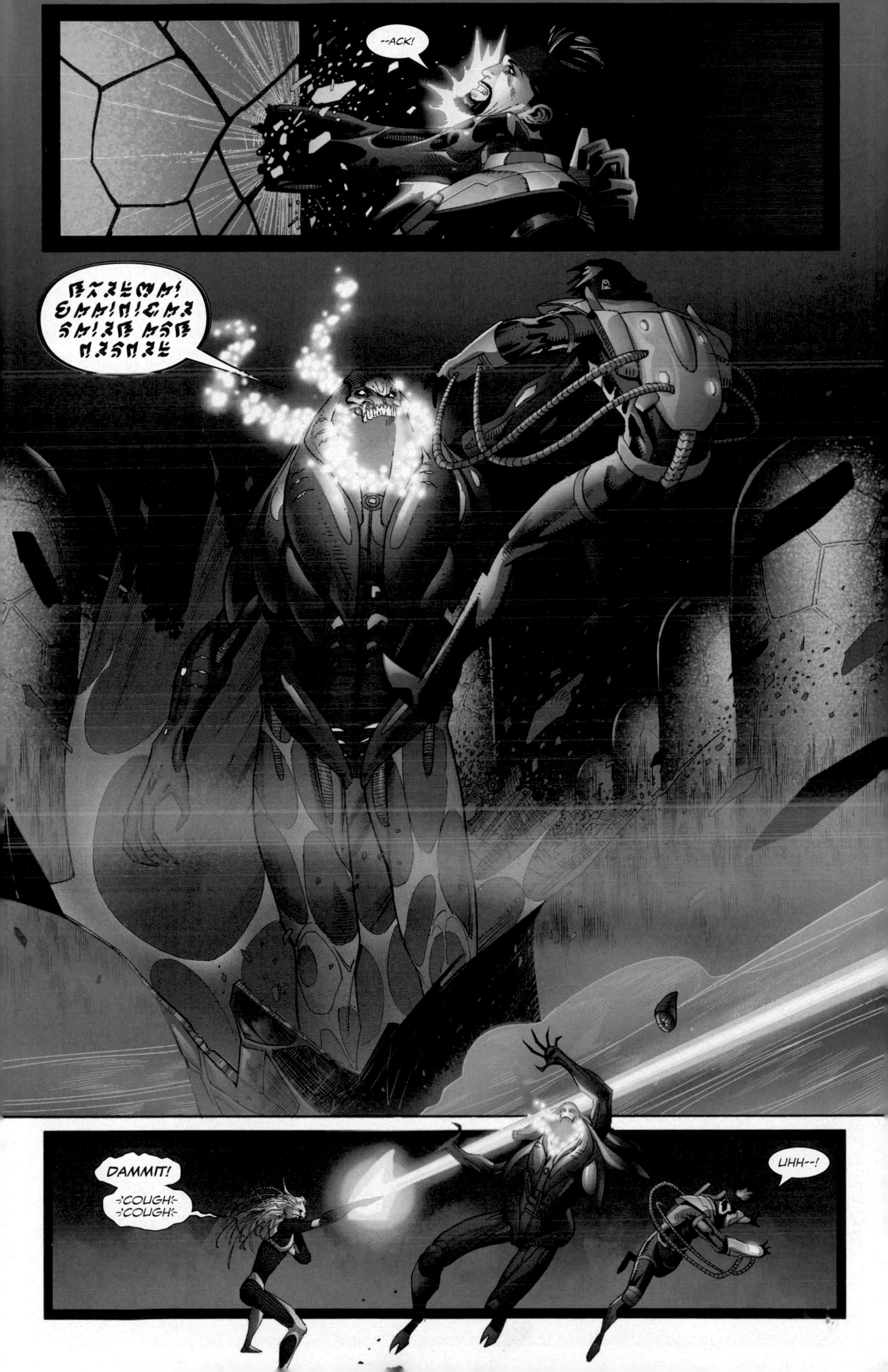
--ACK!
DAMMIT!
COUGH
COUGH
UHH--!

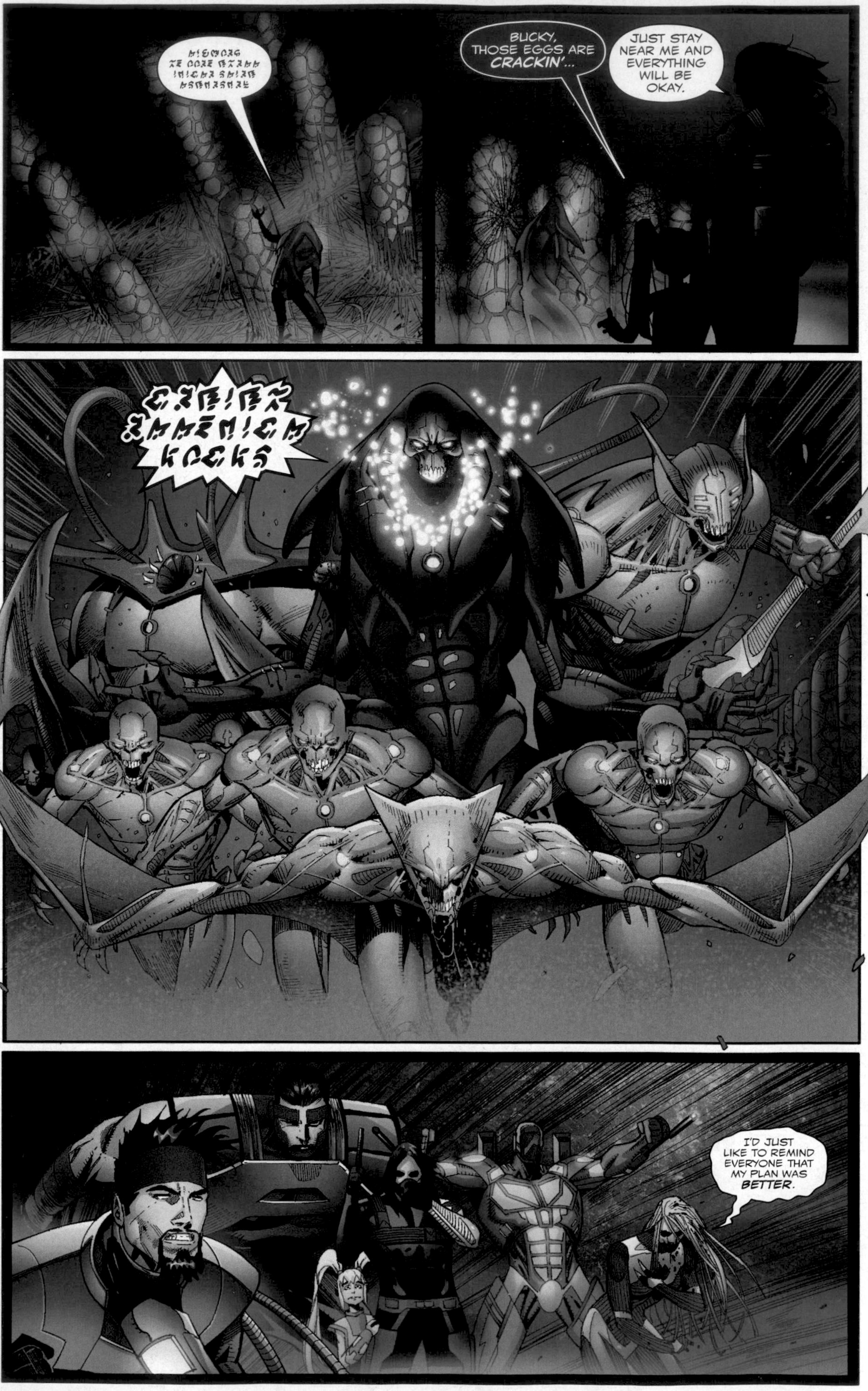
BUCKY, THOSE EGGS ARE CRACKIN'...
JUST STAY NEAR ME AND EVERYTHING WILL BE OKAY.
I'D JUST LIKE TO REMIND EVERYONE THAT MY PLAN WAS BETTER.

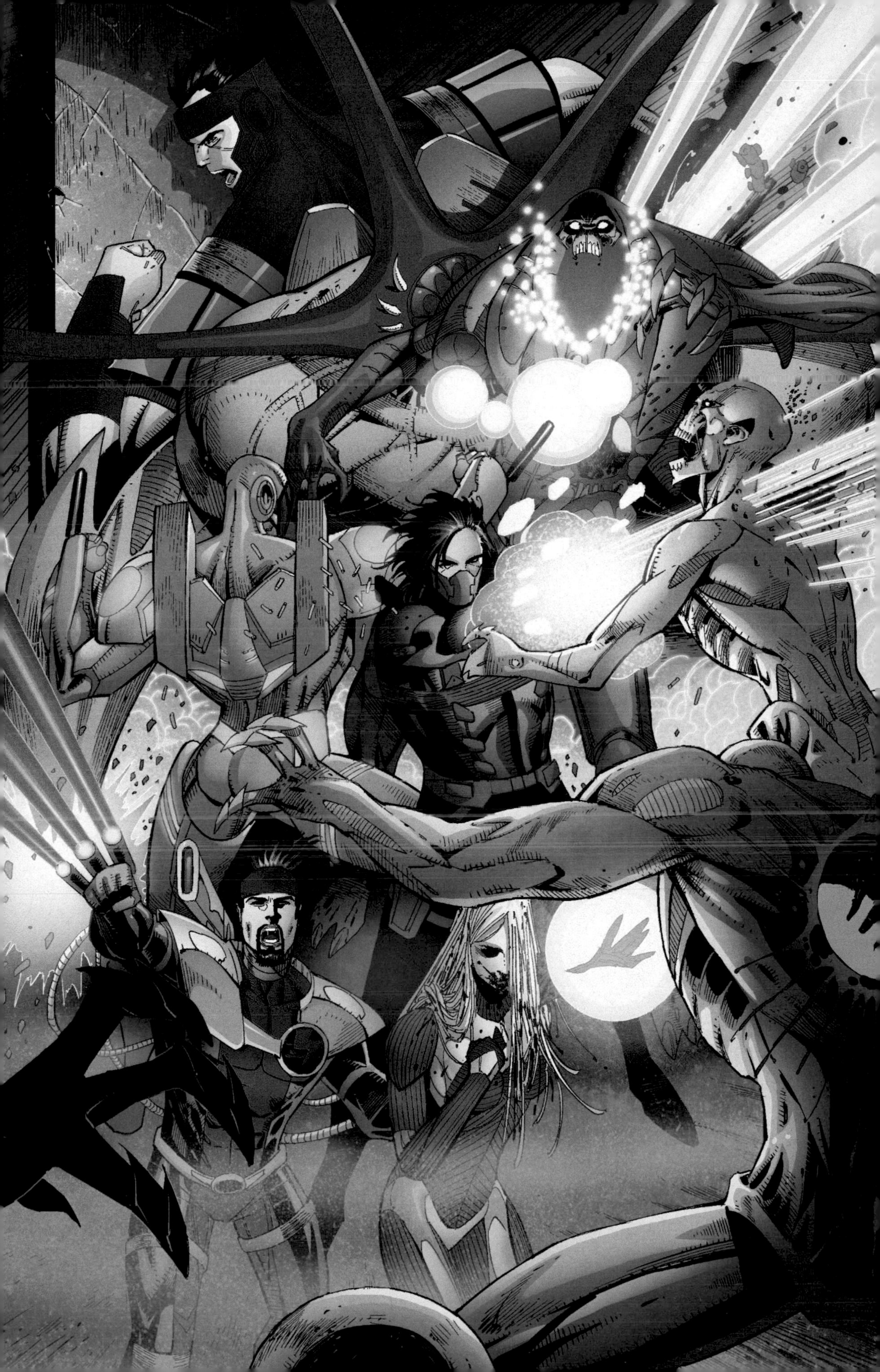

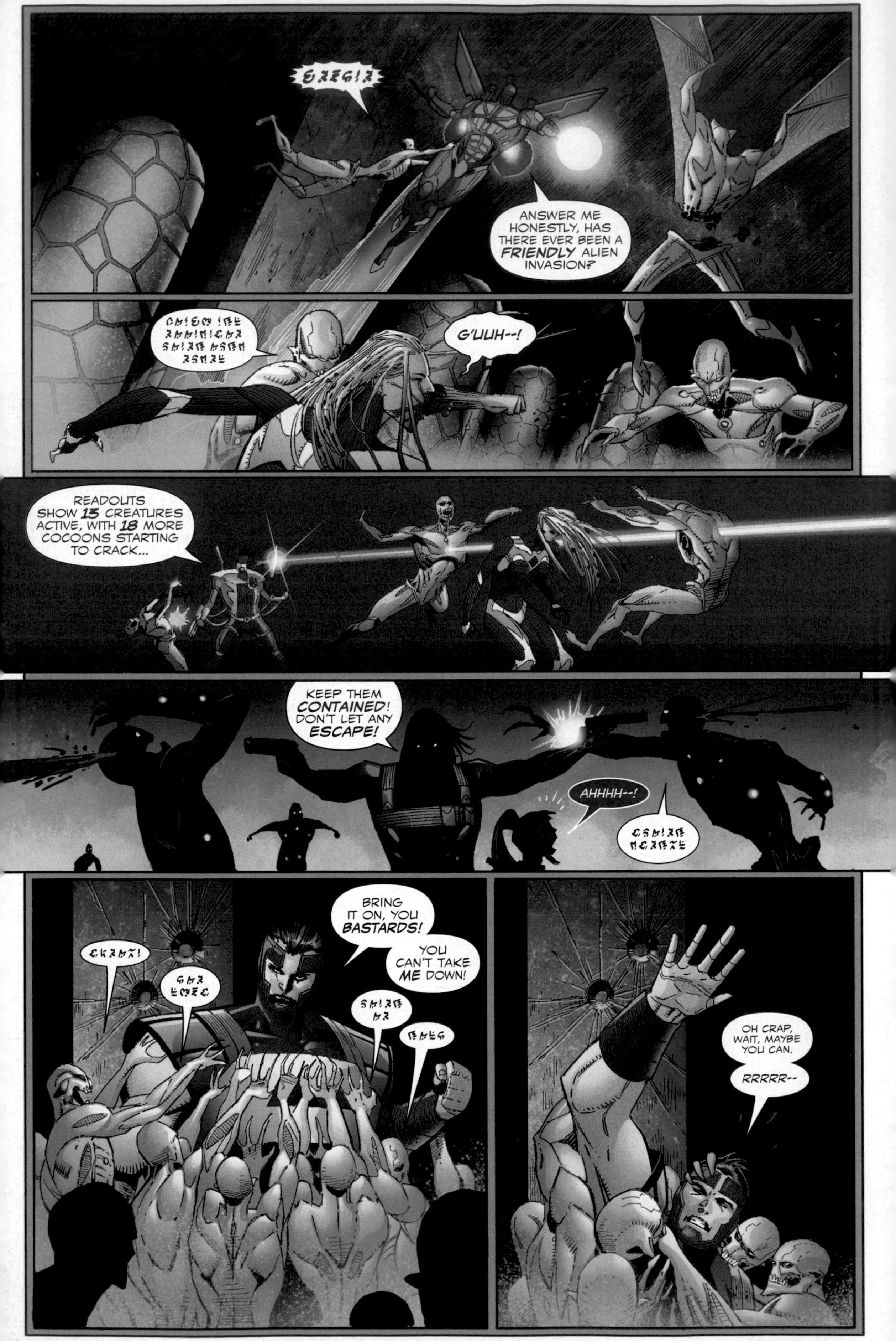

ANSWER ME HONESTLY, HAS THERE EVER BEEN A FRIENDLY ALIEN INVASION?
G'UUH--!
READOUTS SHOW 13 CREATURES ACTIVE, WITH 18 MORE COCOONS STARTING TO CRACK...
KEEP THEM CONTAINED! DON'T LET ANY ESCAPE!
AHHHH--!
BRING IT ON, YOU BASTARDS!
YOU CAN'T TAKE ME DOWN!
OH CRAP, WAIT, MAYBE YOU CAN.
RRRRR--

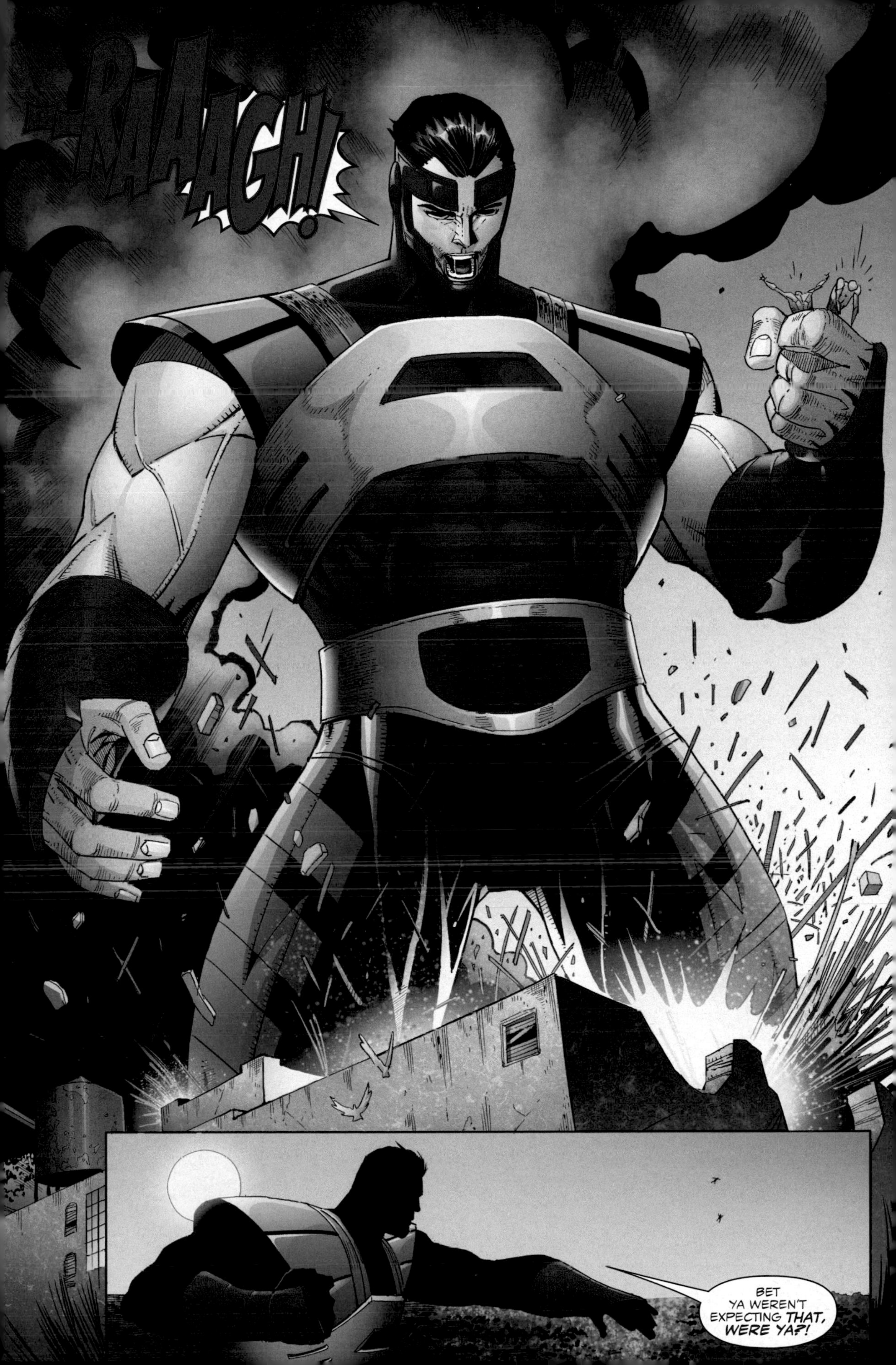
RAAAGH!
BET YA WEREN'T EXPECTING THAT, WERE YA?!

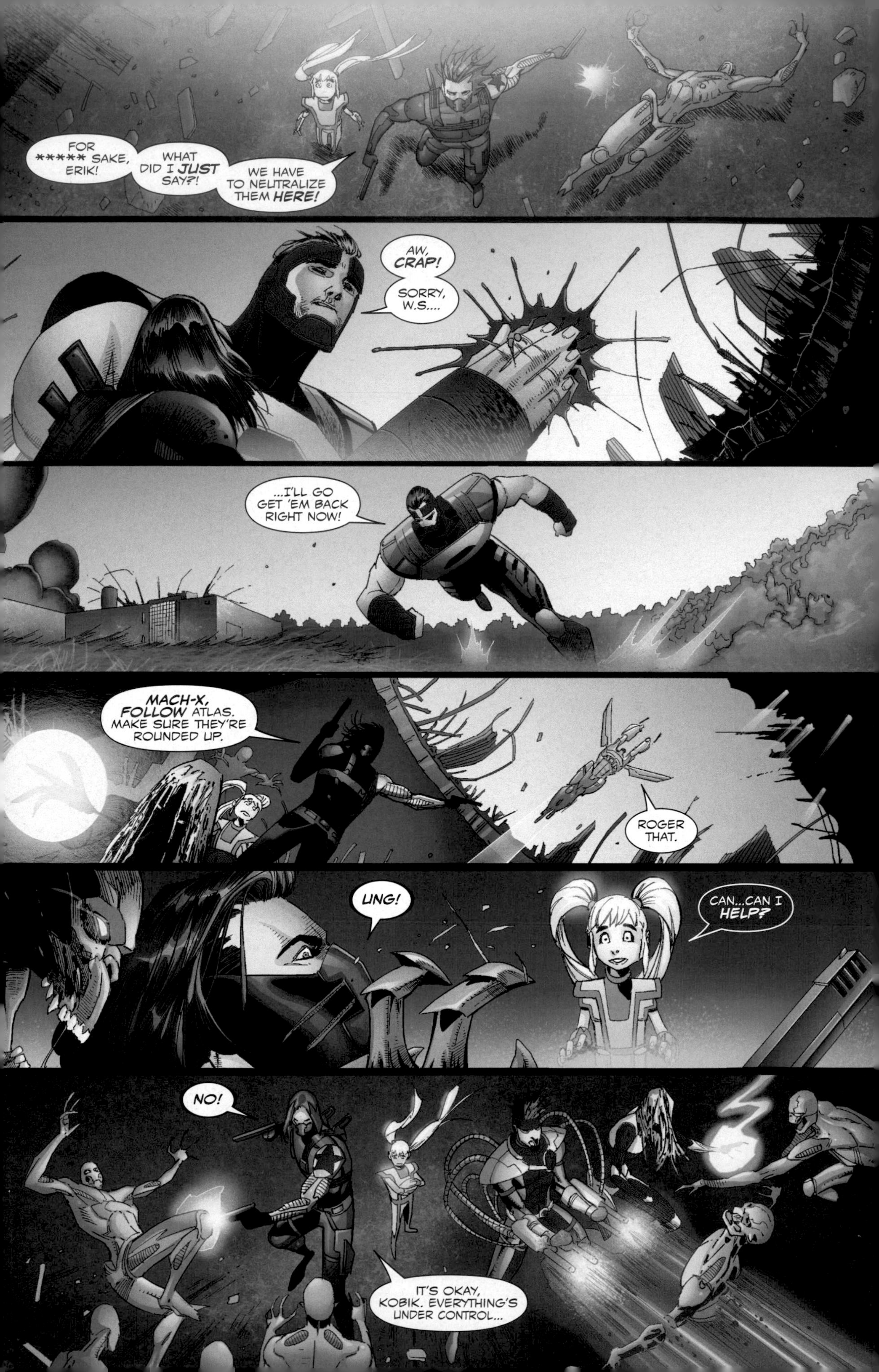
FOR ***** SAKE, ERIK!
WHAT DID I JUST SAY?!
WE HAVE TO NEUTRALIZE THEM HERE!
AW, CRAP!
SORRY, W.S....
...I'LL GO GET 'EM BACK RIGHT NOW!
MACH-X, FOLLOW ATLAS. MAKE SURE THEY'RE ROUNDED UP.
ROGER THAT.
UNG!
CAN...CAN I HELP?
NO!
IT'S OKAY, KOBIK. EVERYTHING'S UNDER CONTROL...

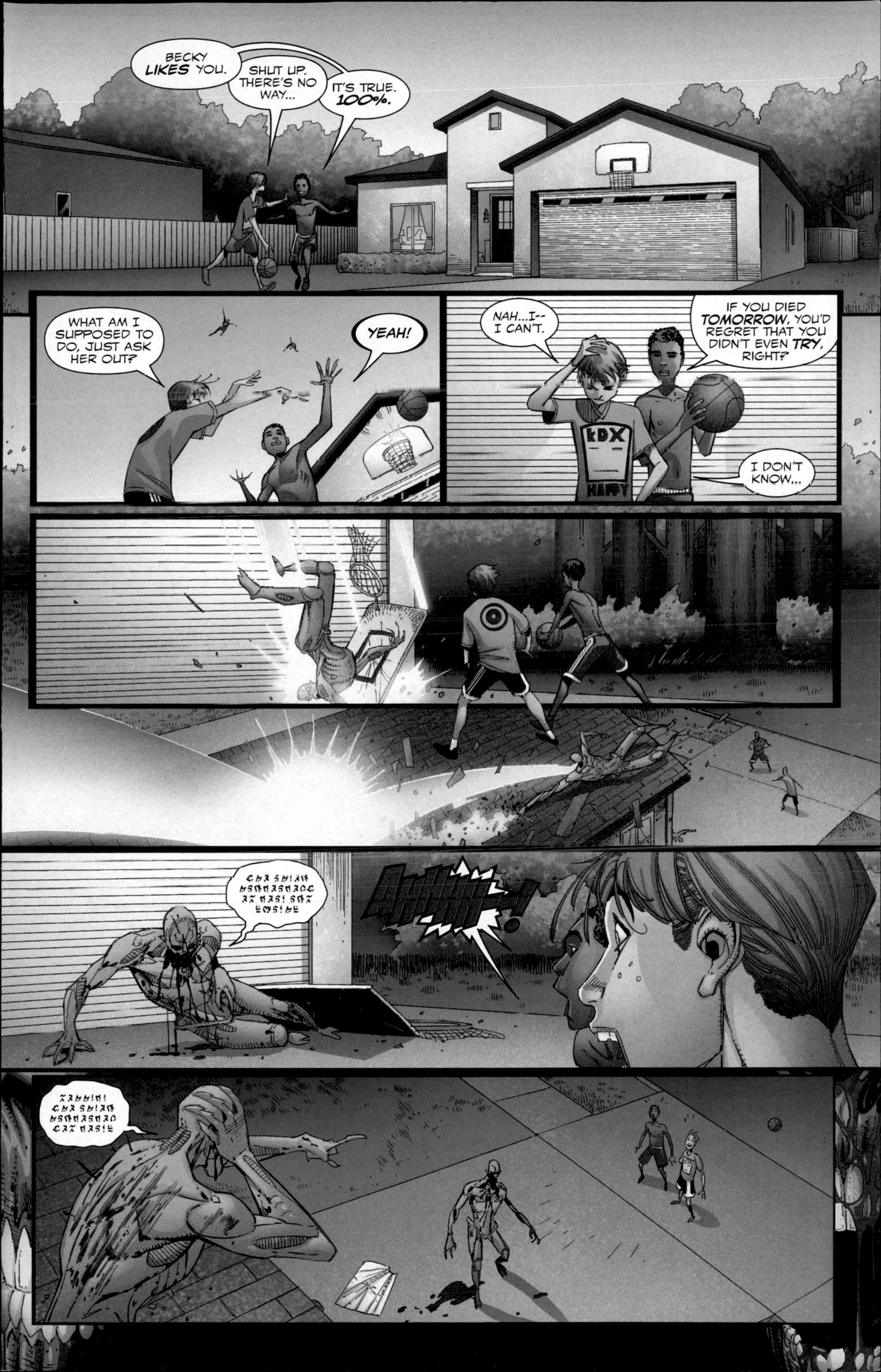
BECKY LIKES YOU.
SHUT UP. THERE'S NO WAY...
IT'S TRUE. 100%.
WHAT AM I SUPPOSED TO DO, JUST ASK HER OUT?
YEAH!
NAH...I-- I CAN'T.
IF YOU DIED TOMORROW, YOU'D REGRET THAT YOU DIDN'T EVEN TRY, RIGHT?
I DON'T KNOW...
kDX
HAPPY
AHHHH--!

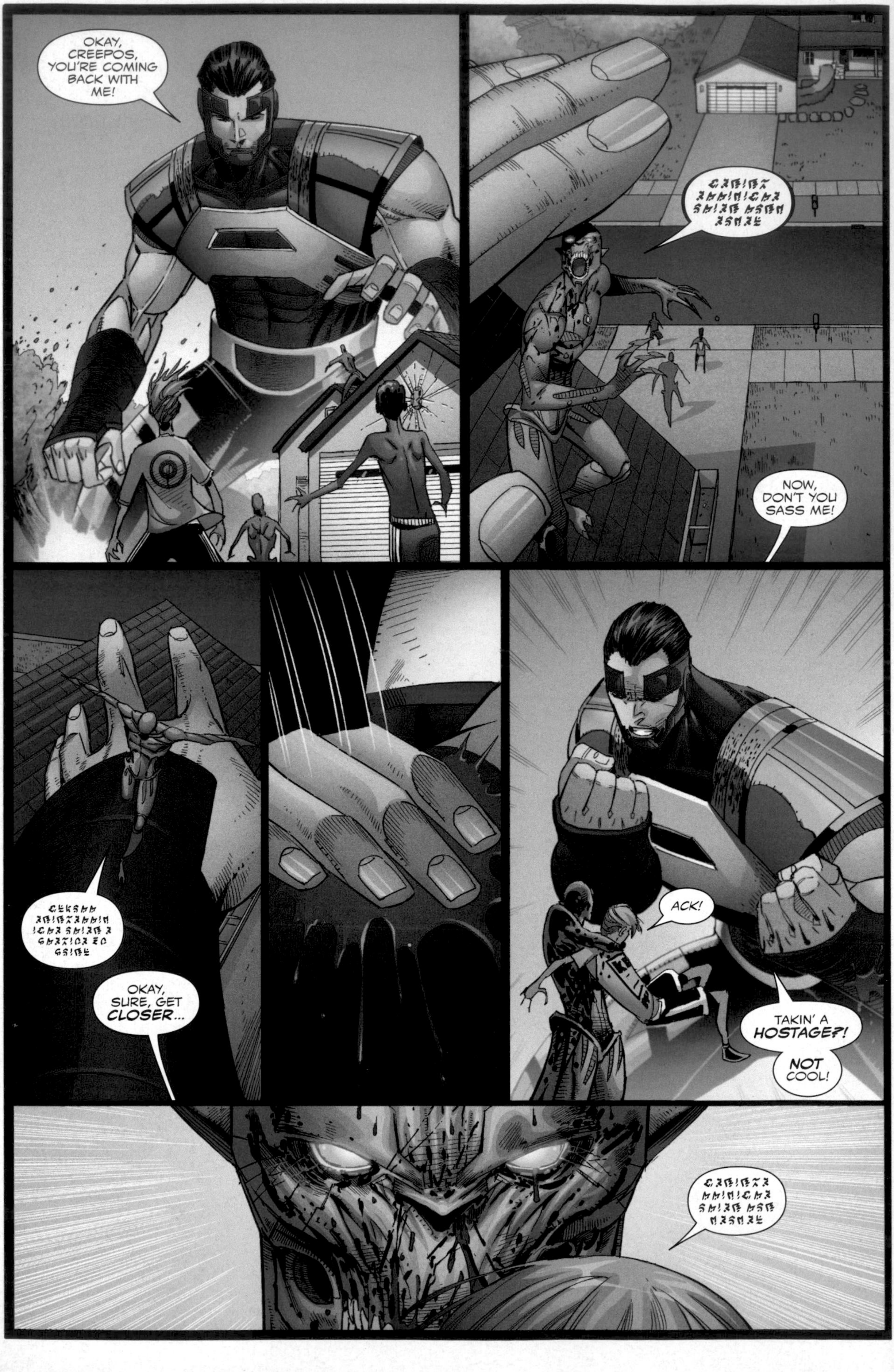
OKAY, CREEPOS, YOU'RE COMING BACK WITH ME!
NOW, DON'T YOU SASS ME!
OKAY, SURE, GET CLOSER...
ACK!
TAKIN' A HOSTAGE?!
NOT COOL!

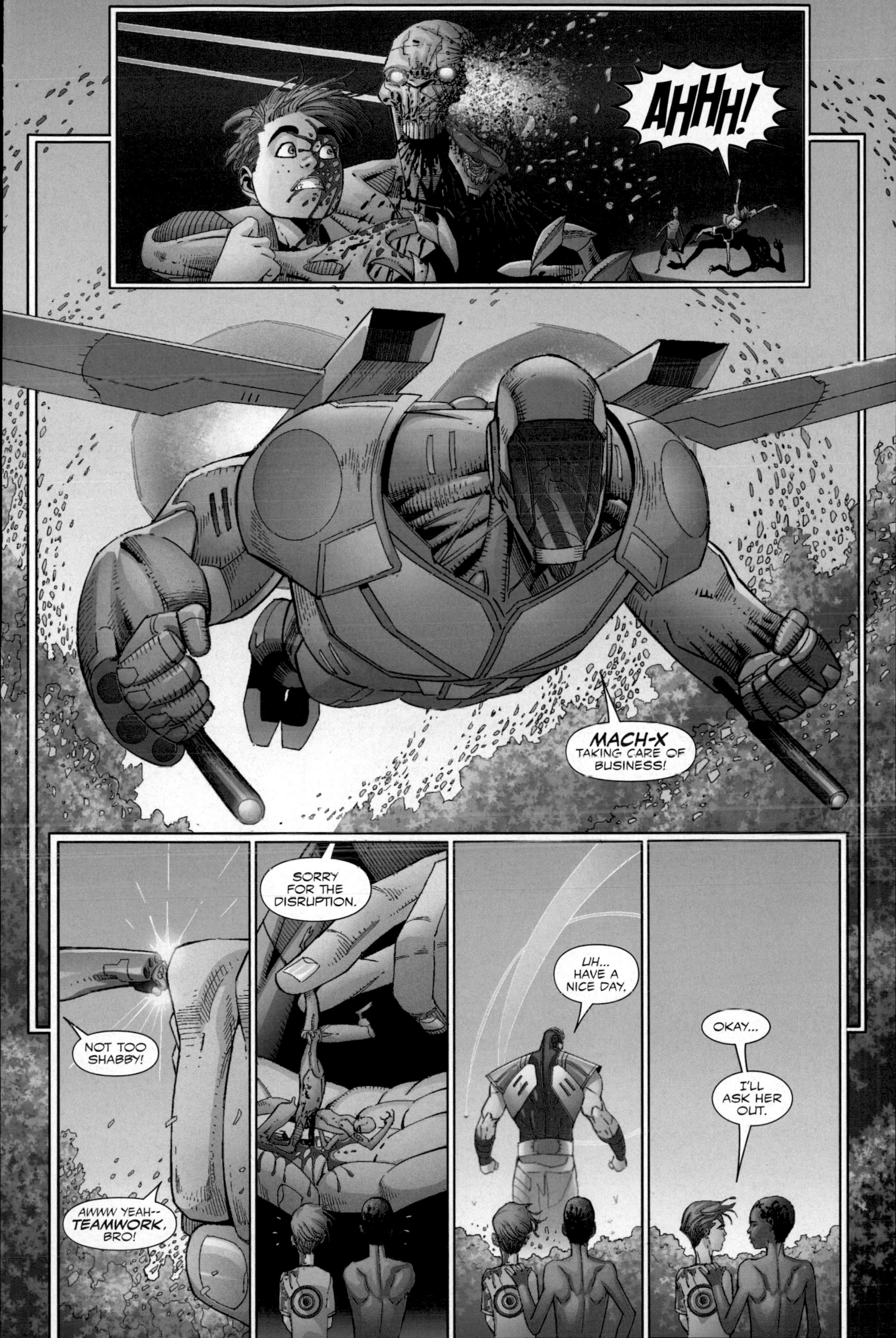
AHHH!
MACH-X TAKING CARE OF BUSINESS!
NOT TOO SHABBY!
AWWW YEAH-- TEAMWORK, BRO!
SORRY FOR THE DISRUPTION.
UH... HAVE A NICE DAY.
OKAY...
I'LL ASK HER OUT.

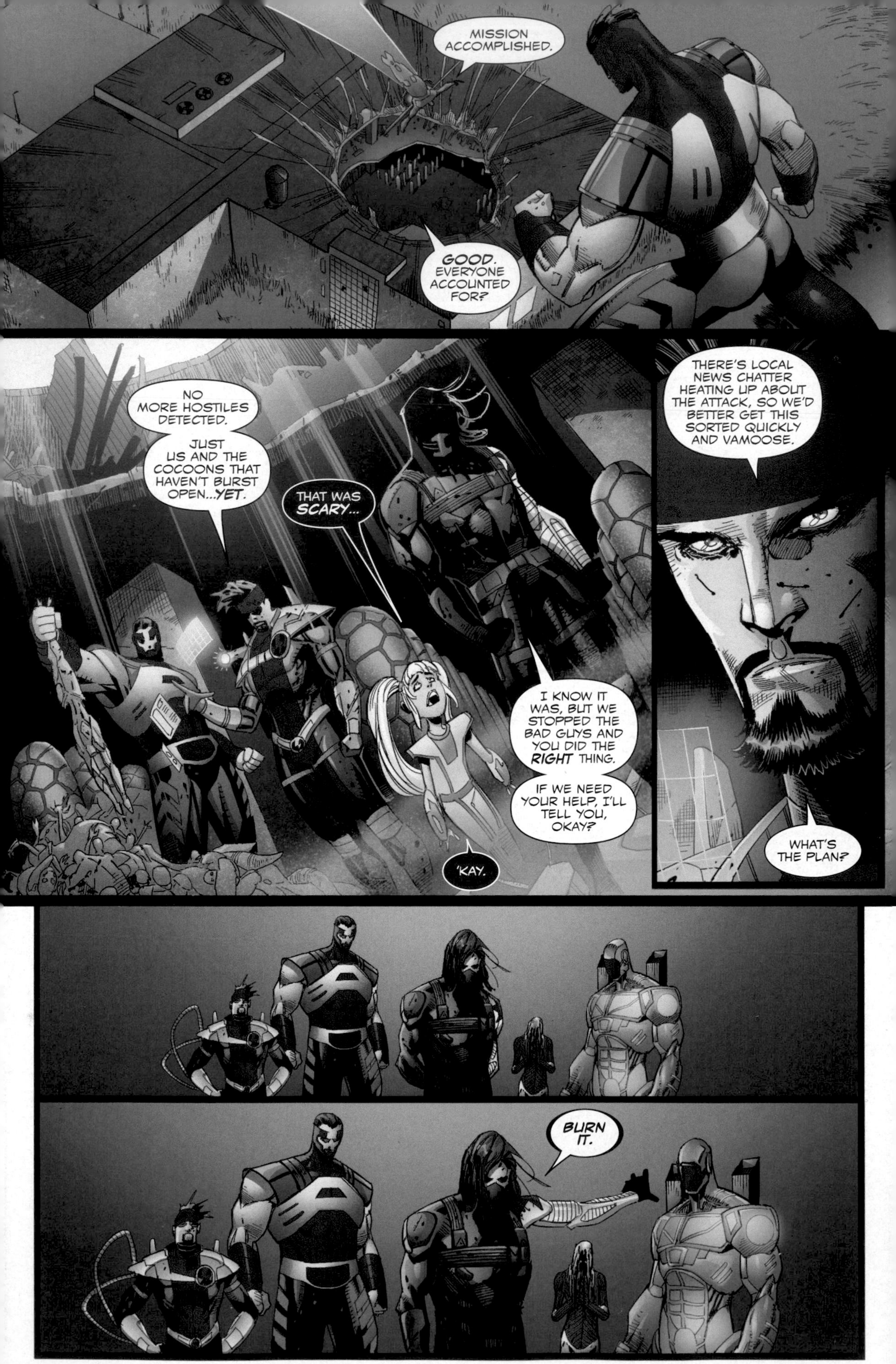
MISSION ACCOMPLISHED.
GOOD. EVERYONE ACCOUNTED FOR?
NO MORE HOSTILES DETECTED.
JUST US AND THE COCOONS THAT HAVEN'T BURST OPEN...YET.
THAT WAS SCARY...
I KNOW IT WAS, BUT WE STOPPED THE BAD GUYS AND YOU DID THE RIGHT THING.
IF WE NEED YOUR HELP, I'LL TELL YOU, OKAY?
'KAY.
THERE'S LOCAL NEWS CHATTER HEATING UP ABOUT THE ATTACK, SO WE'D BETTER GET THIS SORTED QUICKLY AND VAMOOSE.
WHAT'S THE PLAN?
BURN IT.

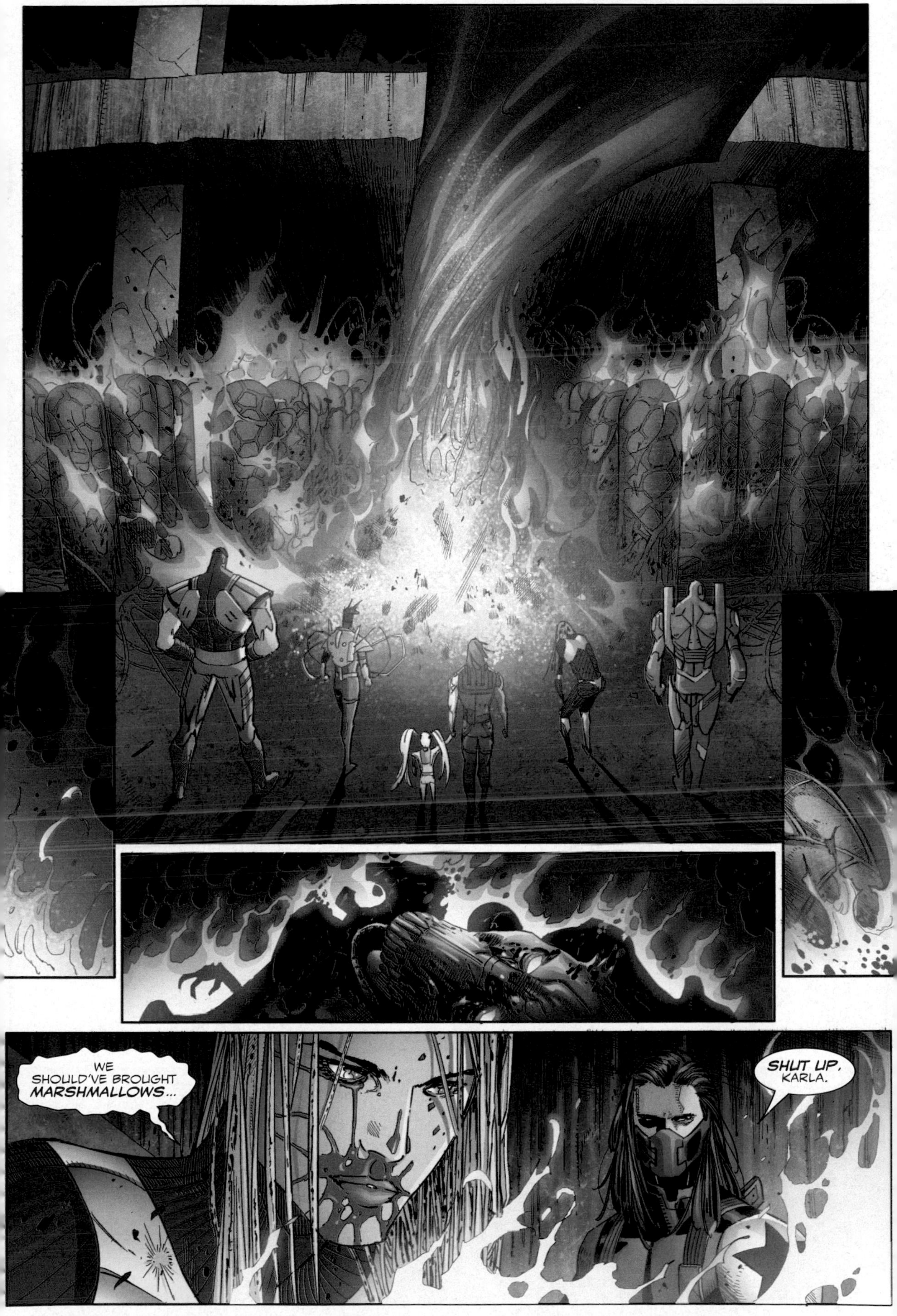
WE SHOULD'VE BROUGHT MARSHMALLOWS...
SHUT UP, KARLA.

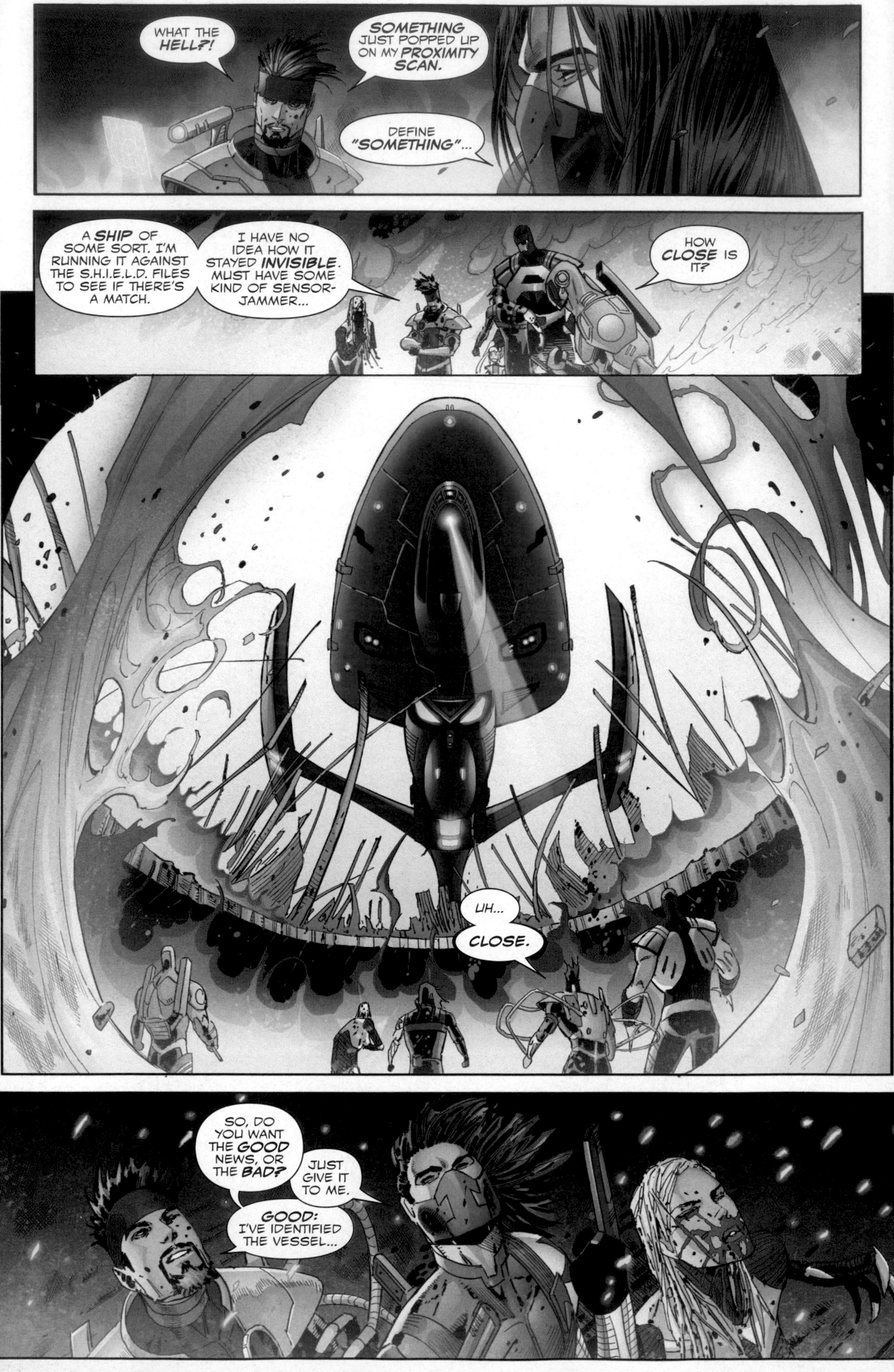
WHAT THE HELL?!
SOMETHING JUST POPPED UP ON MY PROXIMITY SCAN.
DEFINE "SOMETHING"...
A SHIP OF SOME SORT. I'M RUNNING IT AGAINST THE S.H.I.E.L.D. FILES TO SEE IF THERE'S A MATCH.
I HAVE NO IDEA HOW IT STAYED INVISIBLE. MUST HAVE SOME KIND OF SENSOR-JAMMER...
HOW CLOSE IS IT?
UH...
CLOSE.
SO, DO YOU WANT THE GOOD NEWS, OR THE BAD?
JUST GIVE IT TO ME.
GOOD: I'VE IDENTIFIED THE VESSEL...

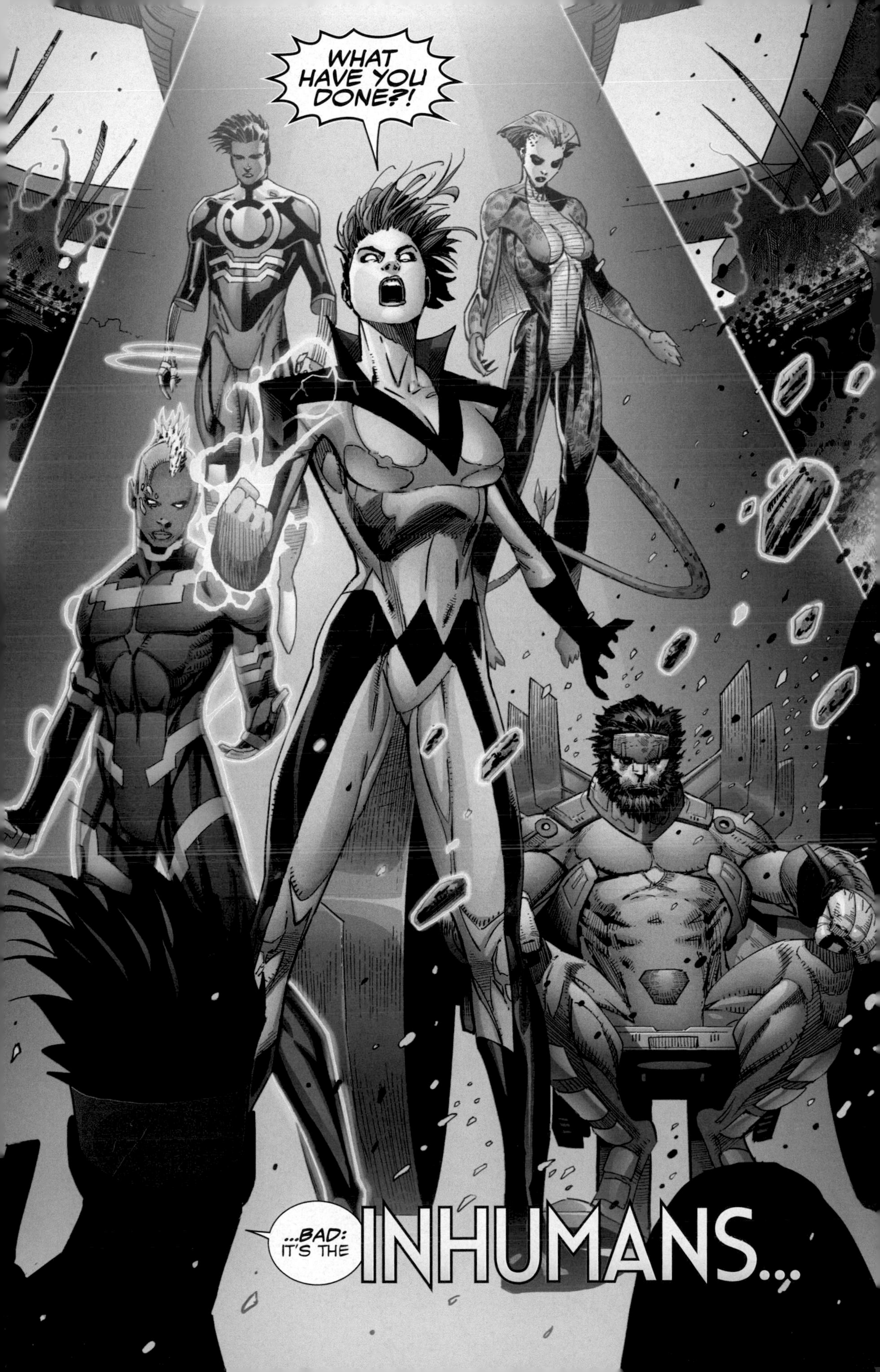
WHAT HAVE YOU DONE?!
...BAD: IT'S THE
INHUMANS...

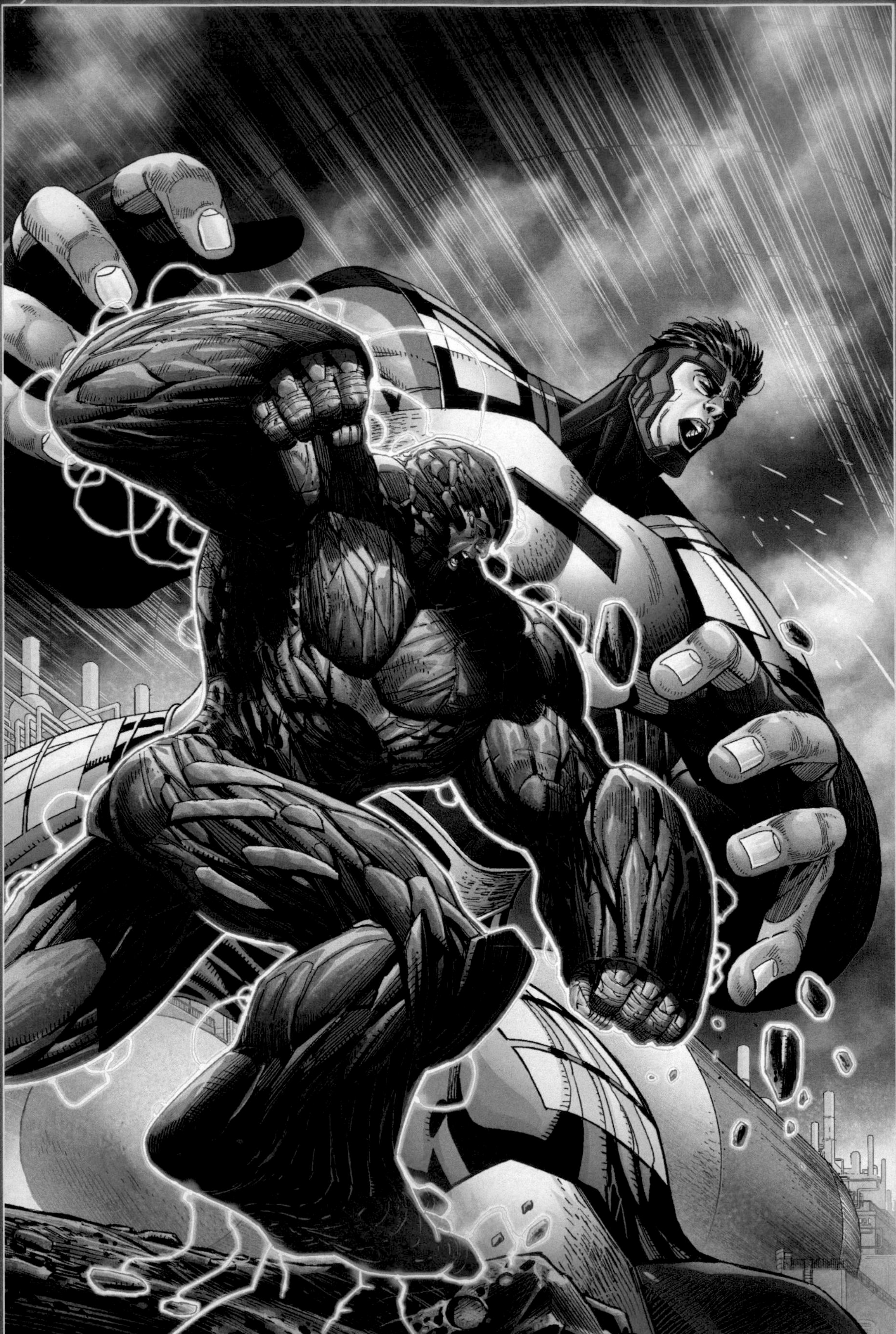

3: MISTAKES WERE MADE

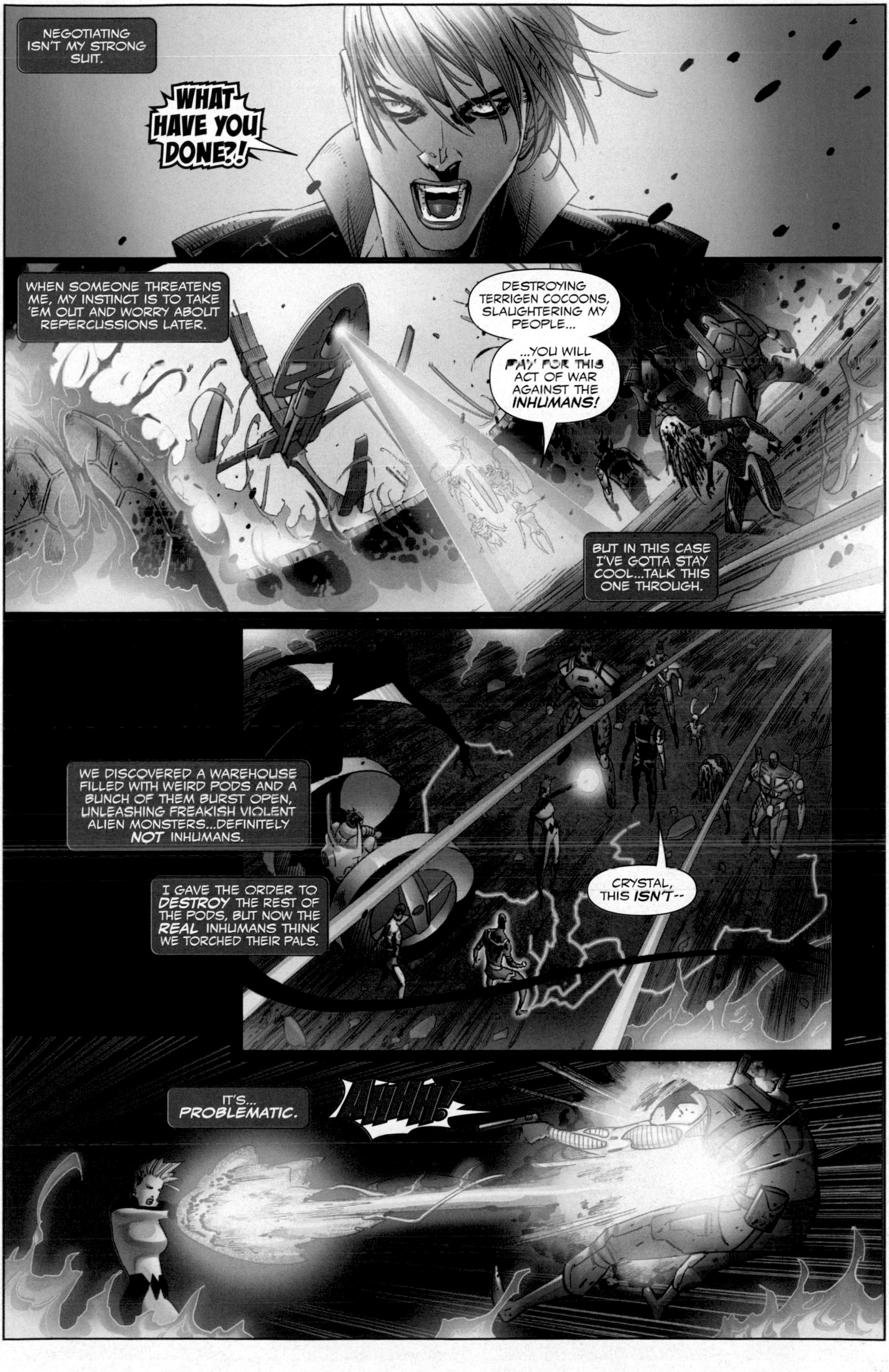
NEGOTIATING ISN'T MY STRONG SUIT.
WHAT HAVE YOU DONE?!
WHEN SOMEONE THREATENS ME, MY INSTINCT IS TO TAKE 'EM OUT AND WORRY ABOUT REPERCUSSIONS LATER.
DESTROYING TERRIGEN COCOONS, SLAUGHTERING MY PEOPLE...
...YOU WILL PAY FOR THIS ACT OF WAR AGAINST THE INHUMANS!
BUT IN THIS CASE I'VE GOTTA STAY COOL...TALK THIS ONE THROUGH.
WE DISCOVERED A WAREHOUSE FILLED WITH WEIRD PODS AND A BUNCH OF THEM BURST OPEN, UNLEASHING FREAKISH VIOLENT ALIEN MONSTERS...DEFINITELY NOT INHUMANS.
I GAVE THE ORDER TO DESTROY THE REST OF THE PODS, BUT NOW THE REAL INHUMANS THINK WE TORCHED THEIR PALS.
CRYSTAL, THIS ISN'T--
IT'S... PROBLEMATIC.
AHHH!

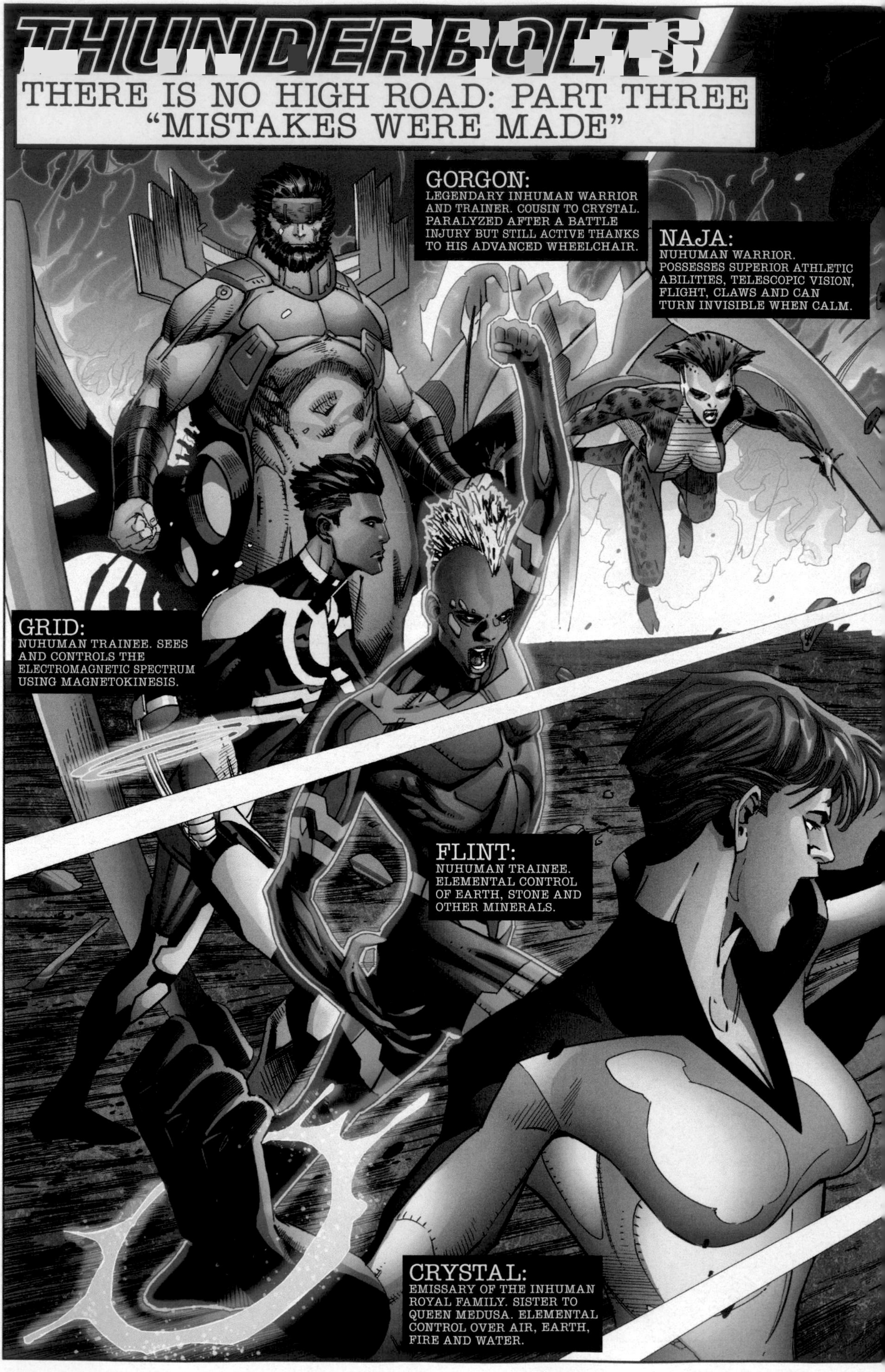
THUNDERBOLTS
THERE IS NO HIGH ROAD: PART THREE
"MISTAKES WERE MADE"
GORGON:
LEGENDARY INHUMAN WARRIOR AND TRAINER. COUSIN TO CRYSTAL. PARALYZED AFTER A BATTLE INJURY BUT STILL ACTIVE THANKS TO HIS ADVANCED WHEELCHAIR.
NAJA:
NUHUMAN WARRIOR. POSSESSES SUPERIOR ATHLETIC ABILITIES, TELESCOPIC VISION, FLIGHT, CLAWS AND CAN TURN INVISIBLE WHEN CALM.
GRID:
NUHUMAN TRAINEE. SEES AND CONTROLS THE ELECTROMAGNETIC SPECTRUM USING MAGNETOKINESIS.
FLINT:
NUHUMAN TRAINEE. ELEMENTAL CONTROL OF EARTH, STONE AND OTHER MINERALS.
CRYSTAL:
EMISSARY OF THE INHUMAN ROYAL FAMILY. SISTER TO QUEEN MEDUSA. ELEMENTAL CONTROL OVER AIR, EARTH, FIRE AND WATER.

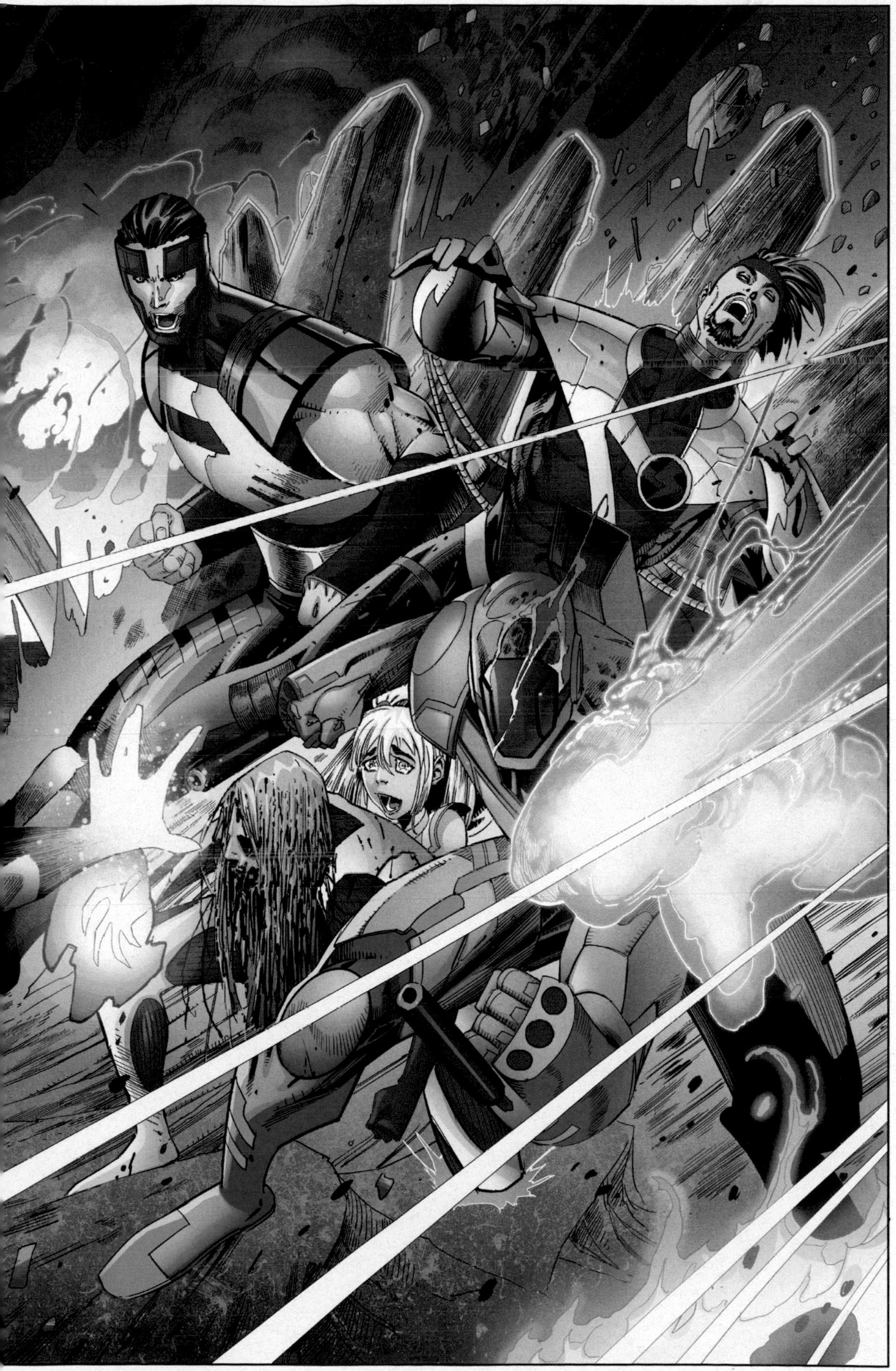

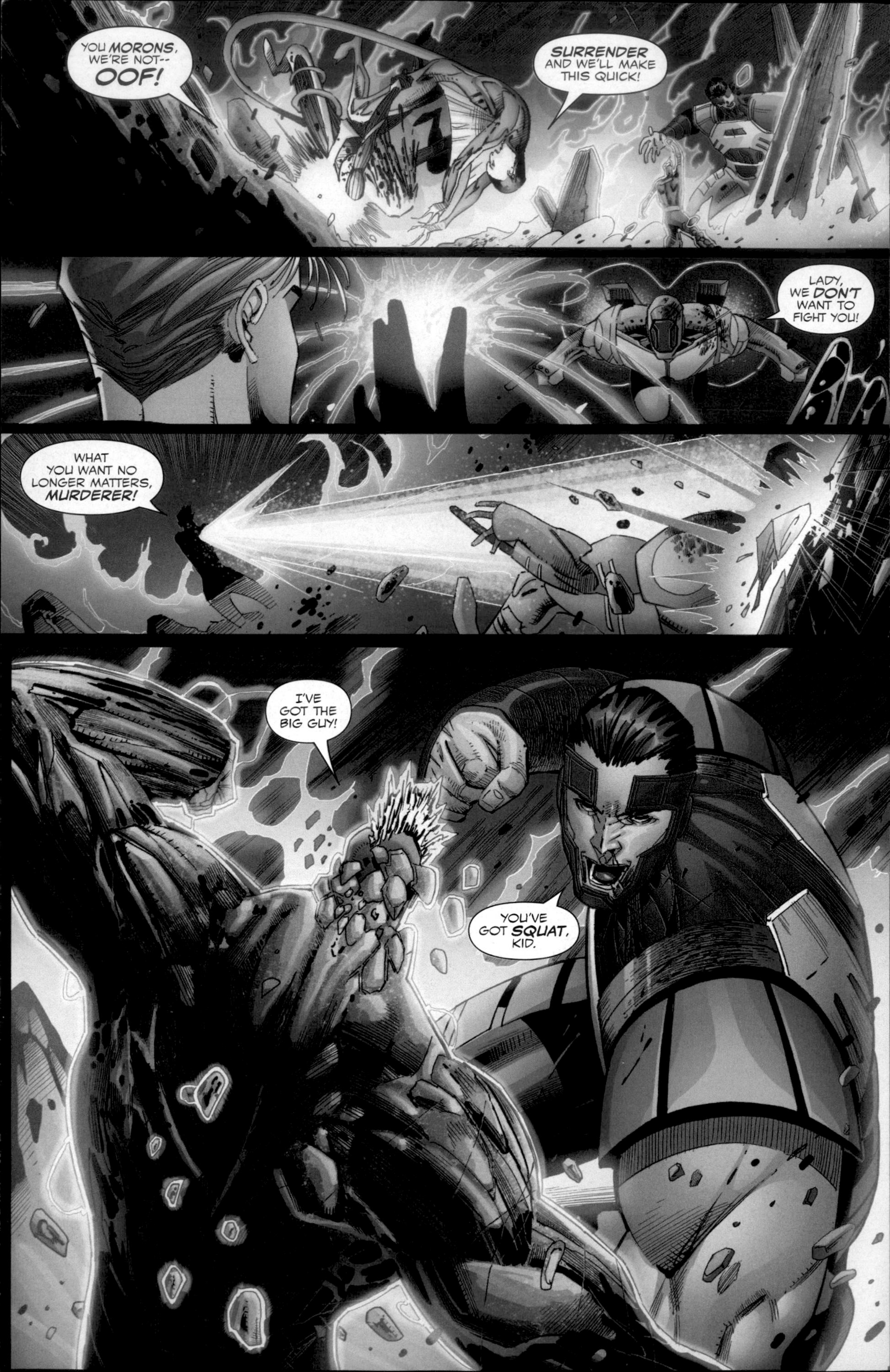
YOU MORONS, WE'RE NOT-- OOF!
SURRENDER AND WE'LL MAKE THIS QUICK!
LADY, WE DON'T WANT TO FIGHT YOU!
WHAT YOU WANT NO LONGER MATTERS, MURDERER!
I'VE GOT THE BIG GUY!
YOU'VE GOT SQUAT, KID.

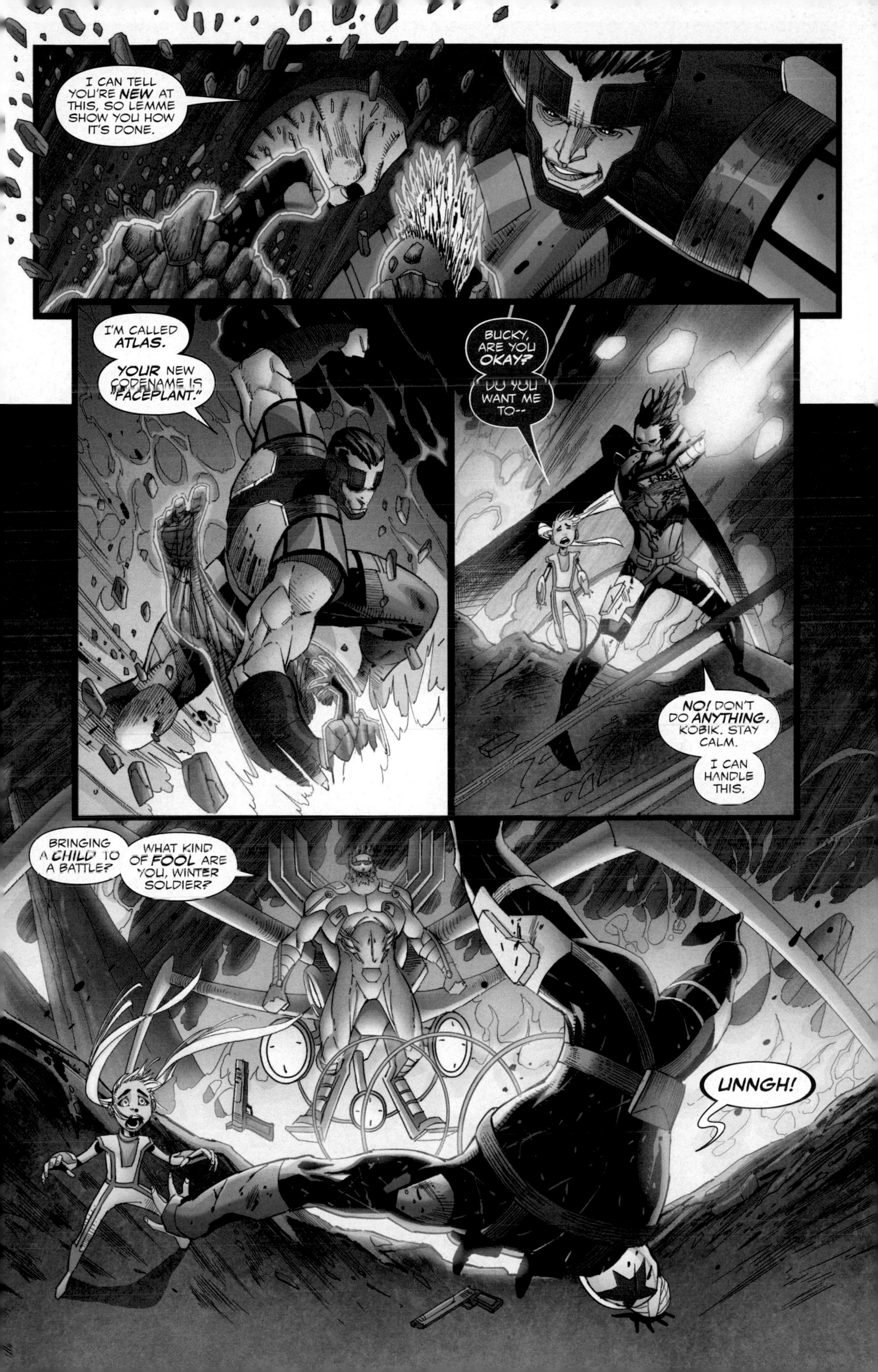
I CAN TELL YOU'RE NEW AT THIS, SO LEMME SHOW YOU HOW IT'S DONE.
I'M CALLED ATLAS.
YOUR NEW CODENAME IS "FACEPLANT."
BUCKY, ARE YOU OKAY?
DO YOU WANT ME TO--
NO! DON'T DO ANYTHING, KOBIK. STAY CALM.
I CAN HANDLE THIS.
BRINGING A CHILD TO A BATTLE?
WHAT KIND OF FOOL ARE YOU, WINTER SOLDIER?
UNNGH!

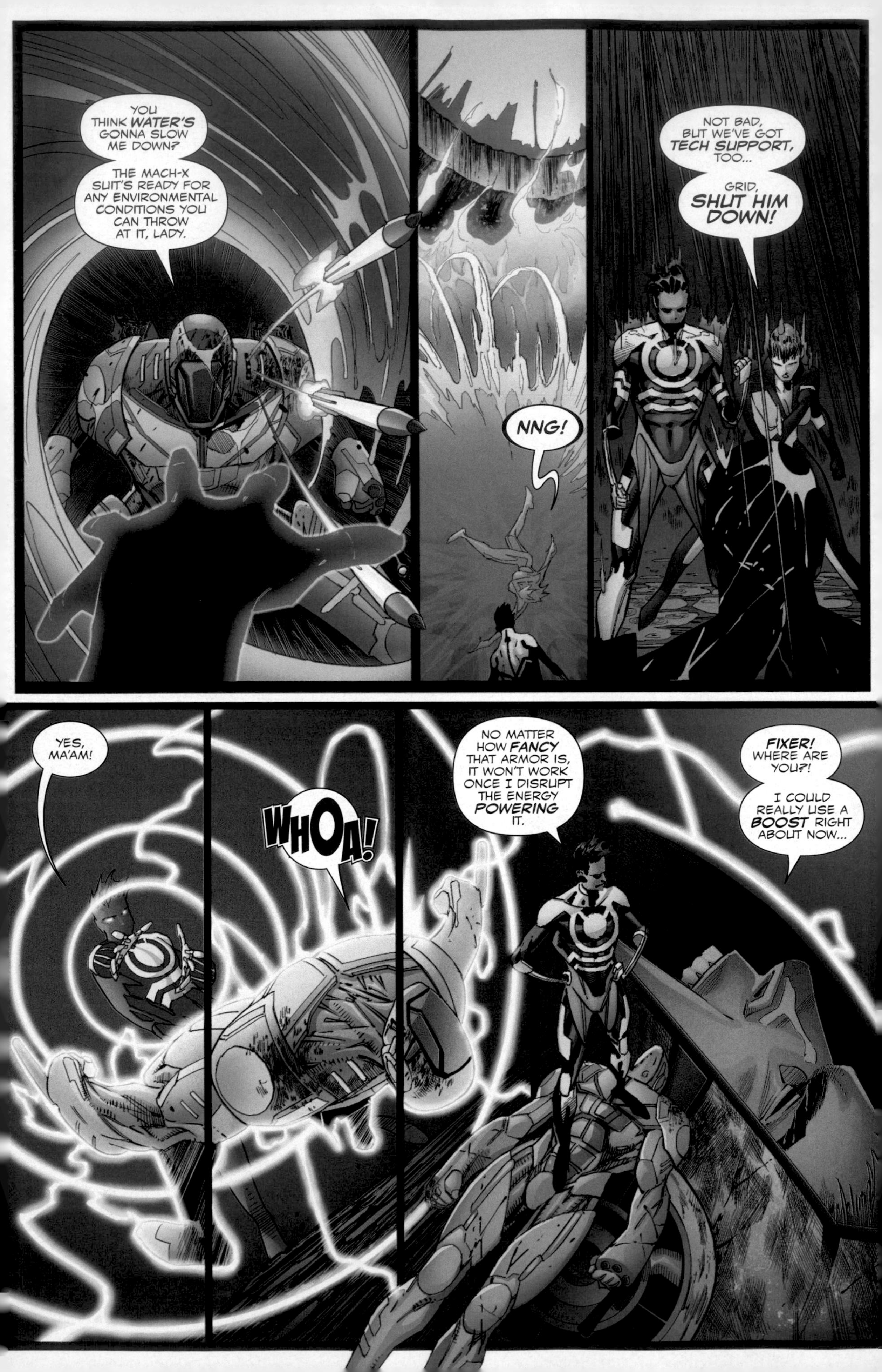
YOU THINK WATER'S GONNA SLOW ME DOWN?
THE MACH-X SUIT'S READY FOR ANY ENVIRONMENTAL CONDITIONS YOU CAN THROW AT IT, LADY.
NNG!
NOT BAD, BUT WE'VE GOT TECH SUPPORT, TOO...
GRID, SHUT HIM DOWN!
YES, MA'AM!
WHOA!
NO MATTER HOW FANCY THAT ARMOR IS, IT WON'T WORK ONCE I DISRUPT THE ENERGY POWERING IT.
FIXER! WHERE ARE YOU?!
I COULD REALLY USE A BOOST RIGHT ABOUT NOW...

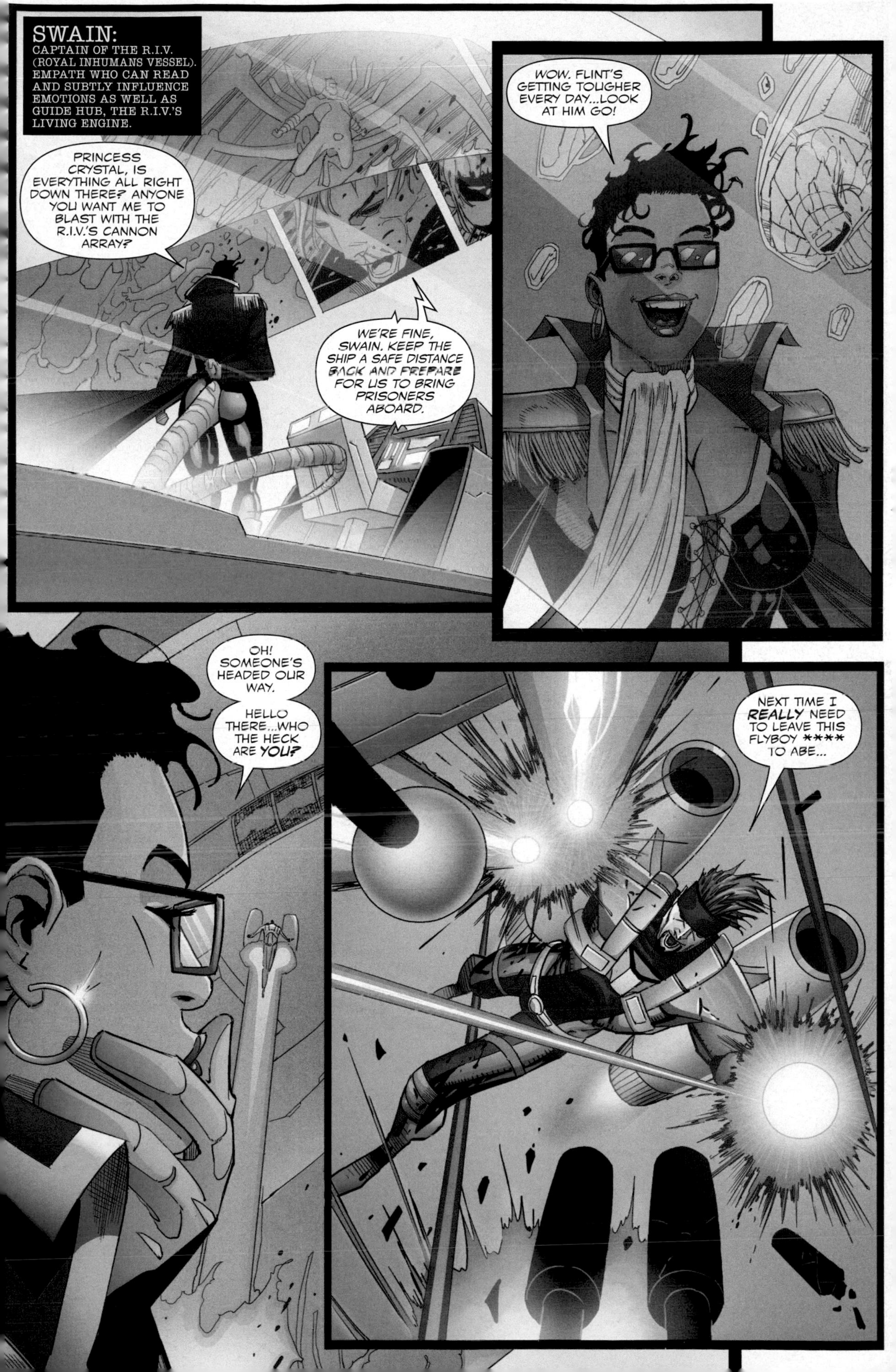
SWAIN:
CAPTAIN OF THE R.I.V. (ROYAL INHUMANS VESSEL). EMPATH WHO CAN READ AND SUBTLY INFLUENCE EMOTIONS AS WELL AS GUIDE HUB, THE R.I.V.'S LIVING ENGINE.
PRINCESS CRYSTAL, IS EVERYTHING ALL RIGHT DOWN THERE? ANYONE YOU WANT ME TO BLAST WITH THE R.I.V.'S CANNON ARRAY?
WE'RE FINE, SWAIN. KEEP THE SHIP A SAFE DISTANCE BACK AND PREPARE FOR US TO BRING PRISONERS ABOARD.
WOW. FLINT'S GETTING TOUGHER EVERY DAY...LOOK AT HIM GO!
OH! SOMEONE'S HEADED OUR WAY.
HELLO THERE...WHO THE HECK ARE YOU?
NEXT TIME I REALLY NEED TO LEAVE THIS FLYBOY **** TO ABE...

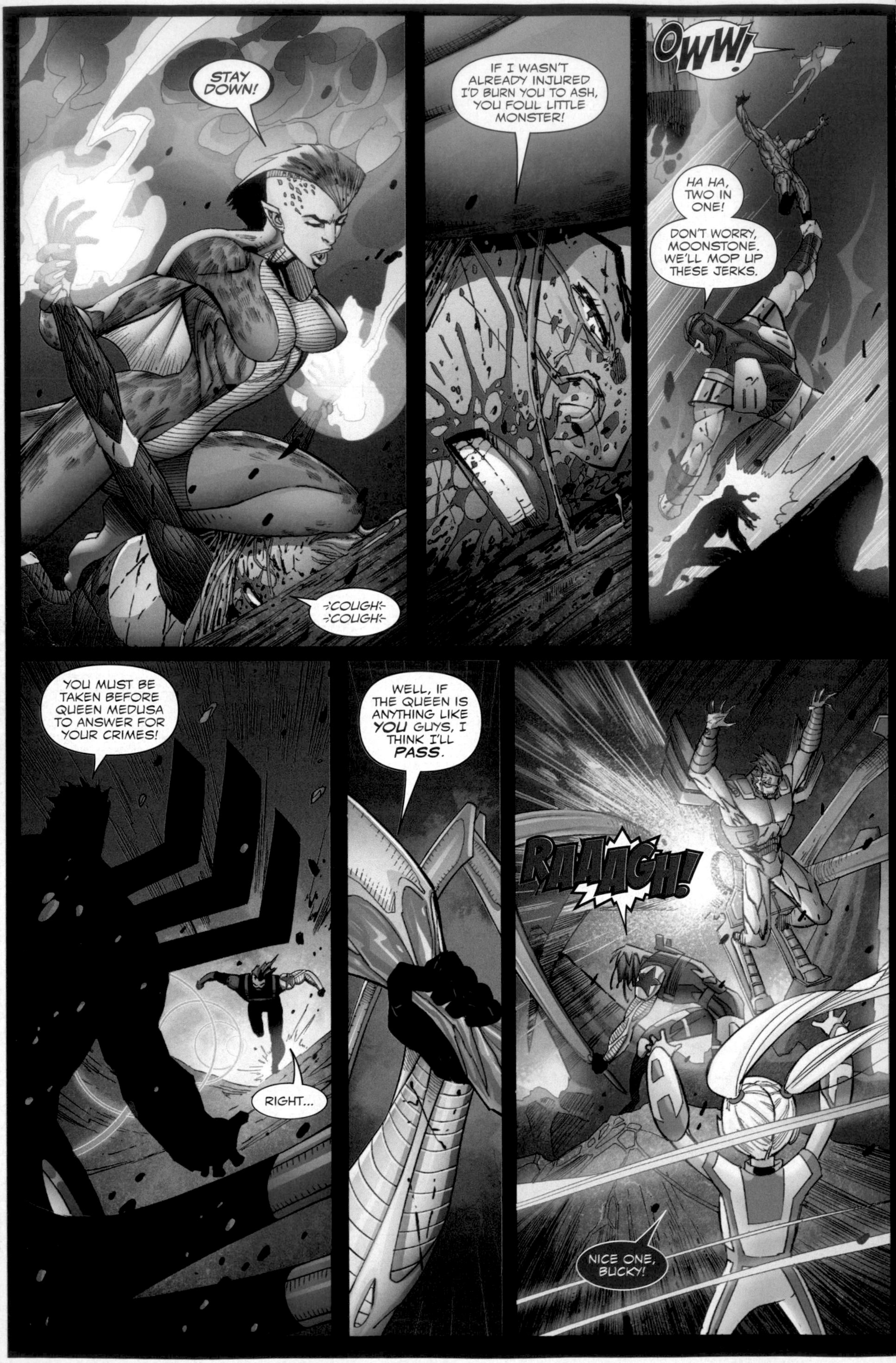
STAY DOWN!
-COUGH- -COUGH-
IF I WASN'T ALREADY INJURED I'D BURN YOU TO ASH, YOU FOUL LITTLE MONSTER!
OWW!
HA HA, TWO IN ONE!
DON'T WORRY, MOONSTONE. WE'LL MOP UP THESE JERKS.
YOU MUST BE TAKEN BEFORE QUEEN MEDUSA TO ANSWER FOR YOUR CRIMES!
RIGHT...
WELL, IF THE QUEEN IS ANYTHING LIKE YOU GUYS, I THINK I'LL PASS.
RAAAAGH!
NICE ONE, BUCKY!

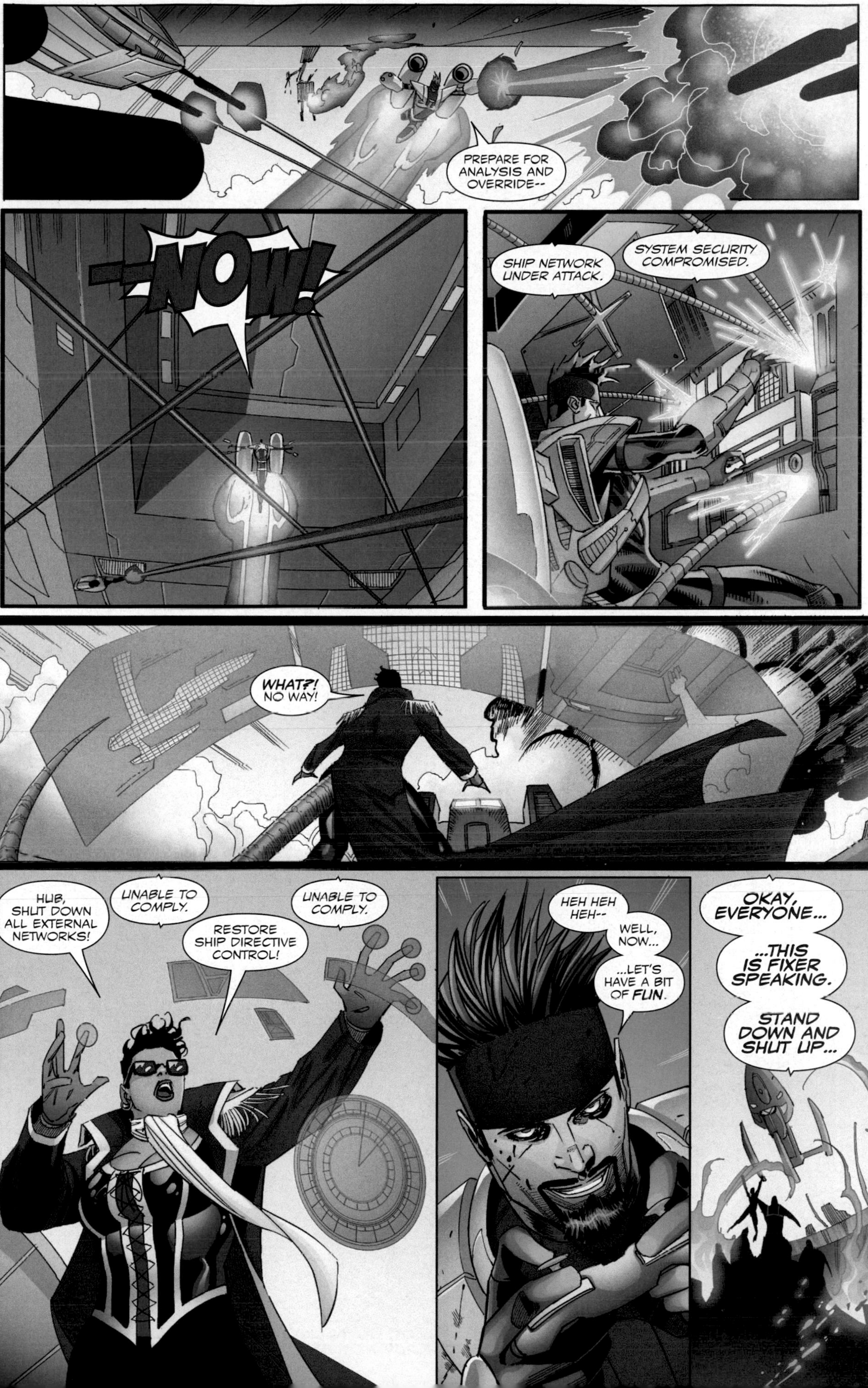
PREPARE FOR ANALYSIS AND OVERRIDE--
--NOW!
SHIP NETWORK UNDER ATTACK.
SYSTEM SECURITY COMPROMISED.
WHAT?! NO WAY!
HUB, SHUT DOWN ALL EXTERNAL NETWORKS!
UNABLE TO COMPLY.
RESTORE SHIP DIRECTIVE CONTROL!
UNABLE TO COMPLY.
HEH HEH HEH--
WELL, NOW...
...LET'S HAVE A BIT OF FUN.
OKAY, EVERYONE...
...THIS IS FIXER SPEAKING.
STAND DOWN AND SHUT UP...

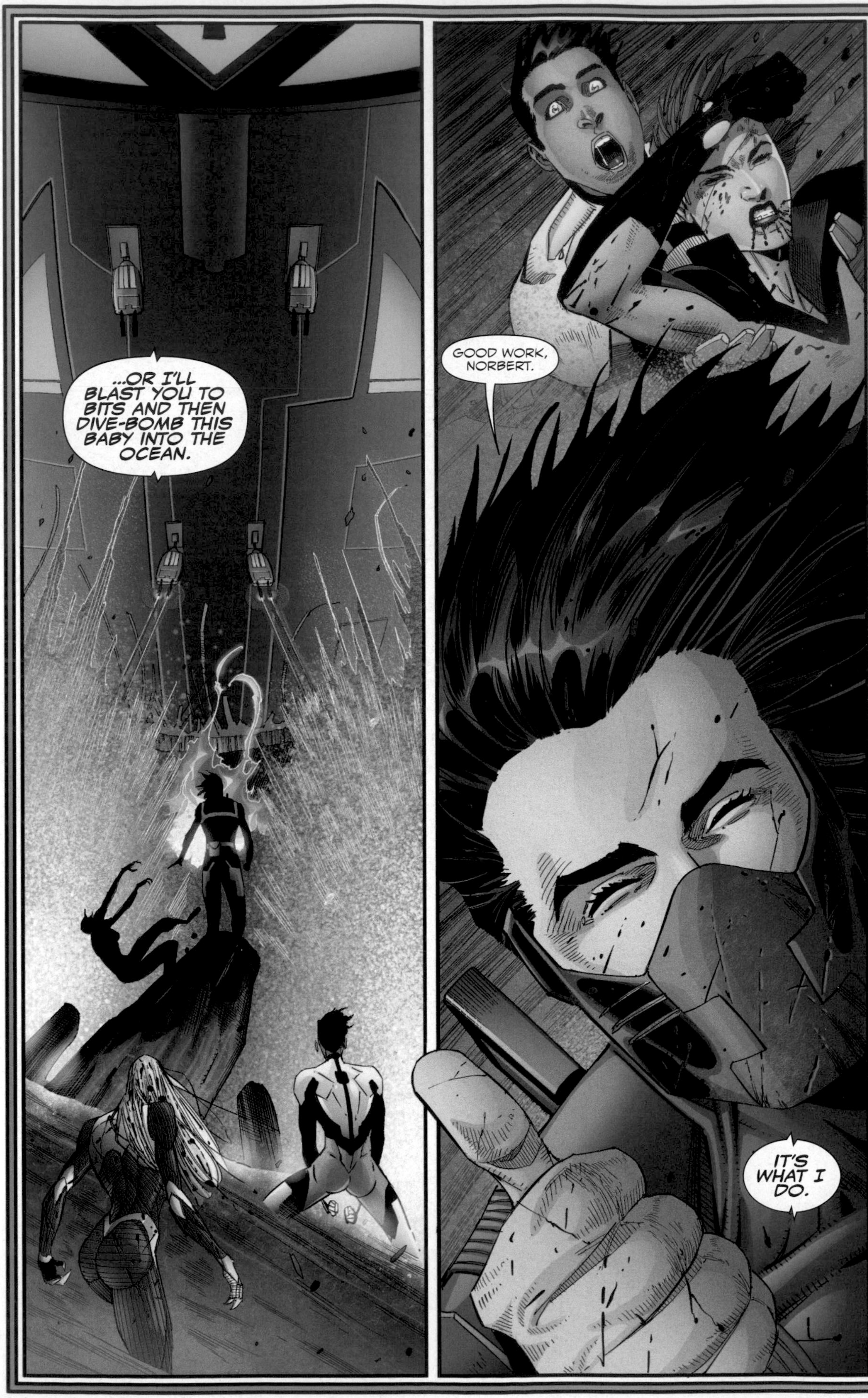
...OR I'LL BLAST YOU TO BITS AND THEN DIVE-BOMB THIS BABY INTO THE OCEAN.
GOOD WORK, NORBERT.
IT'S WHAT I DO.

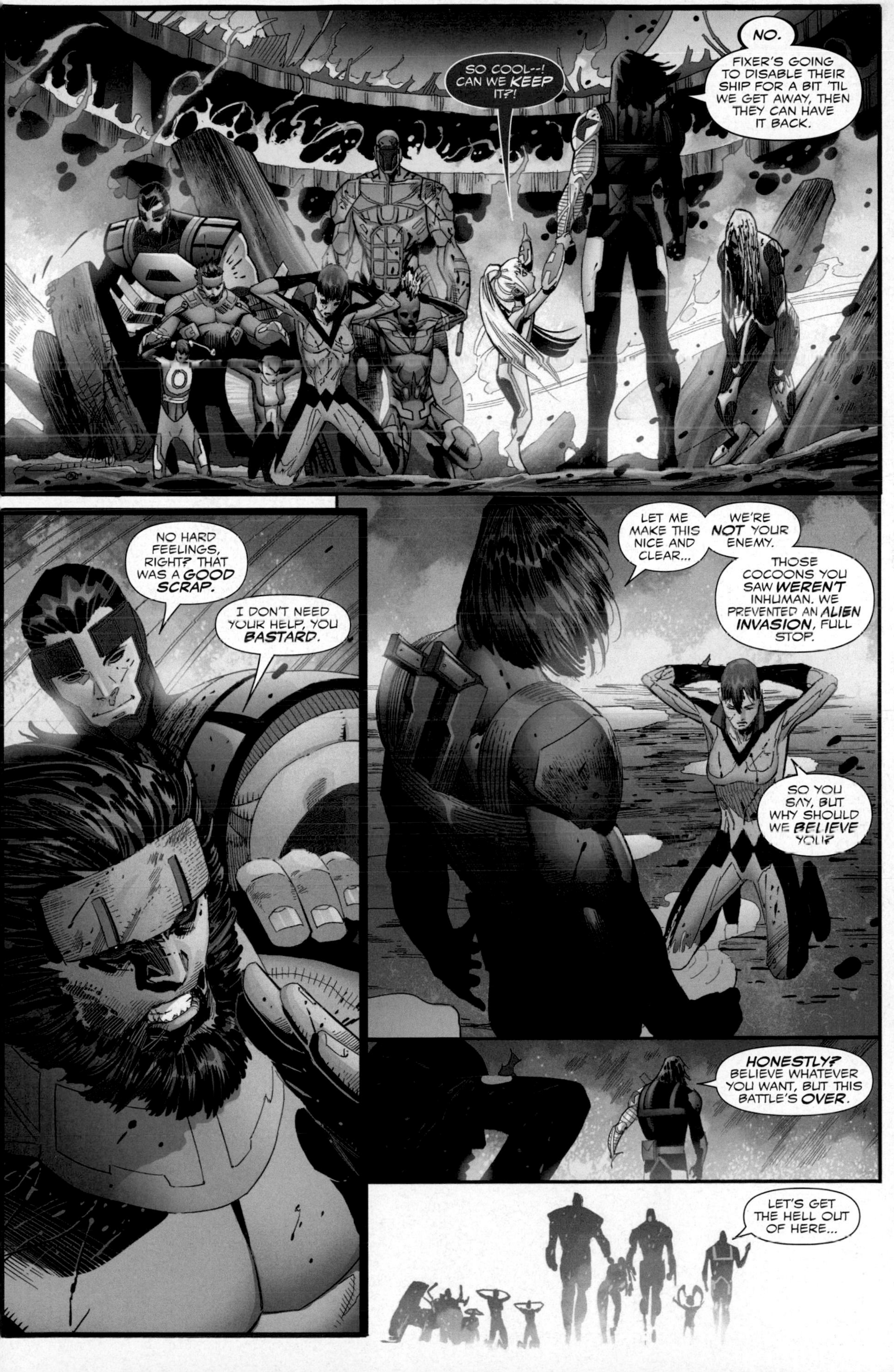
SO COOL--! CAN WE KEEP IT?!
NO.
FIXER'S GOING TO DISABLE THEIR SHIP FOR A BIT 'TIL WE GET AWAY, THEN THEY CAN HAVE IT BACK.
NO HARD FEELINGS, RIGHT? THAT WAS A GOOD SCRAP.
I DON'T NEED YOUR HELP, YOU BASTARD.
LET ME MAKE THIS NICE AND CLEAR...
WE'RE NOT YOUR ENEMY.
THOSE COCOONS YOU SAW WEREN'T INHUMAN. WE PREVENTED AN ALIEN INVASION, FULL STOP.
SO YOU SAY, BUT WHY SHOULD WE BELIEVE YOU?
HONESTLY? BELIEVE WHATEVER YOU WANT, BUT THIS BATTLE'S OVER.
LET'S GET THE HELL OUT OF HERE...

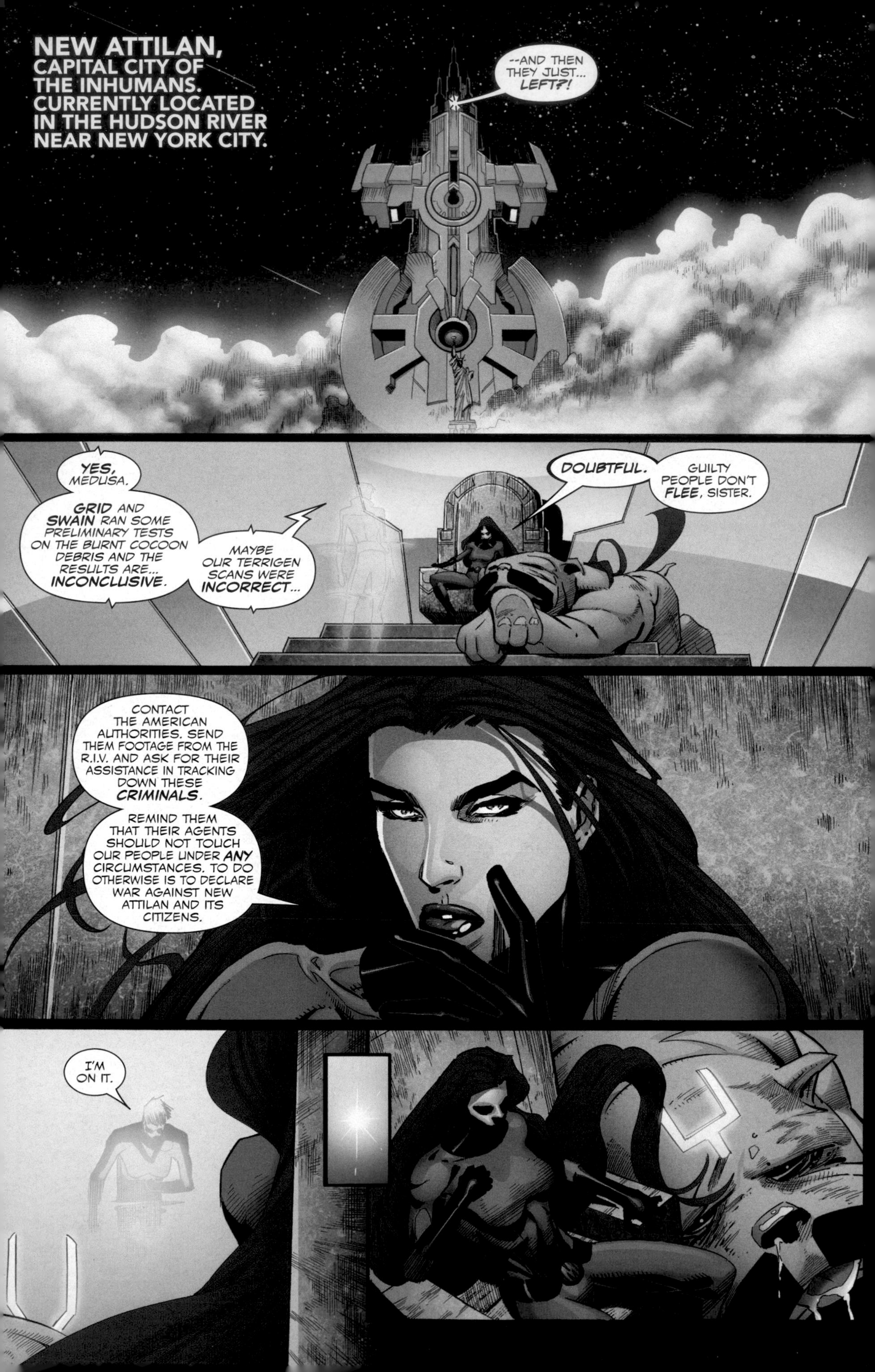
NEW ATTILAN, CAPITAL CITY OF THE INHUMANS. CURRENTLY LOCATED IN THE HUDSON RIVER NEAR NEW YORK CITY.
--AND THEN THEY JUST... LEFT?!
YES, MEDUSA.
GRID AND SWAIN RAN SOME PRELIMINARY TESTS ON THE BURNT COCOON DEBRIS AND THE RESULTS ARE... INCONCLUSIVE.
MAYBE OUR TERRIGEN SCANS WERE INCORRECT...
DOUBTFUL.
GUILTY PEOPLE DON'T FLEE, SISTER.
CONTACT THE AMERICAN AUTHORITIES. SEND THEM FOOTAGE FROM THE R.I.V. AND ASK FOR THEIR ASSISTANCE IN TRACKING DOWN THESE CRIMINALS.
REMIND THEM THAT THEIR AGENTS SHOULD NOT TOUCH OUR PEOPLE UNDER ANY CIRCUMSTANCES. TO DO OTHERWISE IS TO DECLARE WAR AGAINST NEW ATTILAN AND ITS CITIZENS.
I'M ON IT.

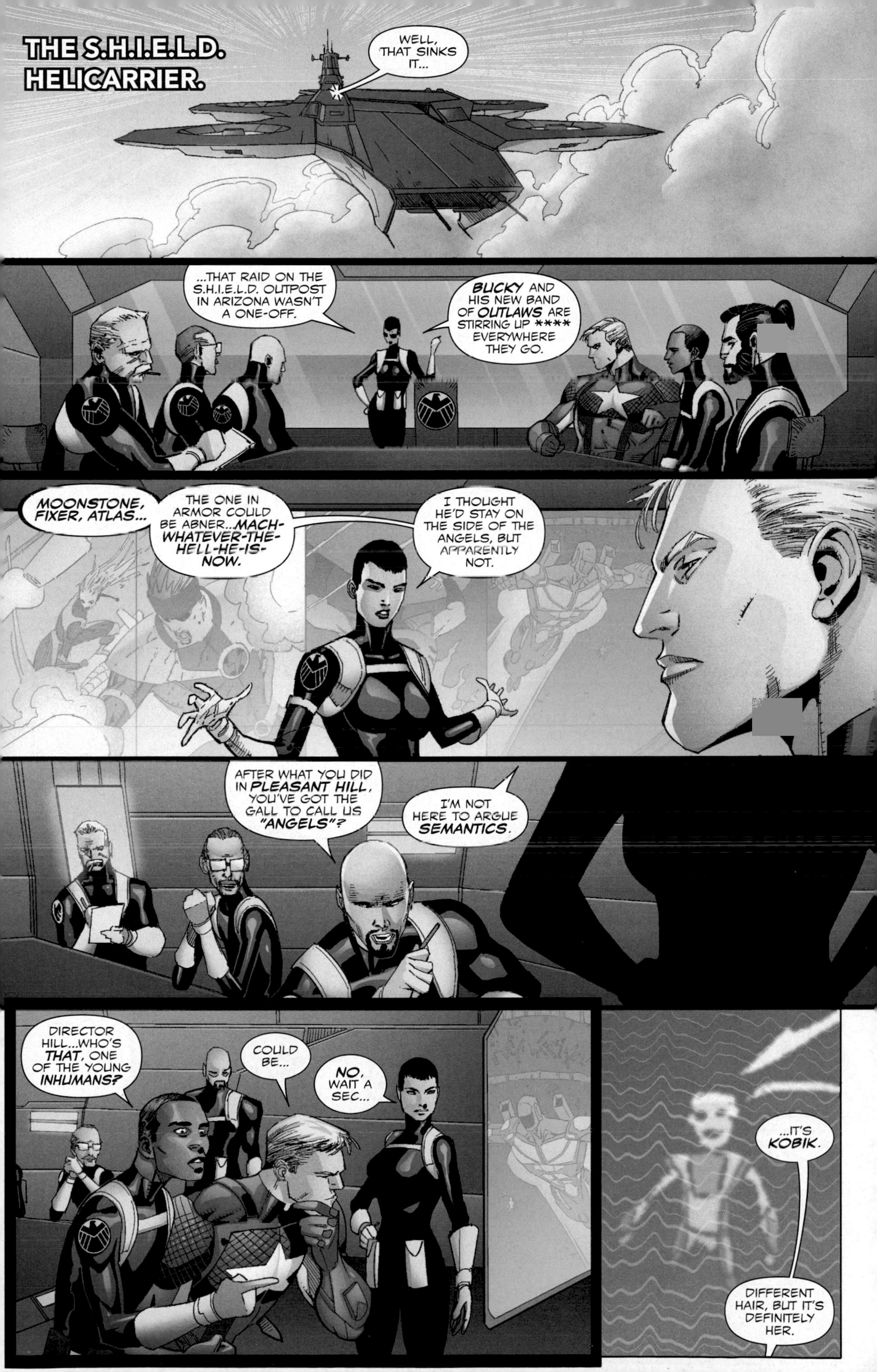
THE S.H.I.E.L.D. HELICARRIER.
WELL, THAT SINKS IT...
...THAT RAID ON THE S.H.I.E.L.D. OUTPOST IN ARIZONA WASN'T A ONE-OFF.
BUCKY AND HIS NEW BAND OF OUTLAWS ARE STIRRING UP **** EVERYWHERE THEY GO.
MOONSTONE, FIXER, ATLAS...
THE ONE IN ARMOR COULD BE ABNER...MACH-WHATEVER-THE-HELL-HE-IS-NOW.
I THOUGHT HE'D STAY ON THE SIDE OF THE ANGELS, BUT APPARENTLY NOT.
AFTER WHAT YOU DID IN PLEASANT HILL, YOU'VE GOT THE GALL TO CALL US "ANGELS"?
I'M NOT HERE TO ARGUE SEMANTICS.
DIRECTOR HILL...WHO'S THAT, ONE OF THE YOUNG INHUMANS?
COULD BE...
NO, WAIT A SEC...
...IT'S KOBIK.
DIFFERENT HAIR, BUT IT'S DEFINITELY HER.

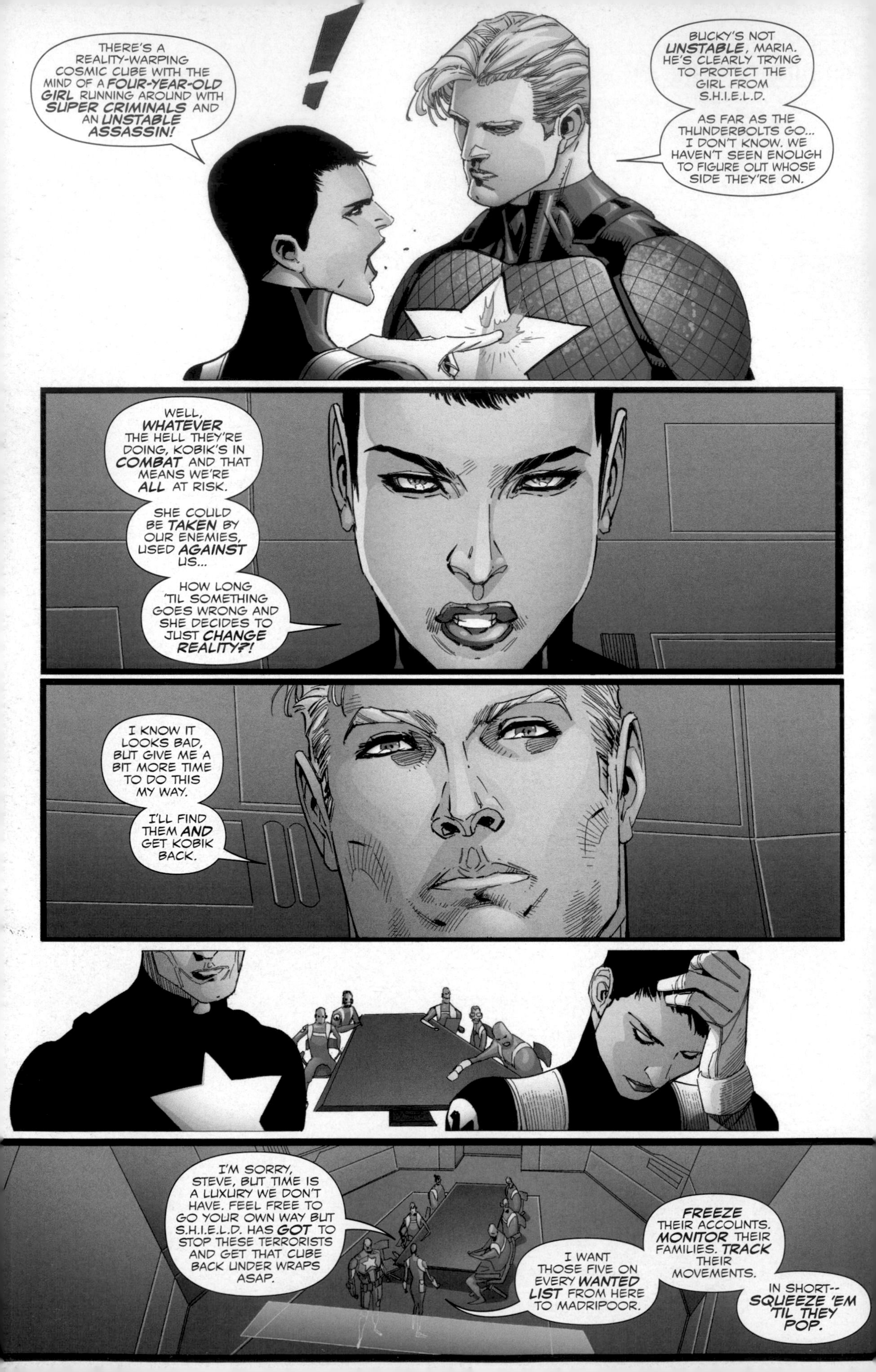

THERE'S A REALITY-WARPING COSMIC CUBE WITH THE MIND OF A FOUR-YEAR-OLD GIRL RUNNING AROUND WITH SUPER CRIMINALS AND AN UNSTABLE ASSASSIN!
!
BUCKY'S NOT UNSTABLE, MARIA. HE'S CLEARLY TRYING TO PROTECT THE GIRL FROM S.H.I.E.L.D.
AS FAR AS THE THUNDERBOLTS GO... I DON'T KNOW. WE HAVEN'T SEEN ENOUGH TO FIGURE OUT WHOSE SIDE THEY'RE ON.
WELL, WHATEVER THE HELL THEY'RE DOING, KOBIK'S IN COMBAT AND THAT MEANS WE'RE ALL AT RISK.
SHE COULD BE TAKEN BY OUR ENEMIES, USED AGAINST US...
HOW LONG 'TIL SOMETHING GOES WRONG AND SHE DECIDES TO JUST CHANGE REALITY?!
I KNOW IT LOOKS BAD, BUT GIVE ME A BIT MORE TIME TO DO THIS MY WAY.
I'LL FIND THEM AND GET KOBIK BACK.
I'M SORRY, STEVE, BUT TIME IS A LUXURY WE DON'T HAVE. FEEL FREE TO GO YOUR OWN WAY BUT S.H.I.E.L.D. HAS GOT TO STOP THESE TERRORISTS AND GET THAT CUBE BACK UNDER WRAPS ASAP.
I WANT THOSE FIVE ON EVERY WANTED LIST FROM HERE TO MADRIPOOR.
FREEZE THEIR ACCOUNTS. MONITOR THEIR FAMILIES. TRACK THEIR MOVEMENTS.
IN SHORT-- SQUEEZE 'EM 'TIL THEY POP.

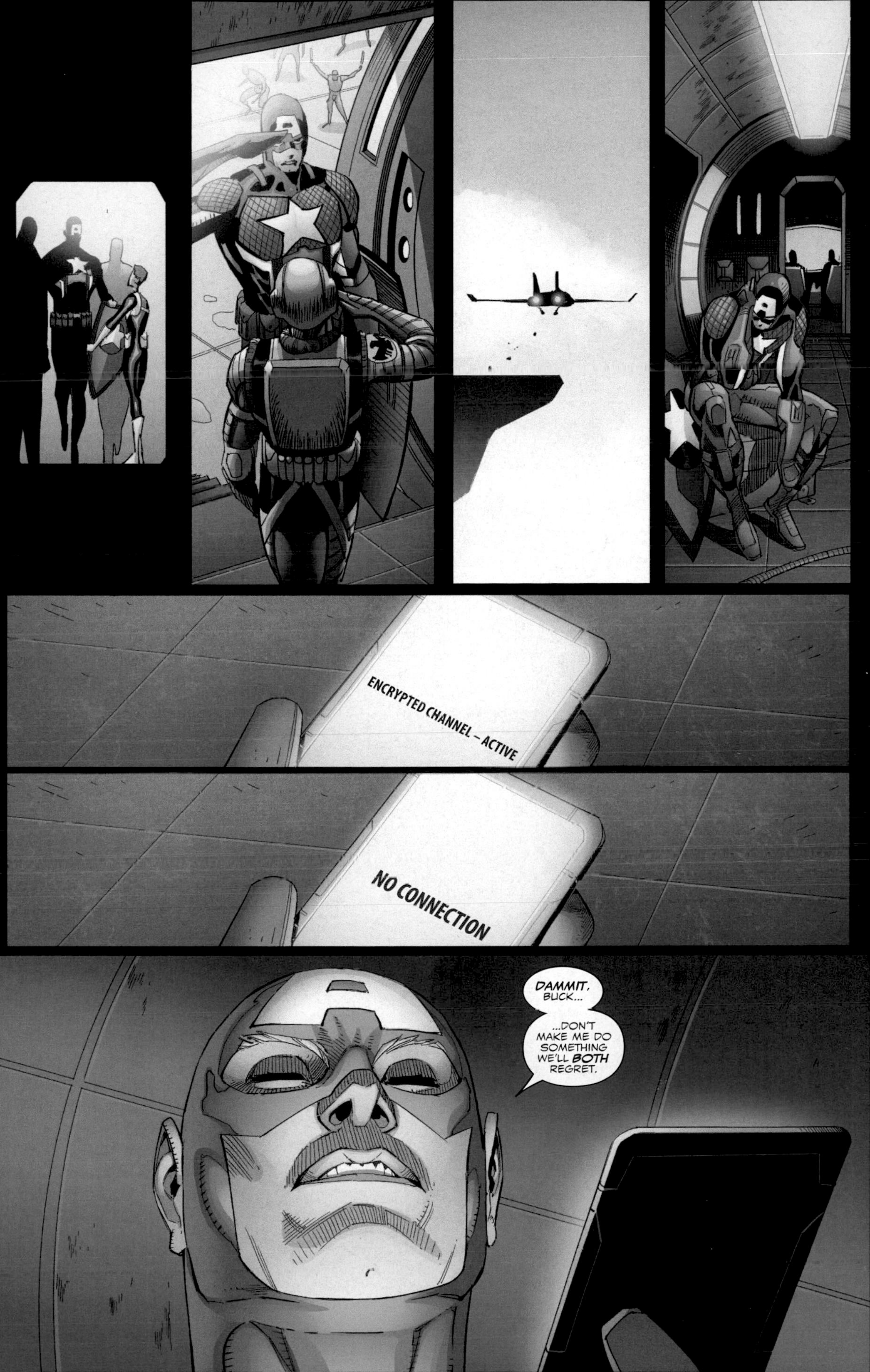
ENCRYPTED CHANNEL – ACTIVE
NO CONNECTION
DAMMIT, BUCK...
...DON'T MAKE ME DO SOMETHING WE'LL BOTH REGRET.

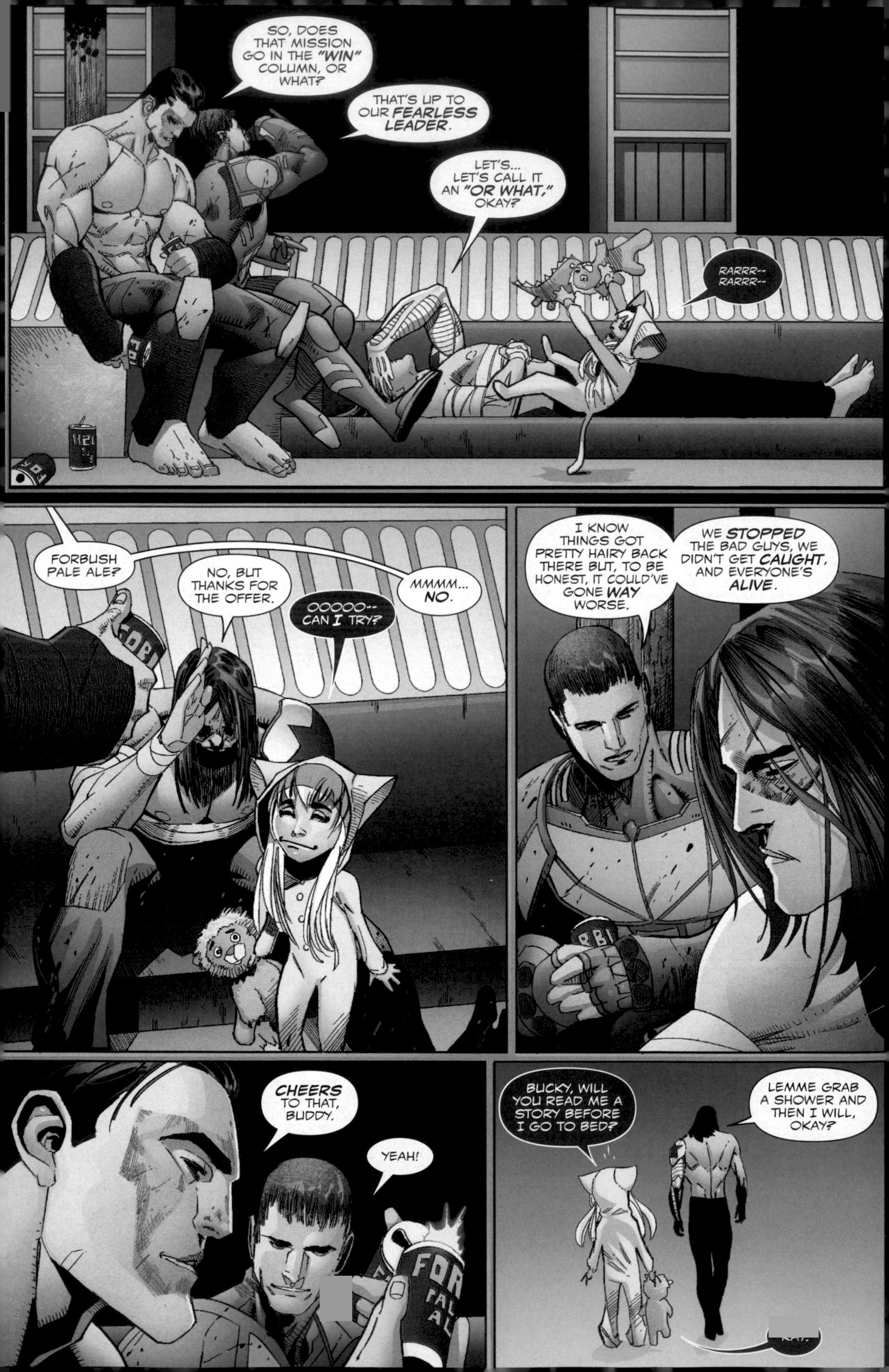
SO, DOES THAT MISSION GO IN THE "WIN" COLUMN, OR WHAT?
THAT'S UP TO OUR FEARLESS LEADER.
LET'S... LET'S CALL IT AN "OR WHAT," OKAY?
RARRR-- RARRR--
FORBUSH PALE ALE?
NO, BUT THANKS FOR THE OFFER.
MMMM... NO.
OOOOO-- CAN I TRY?
I KNOW THINGS GOT PRETTY HAIRY BACK THERE BUT, TO BE HONEST, IT COULD'VE GONE WAY WORSE.
WE STOPPED THE BAD GUYS, WE DIDN'T GET CAUGHT, AND EVERYONE'S ALIVE.
CHEERS TO THAT, BUDDY.
YEAH!
BUCKY, WILL YOU READ ME A STORY BEFORE I GO TO BED?
LEMME GRAB A SHOWER AND THEN I WILL, OKAY?

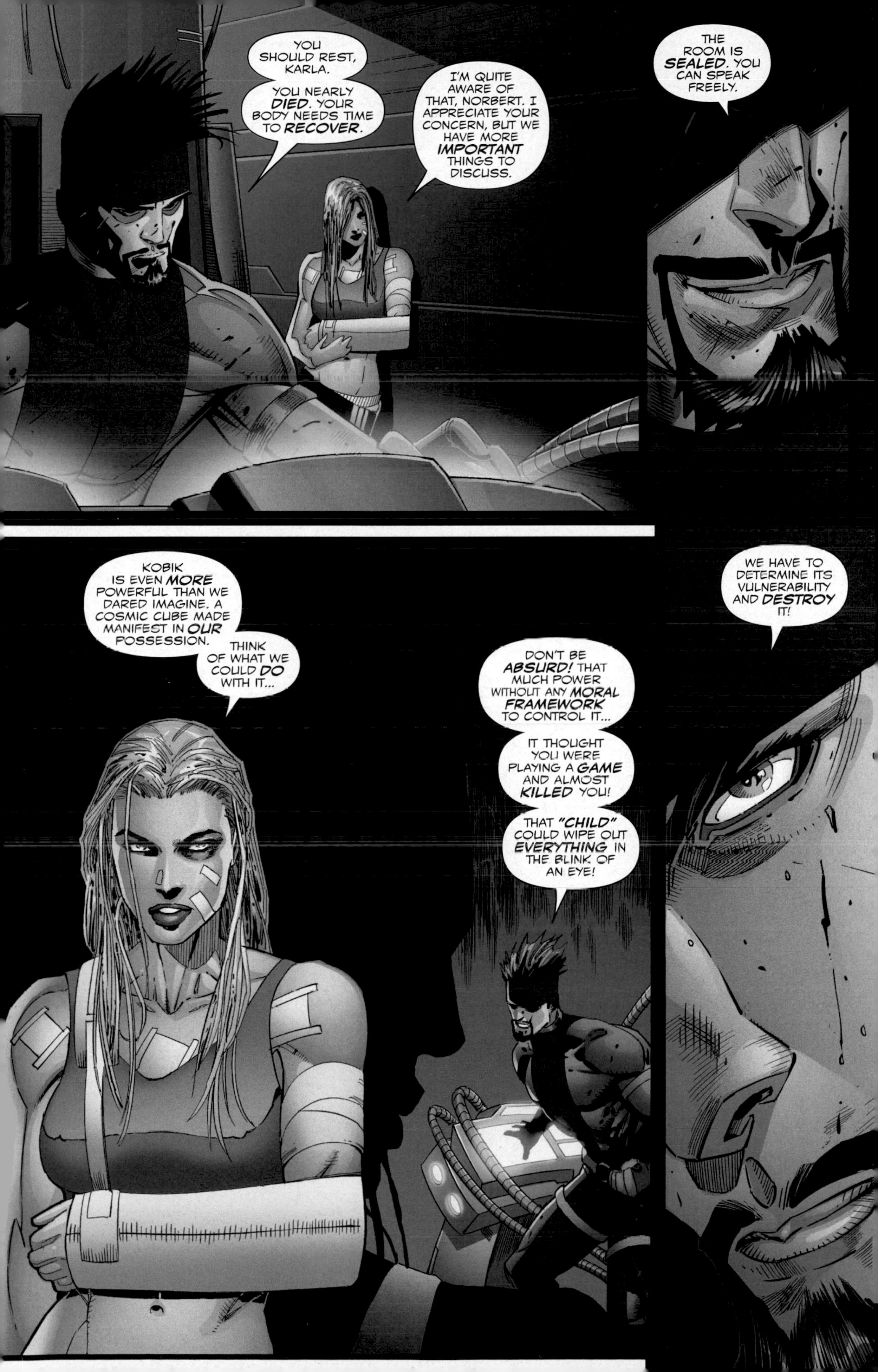

YOU SHOULD REST, KARLA.
YOU NEARLY DIED. YOUR BODY NEEDS TIME TO RECOVER.
I'M QUITE AWARE OF THAT, NORBERT. I APPRECIATE YOUR CONCERN, BUT WE HAVE MORE IMPORTANT THINGS TO DISCUSS.
THE ROOM IS SEALED. YOU CAN SPEAK FREELY.
KOBIK IS EVEN MORE POWERFUL THAN WE DARED IMAGINE. A COSMIC CUBE MADE MANIFEST IN OUR POSSESSION.
THINK OF WHAT WE COULD DO WITH IT...
DON'T BE ABSURD! THAT MUCH POWER WITHOUT ANY MORAL FRAMEWORK TO CONTROL IT...
IT THOUGHT YOU WERE PLAYING A GAME AND ALMOST KILLED YOU!
THAT "CHILD" COULD WIPE OUT EVERYTHING IN THE BLINK OF AN EYE!
WE HAVE TO DETERMINE ITS VULNERABILITY AND DESTROY IT!

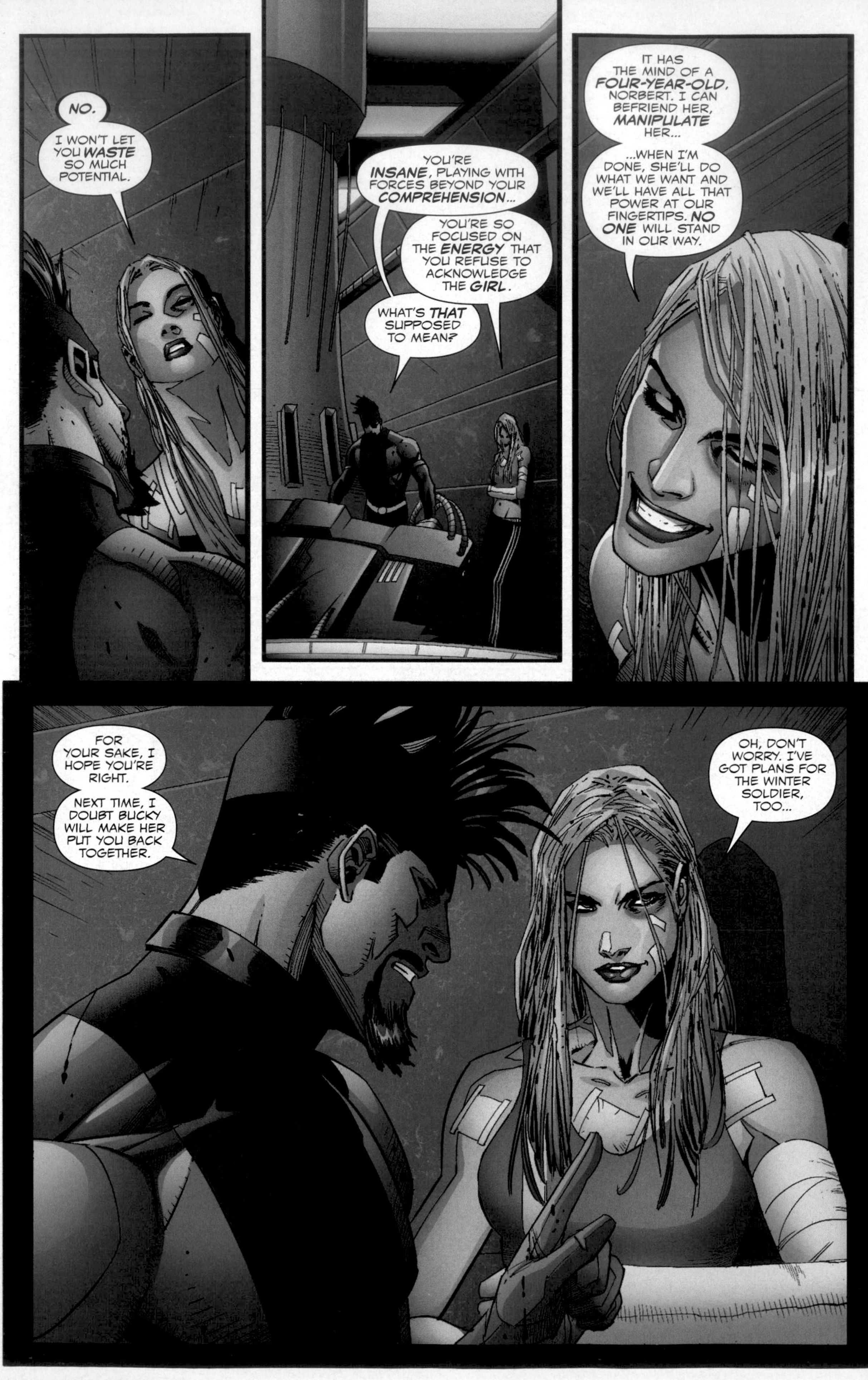
NO.
I WON'T LET YOU WASTE SO MUCH POTENTIAL.
YOU'RE INSANE, PLAYING WITH FORCES BEYOND YOUR COMPREHENSION...
YOU'RE SO FOCUSED ON THE ENERGY THAT YOU REFUSE TO ACKNOWLEDGE THE GIRL.
WHAT'S THAT SUPPOSED TO MEAN?
IT HAS THE MIND OF A FOUR-YEAR-OLD, NORBERT. I CAN BEFRIEND HER, MANIPULATE HER...
...WHEN I'M DONE, SHE'LL DO WHAT WE WANT AND WE'LL HAVE ALL THAT POWER AT OUR FINGERTIPS. NO ONE WILL STAND IN OUR WAY.
FOR YOUR SAKE, I HOPE YOU'RE RIGHT.
NEXT TIME, I DOUBT BUCKY WILL MAKE HER PUT YOU BACK TOGETHER.
OH, DON'T WORRY. I'VE GOT PLANS FOR THE WINTER SOLDIER, TOO...

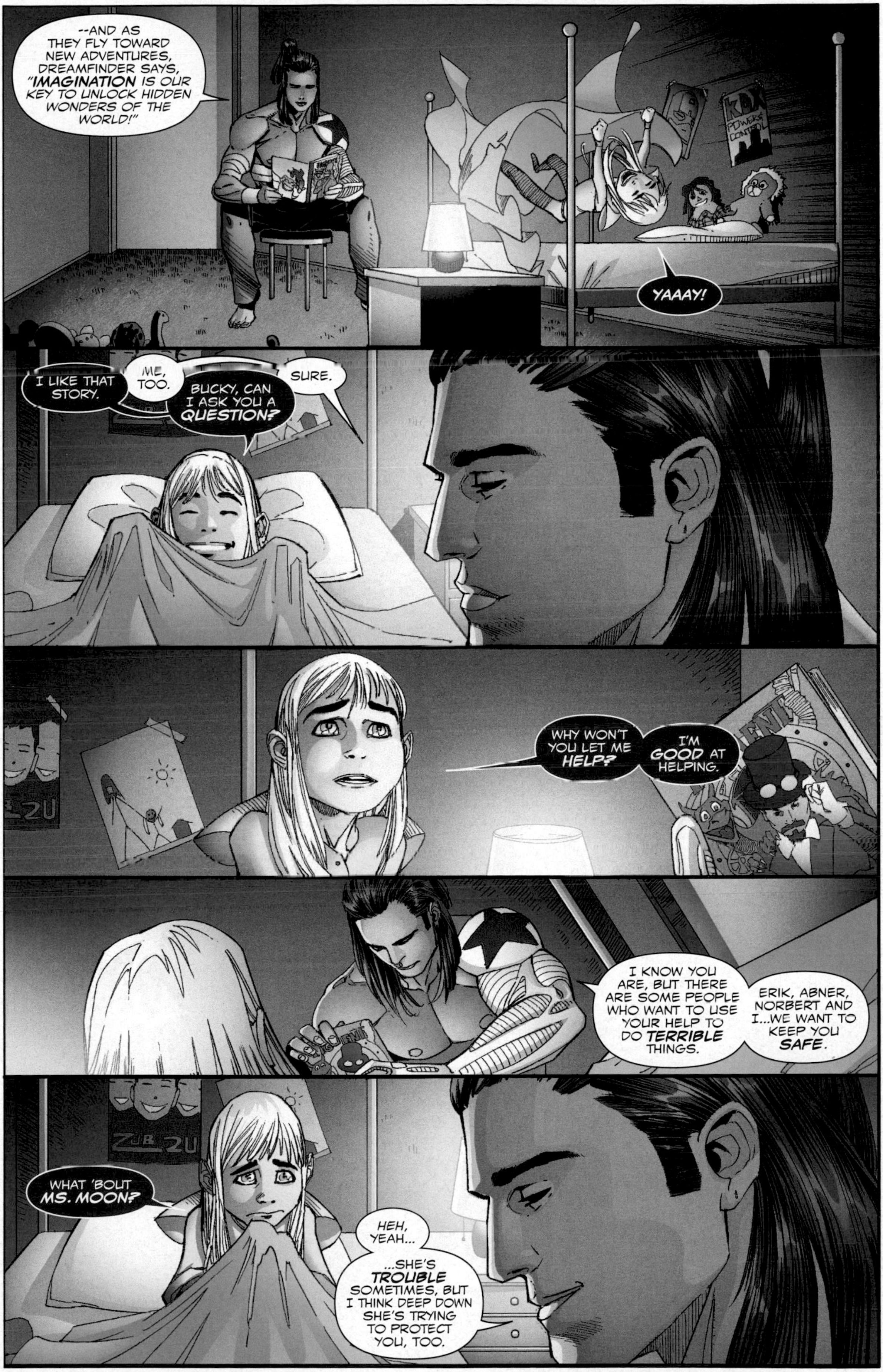
--AND AS THEY FLY TOWARD NEW ADVENTURES, DREAMFINDER SAYS, "IMAGINATION IS OUR KEY TO UNLOCK HIDDEN WONDERS OF THE WORLD!"
KDX POWERS CONTROL
YAAAY!
I LIKE THAT STORY.
ME, TOO.
BUCKY, CAN I ASK YOU A QUESTION?
SURE.
WHY WON'T YOU LET ME HELP?
I'M GOOD AT HELPING.
I KNOW YOU ARE, BUT THERE ARE SOME PEOPLE WHO WANT TO USE YOUR HELP TO DO TERRIBLE THINGS.
ERIK, ABNER, NORBERT AND I...WE WANT TO KEEP YOU SAFE.
ZUB ZU
WHAT 'BOUT MS. MOON?
HEH, YEAH...
...SHE'S TROUBLE SOMETIMES, BUT I THINK DEEP DOWN SHE'S TRYING TO PROTECT YOU, TOO.

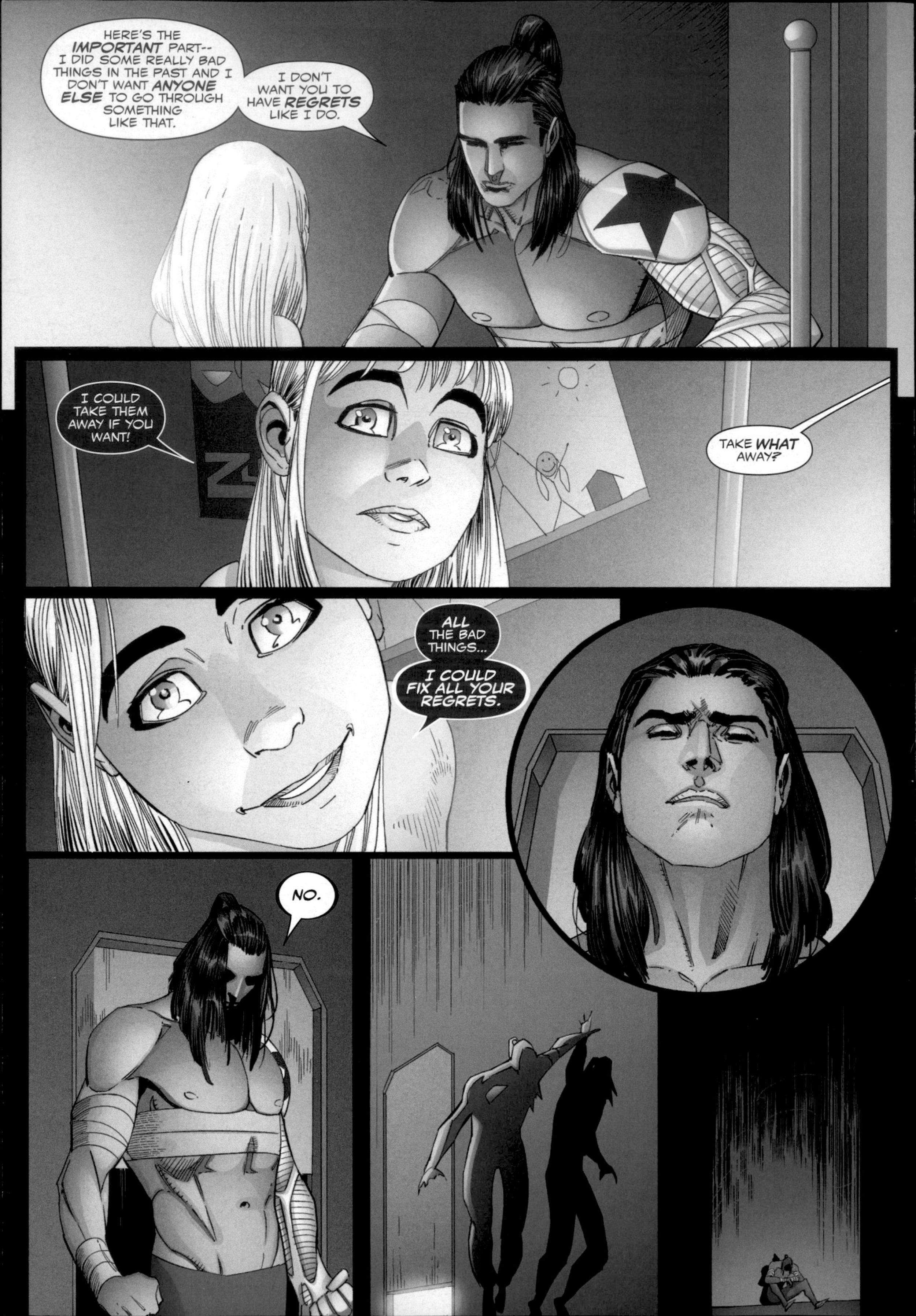
HERE'S THE IMPORTANT PART-- I DID SOME REALLY BAD THINGS IN THE PAST AND I DON'T WANT ANYONE ELSE TO GO THROUGH SOMETHING LIKE THAT.
I DON'T WANT YOU TO HAVE REGRETS LIKE I DO.
I COULD TAKE THEM AWAY IF YOU WANT!
TAKE WHAT AWAY?
ALL THE BAD THINGS...
I COULD FIX ALL YOUR REGRETS.
NO.

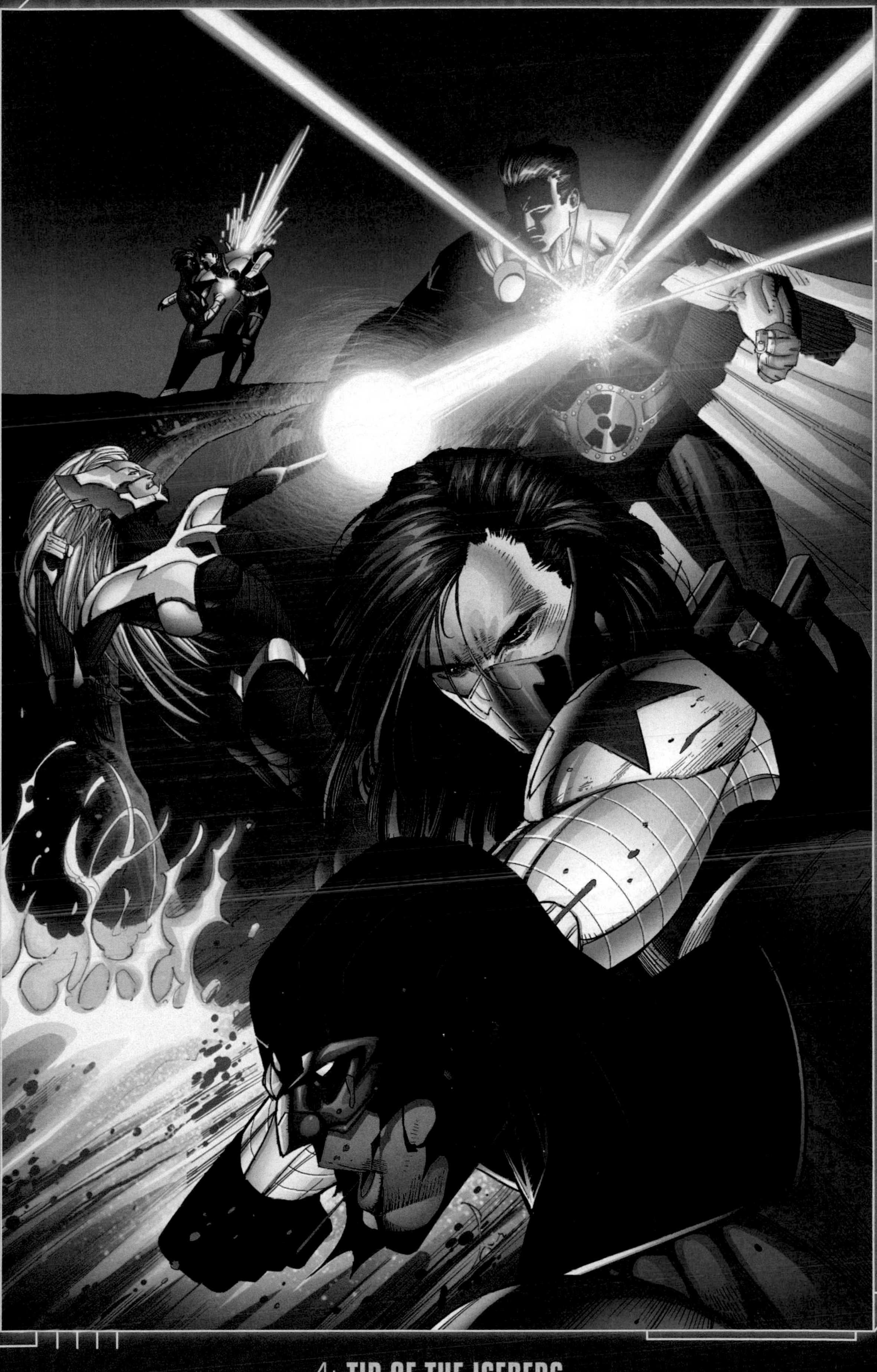

4: TIP OF THE ICEBERG

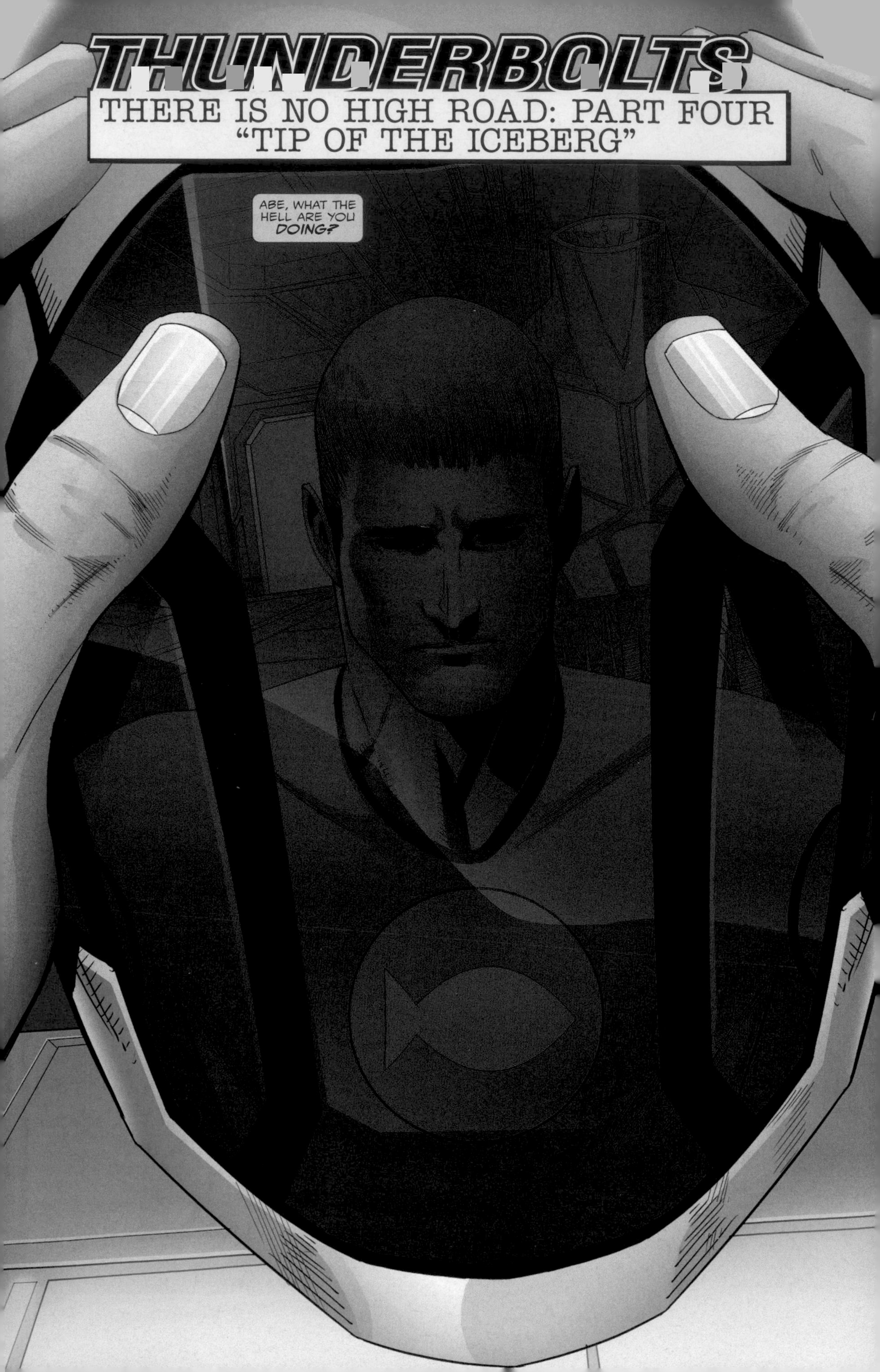
THUNDERBOLTS
THERE IS NO HIGH ROAD: PART FOUR
"TIP OF THE ICEBERG"
ABE, WHAT THE HELL ARE YOU DOING?

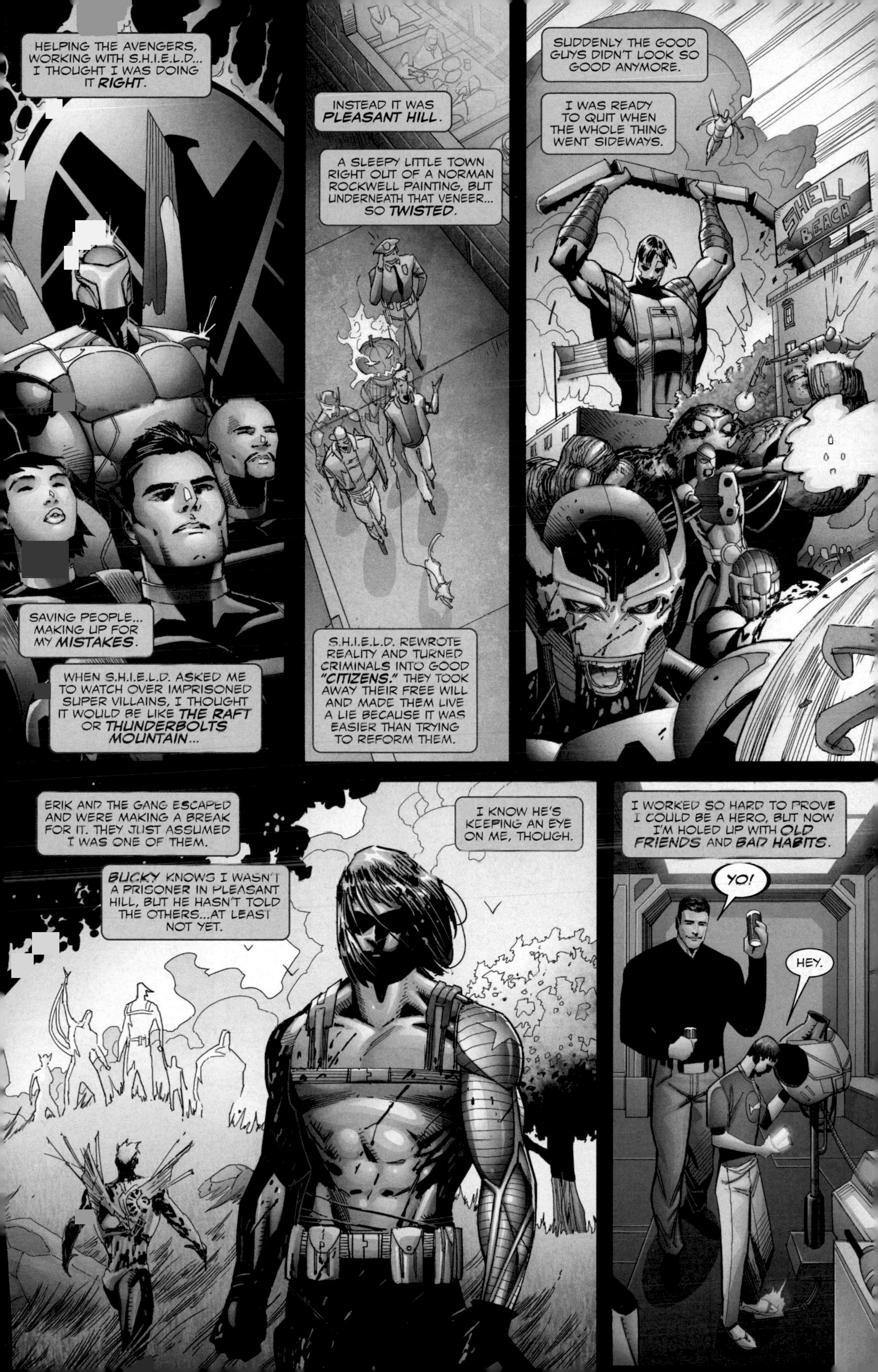
HELPING THE AVENGERS, WORKING WITH S.H.I.E.L.D.... I THOUGHT I WAS DOING IT RIGHT.
SAVING PEOPLE... MAKING UP FOR MY MISTAKES.
WHEN S.H.I.E.L.D. ASKED ME TO WATCH OVER IMPRISONED SUPER VILLAINS, I THOUGHT IT WOULD BE LIKE THE RAFT OR THUNDERBOLTS MOUNTAIN...
INSTEAD IT WAS PLEASANT HILL.
A SLEEPY LITTLE TOWN RIGHT OUT OF A NORMAN ROCKWELL PAINTING, BUT UNDERNEATH THAT VENEER... SO TWISTED.
S.H.I.E.L.D. REWROTE REALITY AND TURNED CRIMINALS INTO GOOD "CITIZENS." THEY TOOK AWAY THEIR FREE WILL AND MADE THEM LIVE A LIE BECAUSE IT WAS EASIER THAN TRYING TO REFORM THEM.
SUDDENLY THE GOOD GUYS DIDN'T LOOK SO GOOD ANYMORE.
I WAS READY TO QUIT WHEN THE WHOLE THING WENT SIDEWAYS.
SHELL BEACH
ERIK AND THE GANG ESCAPED AND WERE MAKING A BREAK FOR IT. THEY JUST ASSUMED I WAS ONE OF THEM.
BUCKY KNOWS I WASN'T A PRISONER IN PLEASANT HILL, BUT HE HASN'T TOLD THE OTHERS...AT LEAST NOT YET.
I KNOW HE'S KEEPING AN EYE ON ME, THOUGH.
I WORKED SO HARD TO PROVE I COULD BE A HERO, BUT NOW I'M HOLED UP WITH OLD FRIENDS AND BAD HABITS.
YO!
HEY.

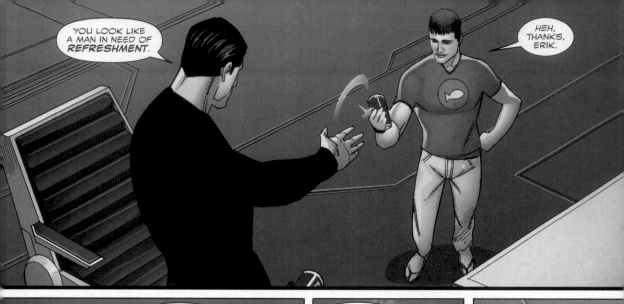

YOU LOOK LIKE A MAN IN NEED OF *REFRESHMENT.*

HEH, THANKS, ERIK.

QUESTION FOR YA.

SHOOT.

WHEN YOU WERE A KID, DIDJA EVER HAVE A *SECRET HIDEOUT?*

SURE. YOU?

HELL, YES.

NOW LOOK *AROUND* US, BUDDY...

...WE ARE *LIVIN' THE DREAM.*

ERIK LOOKS HAPPIER THAN I'VE SEEN HIM IN A *LONG* TIME.

HE'S LOVING THIS *MERRY BAND OF OUTLAWS.*

I NEED TO BE MORE LIKE THAT.

LESS STRESSED... EASY TO PLEASE...

RELAXED AND--

BOYS, YOU BETTER CHECK THIS OUT.

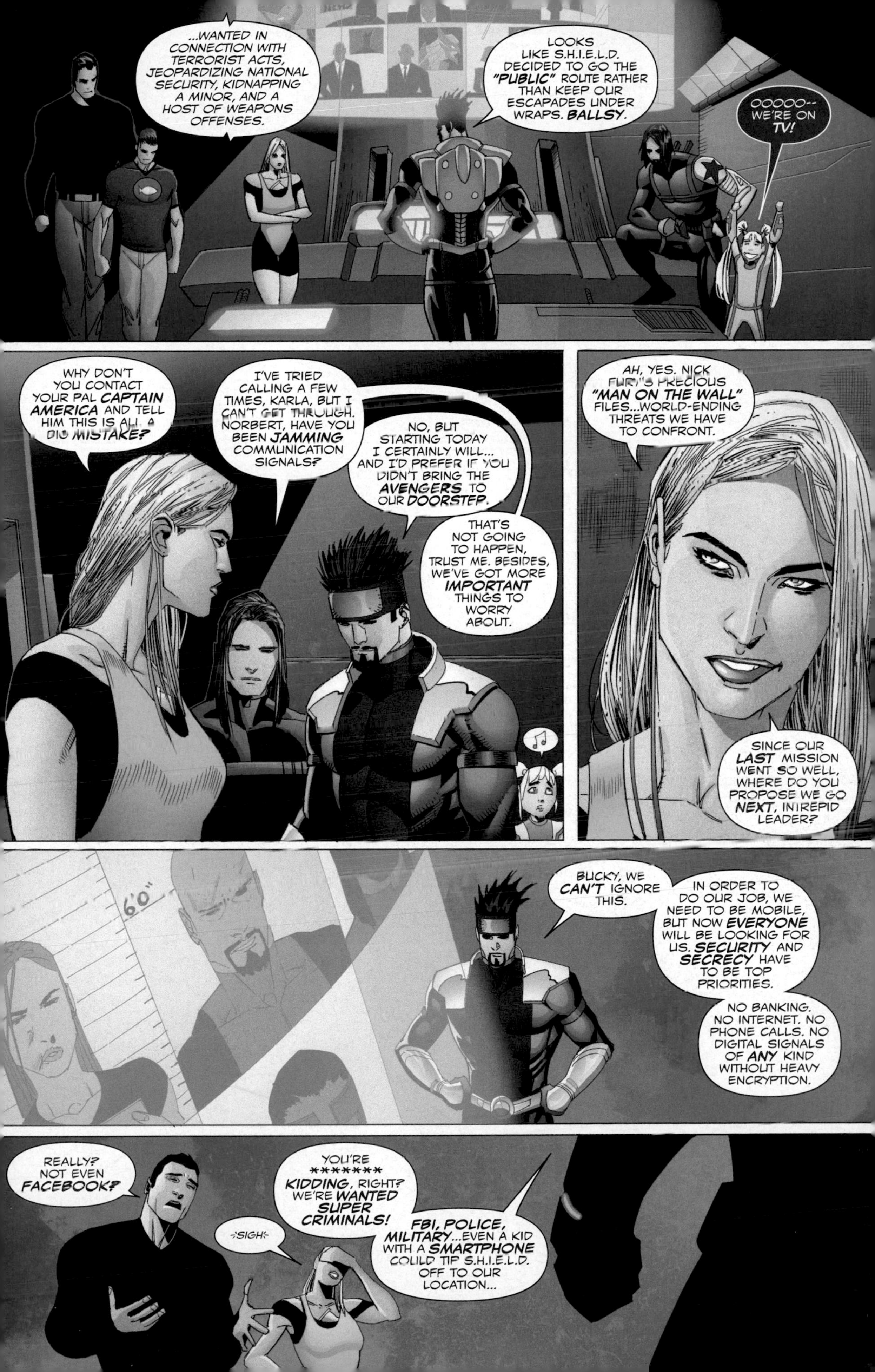
...WANTED IN CONNECTION WITH TERRORIST ACTS, JEOPARDIZING NATIONAL SECURITY, KIDNAPPING A MINOR, AND A HOST OF WEAPONS OFFENSES.
LOOKS LIKE S.H.I.E.L.D. DECIDED TO GO THE "PUBLIC" ROUTE RATHER THAN KEEP OUR ESCAPADES UNDER WRAPS. BALLSY.
OOOOO-- WE'RE ON TV!
WHY DON'T YOU CONTACT YOUR PAL CAPTAIN AMERICA AND TELL HIM THIS IS ALL A BIG MISTAKE?
I'VE TRIED CALLING A FEW TIMES, KARLA, BUT I CAN'T GET THROUGH. NORBERT, HAVE YOU BEEN JAMMING COMMUNICATION SIGNALS?
NO, BUT STARTING TODAY I CERTAINLY WILL... AND I'D PREFER IF YOU DIDN'T BRING THE AVENGERS TO OUR DOORSTEP.
THAT'S NOT GOING TO HAPPEN, TRUST ME. BESIDES, WE'VE GOT MORE IMPORTANT THINGS TO WORRY ABOUT.
AH, YES. NICK FURY'S PRECIOUS "MAN ON THE WALL" FILES...WORLD-ENDING THREATS WE HAVE TO CONFRONT.
SINCE OUR LAST MISSION WENT SO WELL, WHERE DO YOU PROPOSE WE GO NEXT, INTREPID LEADER?
6'0"
BUCKY, WE CAN'T IGNORE THIS.
IN ORDER TO DO OUR JOB, WE NEED TO BE MOBILE, BUT NOW EVERYONE WILL BE LOOKING FOR US. SECURITY AND SECRECY HAVE TO BE TOP PRIORITIES.
NO BANKING. NO INTERNET. NO PHONE CALLS. NO DIGITAL SIGNALS OF ANY KIND WITHOUT HEAVY ENCRYPTION.
REALLY? NOT EVEN FACEBOOK?
YOU'RE ******* KIDDING, RIGHT? WE'RE WANTED SUPER CRIMINALS!
SIGH
FBI, POLICE, MILITARY...EVEN A KID WITH A SMARTPHONE COULD TIP S.H.I.E.L.D. OFF TO OUR LOCATION...

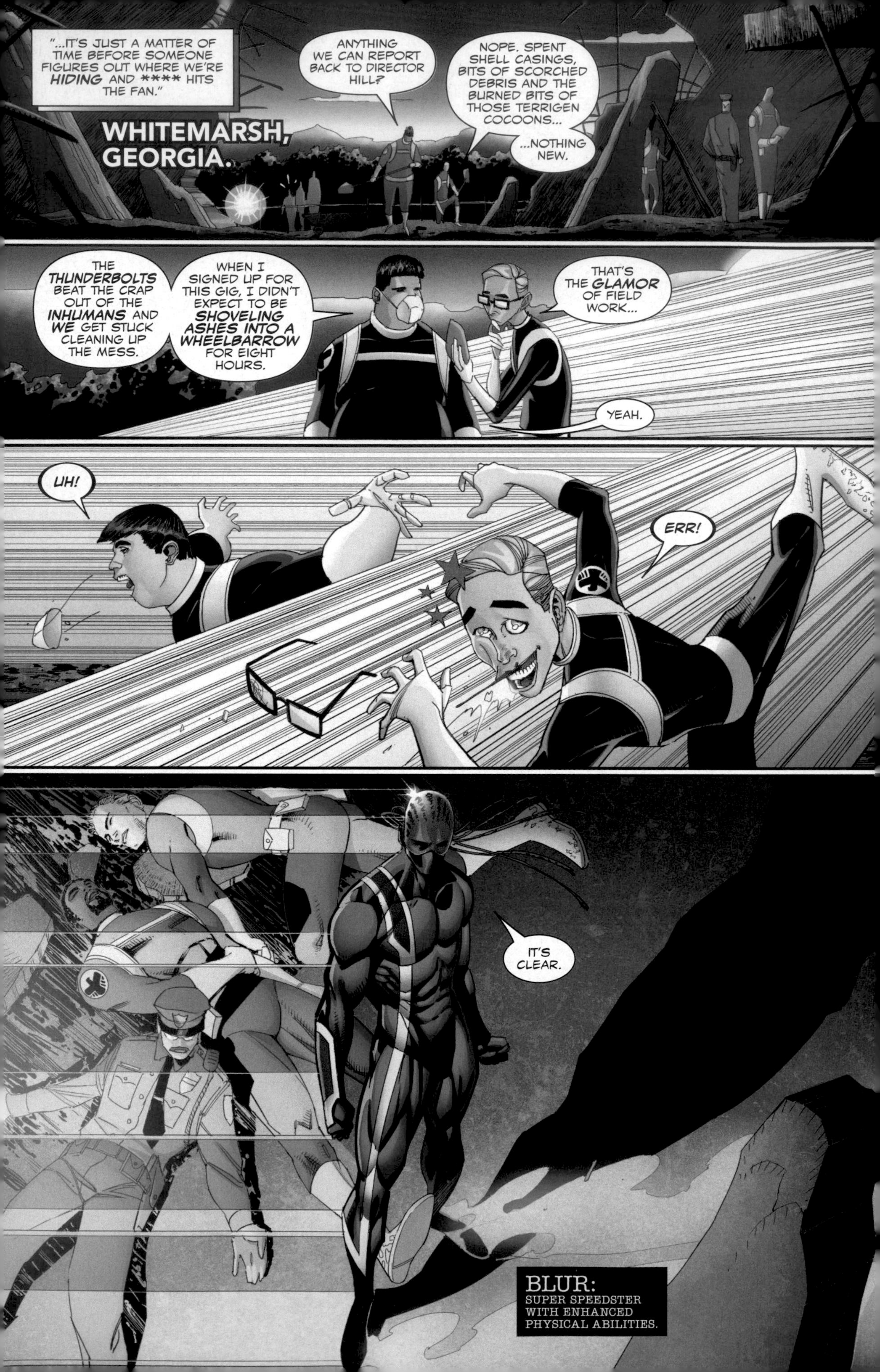
"...IT'S JUST A MATTER OF TIME BEFORE SOMEONE FIGURES OUT WHERE WE'RE HIDING AND **** HITS THE FAN."
WHITEMARSH, GEORGIA.
ANYTHING WE CAN REPORT BACK TO DIRECTOR HILL?
NOPE. SPENT SHELL CASINGS, BITS OF SCORCHED DEBRIS AND THE BURNED BITS OF THOSE TERRIGEN COCOONS...
...NOTHING NEW.
THE THUNDERBOLTS BEAT THE CRAP OUT OF THE INHUMANS AND WE GET STUCK CLEANING UP THE MESS.
WHEN I SIGNED UP FOR THIS GIG, I DIDN'T EXPECT TO BE SHOVELING ASHES INTO A WHEELBARROW FOR EIGHT HOURS.
THAT'S THE GLAMOR OF FIELD WORK...
YEAH.
UH!
ERR!
IT'S CLEAR.
BLUR:
SUPER SPEEDSTER WITH ENHANCED PHYSICAL ABILITIES.

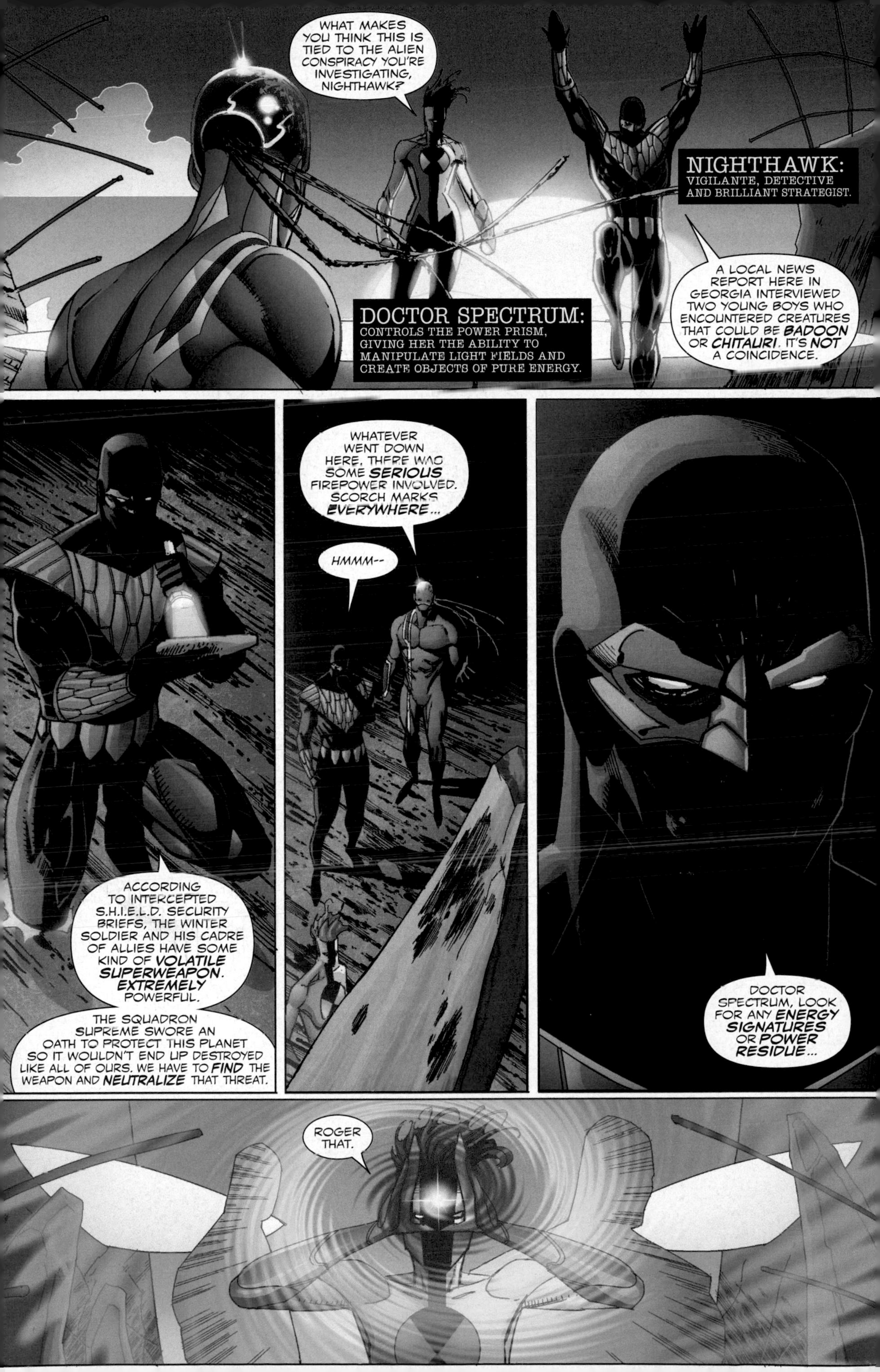
WHAT MAKES YOU THINK THIS IS TIED TO THE ALIEN CONSPIRACY YOU'RE INVESTIGATING, NIGHTHAWK?
NIGHTHAWK: VIGILANTE, DETECTIVE AND BRILLIANT STRATEGIST.
A LOCAL NEWS REPORT HERE IN GEORGIA INTERVIEWED TWO YOUNG BOYS WHO ENCOUNTERED CREATURES THAT COULD BE BADOON OR CHITAURI. IT'S NOT A COINCIDENCE.
DOCTOR SPECTRUM: CONTROLS THE POWER PRISM, GIVING HER THE ABILITY TO MANIPULATE LIGHT FIELDS AND CREATE OBJECTS OF PURE ENERGY.
ACCORDING TO INTERCEPTED S.H.I.E.L.D. SECURITY BRIEFS, THE WINTER SOLDIER AND HIS CADRE OF ALLIES HAVE SOME KIND OF VOLATILE SUPERWEAPON. EXTREMELY POWERFUL.
THE SQUADRON SUPREME SWORE AN OATH TO PROTECT THIS PLANET SO IT WOULDN'T END UP DESTROYED LIKE ALL OF OURS. WE HAVE TO FIND THE WEAPON AND NEUTRALIZE THAT THREAT.
WHATEVER WENT DOWN HERE, THERE WAS SOME SERIOUS FIREPOWER INVOLVED. SCORCH MARKS EVERYWHERE...
HMMM--
DOCTOR SPECTRUM, LOOK FOR ANY ENERGY SIGNATURES OR POWER RESIDUE...
ROGER THAT.

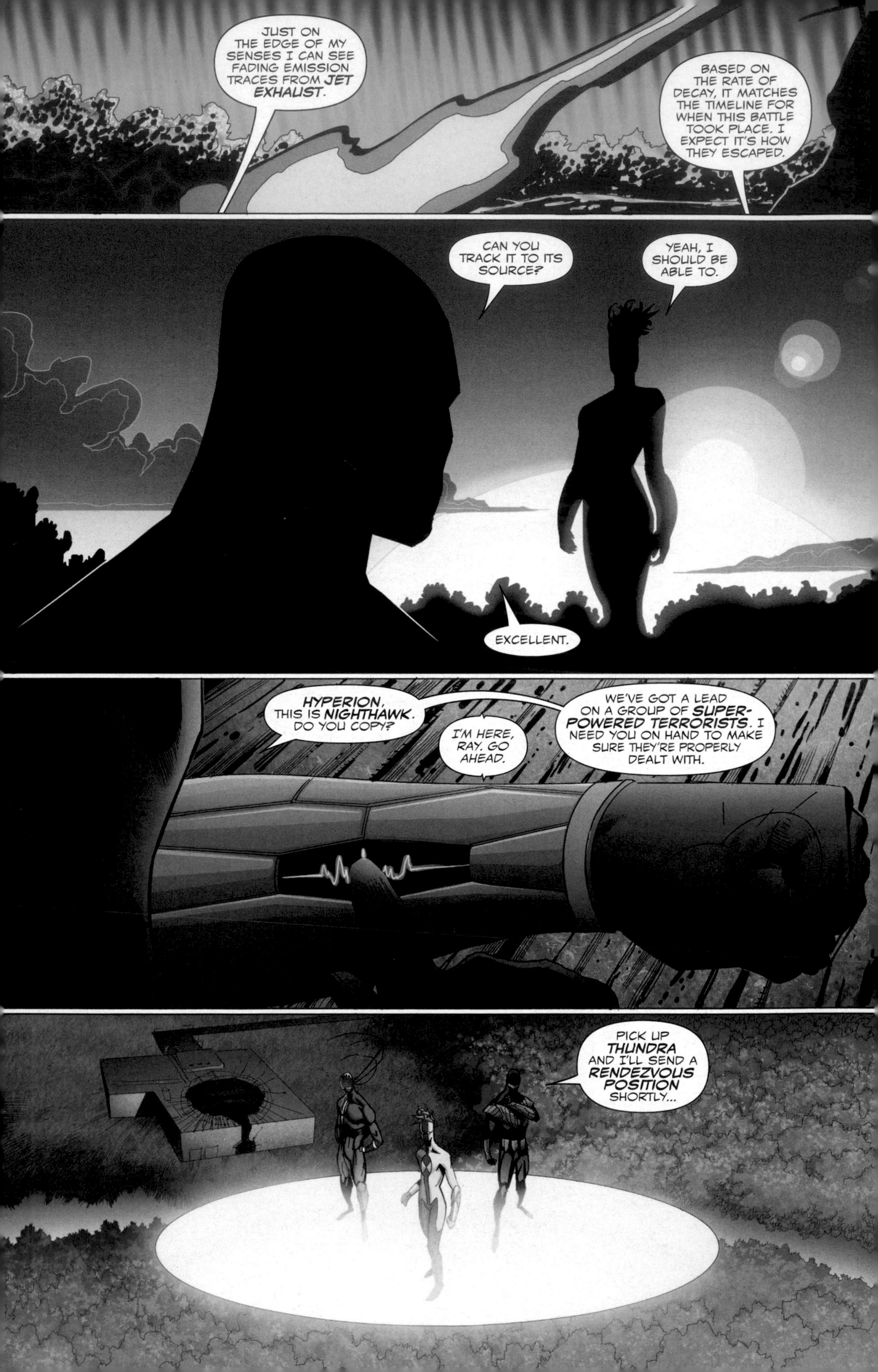
JUST ON THE EDGE OF MY SENSES I CAN SEE FADING EMISSION TRACES FROM JET EXHAUST.
BASED ON THE RATE OF DECAY, IT MATCHES THE TIMELINE FOR WHEN THIS BATTLE TOOK PLACE. I EXPECT IT'S HOW THEY ESCAPED.
CAN YOU TRACK IT TO ITS SOURCE?
YEAH, I SHOULD BE ABLE TO.
EXCELLENT.
HYPERION, THIS IS NIGHTHAWK. DO YOU COPY?
I'M HERE, RAY. GO AHEAD.
WE'VE GOT A LEAD ON A GROUP OF SUPER-POWERED TERRORISTS. I NEED YOU ON HAND TO MAKE SURE THEY'RE PROPERLY DEALT WITH.
PICK UP THUNDRA AND I'LL SEND A RENDEZVOUS POSITION SHORTLY...

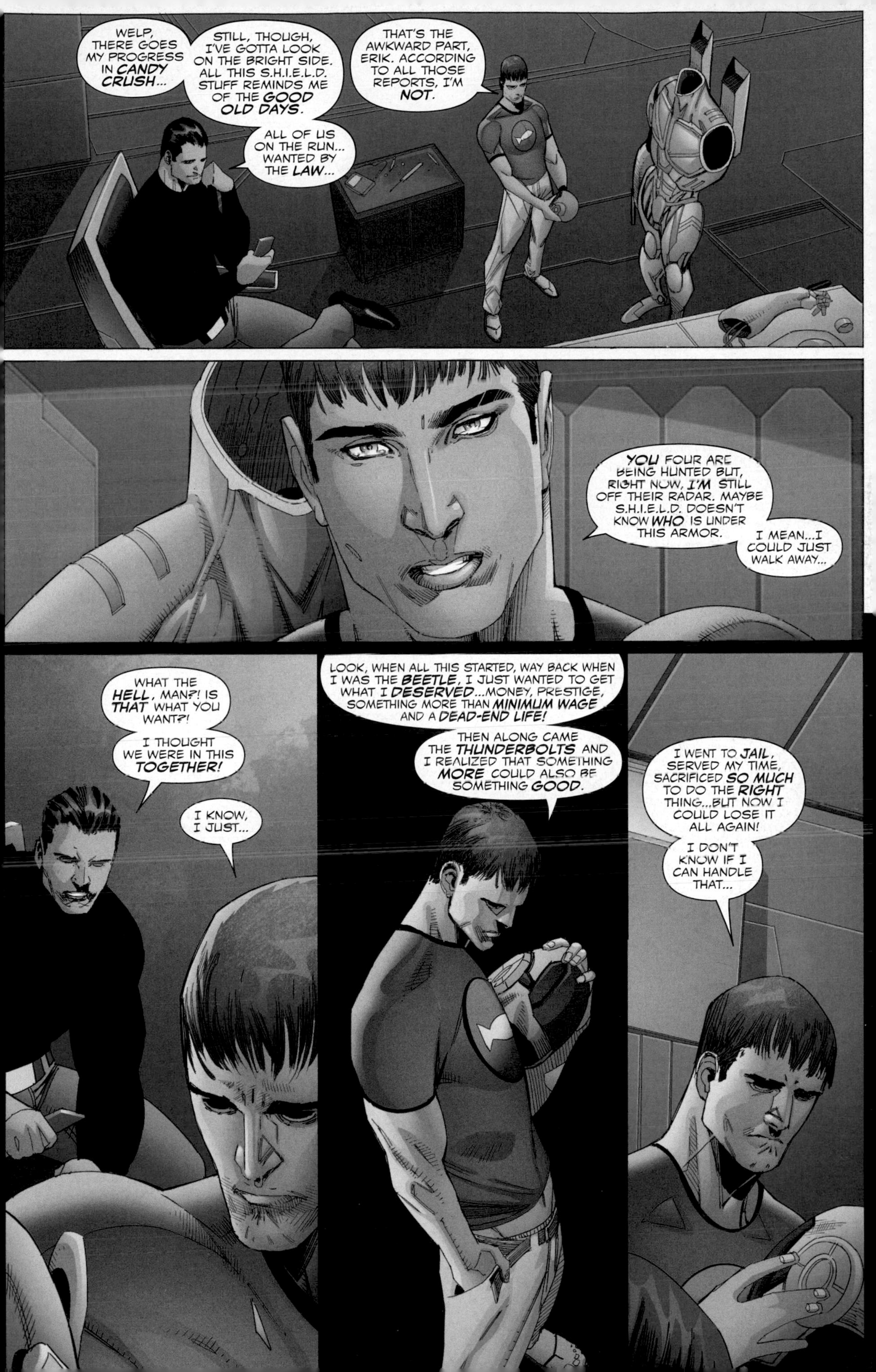
WELP, THERE GOES MY PROGRESS IN CANDY CRUSH...
STILL, THOUGH, I'VE GOTTA LOOK ON THE BRIGHT SIDE. ALL THIS S.H.I.E.L.D. STUFF REMINDS ME OF THE GOOD OLD DAYS.
ALL OF US ON THE RUN... WANTED BY THE LAW...
THAT'S THE AWKWARD PART, ERIK. ACCORDING TO ALL THOSE REPORTS, I'M NOT.
YOU FOUR ARE BEING HUNTED BUT, RIGHT NOW, I'M STILL OFF THEIR RADAR. MAYBE S.H.I.E.L.D. DOESN'T KNOW WHO IS UNDER THIS ARMOR.
I MEAN...I COULD JUST WALK AWAY...
WHAT THE HELL, MAN?! IS THAT WHAT YOU WANT?!
I THOUGHT WE WERE IN THIS TOGETHER!
I KNOW, I JUST...
LOOK, WHEN ALL THIS STARTED, WAY BACK WHEN I WAS THE BEETLE, I JUST WANTED TO GET WHAT I DESERVED...MONEY, PRESTIGE, SOMETHING MORE THAN MINIMUM WAGE AND A DEAD-END LIFE!
THEN ALONG CAME THE THUNDERBOLTS AND I REALIZED THAT SOMETHING MORE COULD ALSO BE SOMETHING GOOD.
I WENT TO JAIL, SERVED MY TIME, SACRIFICED SO MUCH TO DO THE RIGHT THING...BUT NOW I COULD LOSE IT ALL AGAIN!
I DON'T KNOW IF I CAN HANDLE THAT...

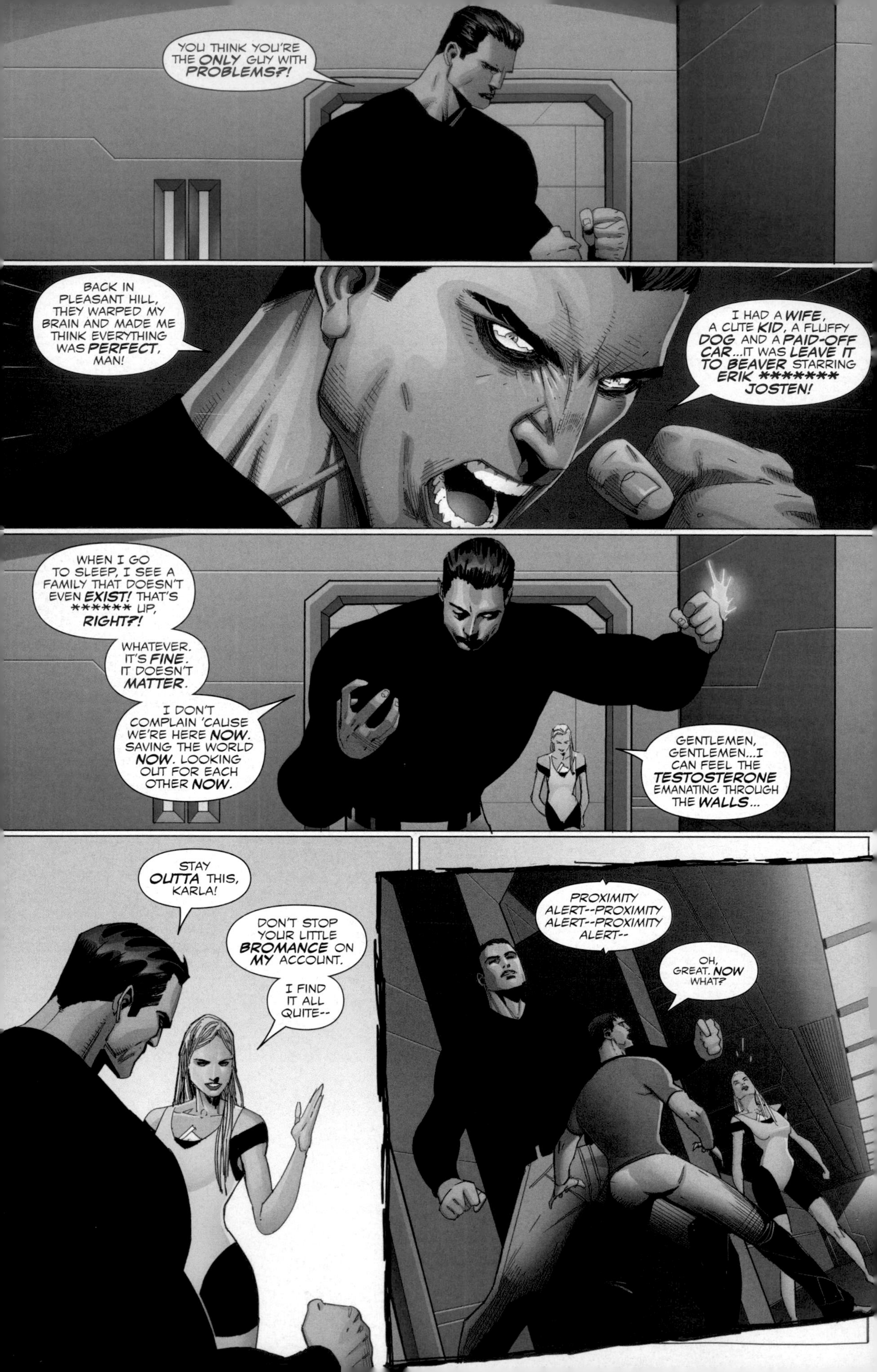

YOU THINK YOU'RE THE ONLY GUY WITH PROBLEMS?!
BACK IN PLEASANT HILL, THEY WARPED MY BRAIN AND MADE ME THINK EVERYTHING WAS PERFECT, MAN!
I HAD A WIFE, A CUTE KID, A FLUFFY DOG AND A PAID-OFF CAR...IT WAS LEAVE IT TO BEAVER STARRING ERIK ******* JOSTEN!
WHEN I GO TO SLEEP, I SEE A FAMILY THAT DOESN'T EVEN EXIST! THAT'S ****** UP, RIGHT?!
WHATEVER. IT'S FINE. IT DOESN'T MATTER.
I DON'T COMPLAIN 'CAUSE WE'RE HERE NOW. SAVING THE WORLD NOW. LOOKING OUT FOR EACH OTHER NOW.
GENTLEMEN, GENTLEMEN...I CAN FEEL THE TESTOSTERONE EMANATING THROUGH THE WALLS...
STAY OUTTA THIS, KARLA!
DON'T STOP YOUR LITTLE BROMANCE ON MY ACCOUNT.
I FIND IT ALL QUITE--
PROXIMITY ALERT--PROXIMITY ALERT--PROXIMITY ALERT--
OH, GREAT. NOW WHAT?

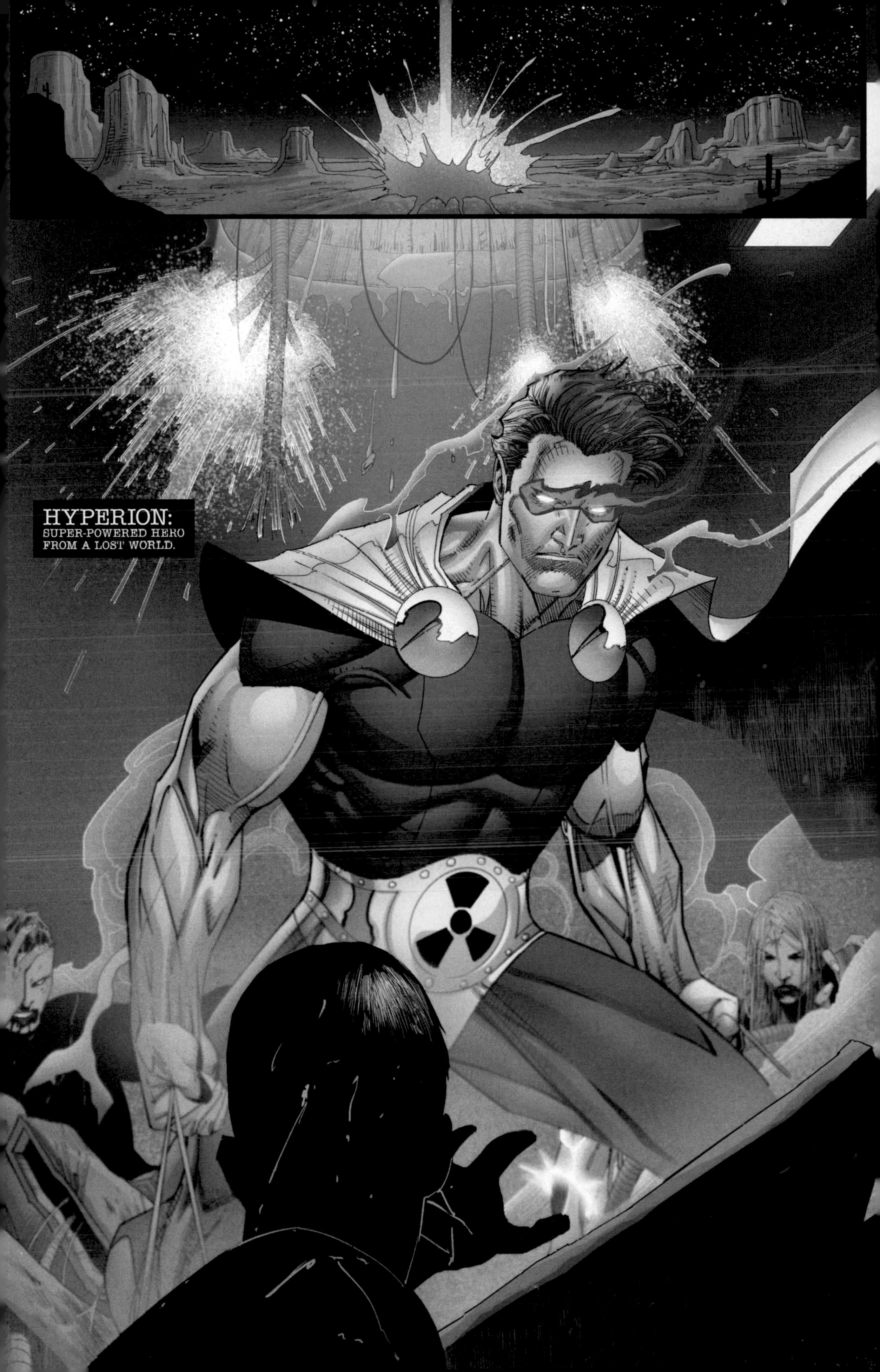
HYPERION:
SUPER-POWERED HERO
FROM A LOST WORLD.

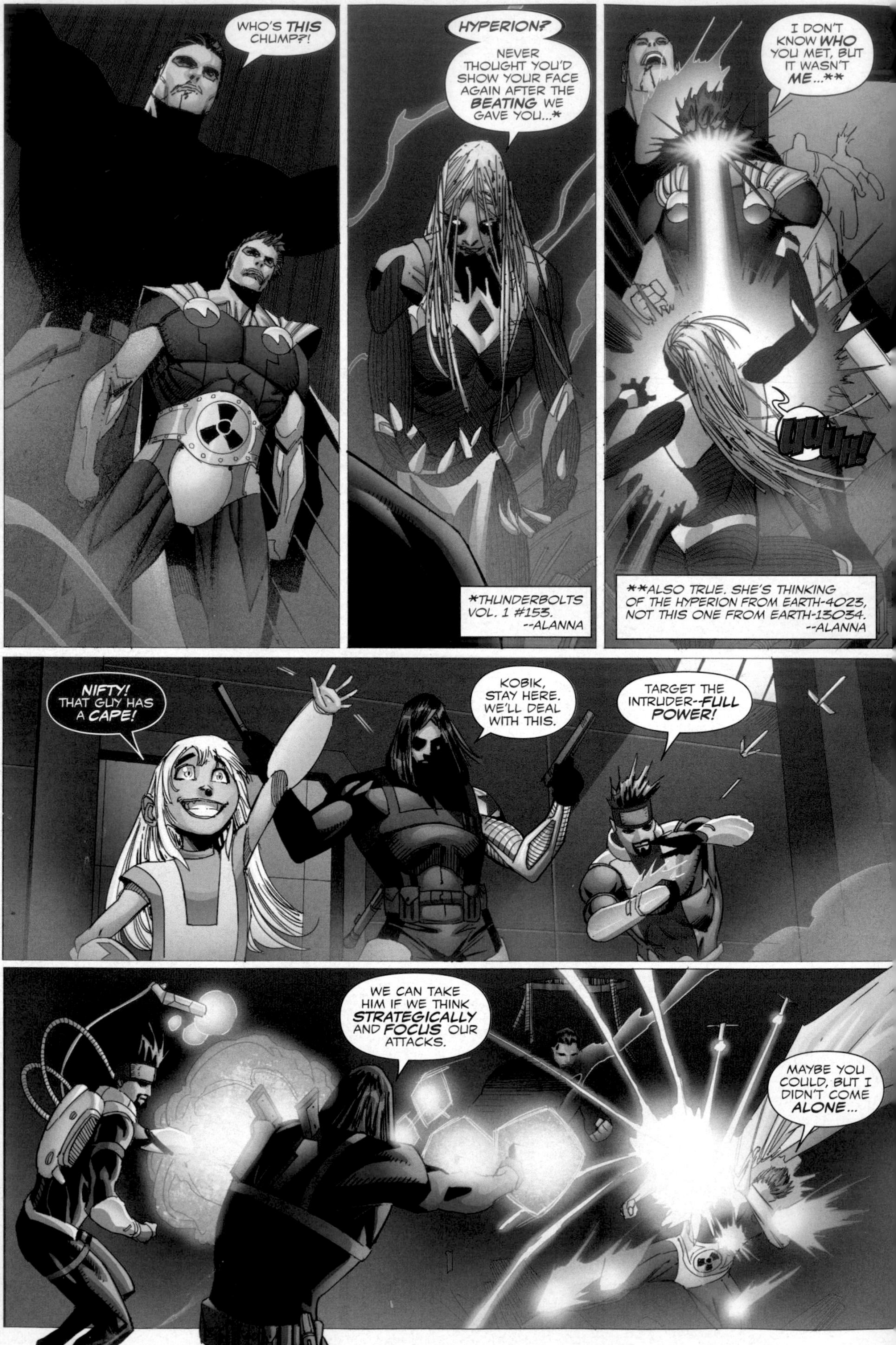
WHO'S THIS CHUMP?!
HYPERION? NEVER THOUGHT YOU'D SHOW YOUR FACE AGAIN AFTER THE BEATING WE GAVE YOU...*
*THUNDERBOLTS VOL. 1 #153. --ALANNA
I DON'T KNOW WHO YOU MET, BUT IT WASN'T ME...**
UUUH!
**ALSO TRUE. SHE'S THINKING OF THE HYPERION FROM EARTH-4023, NOT THIS ONE FROM EARTH-13034. --ALANNA
NIFTY! THAT GUY HAS A CAPE!
KOBIK, STAY HERE. WE'LL DEAL WITH THIS.
TARGET THE INTRUDER--FULL POWER!
WE CAN TAKE HIM IF WE THINK STRATEGICALLY AND FOCUS OUR ATTACKS.
MAYBE YOU COULD, BUT I DIDN'T COME ALONE...

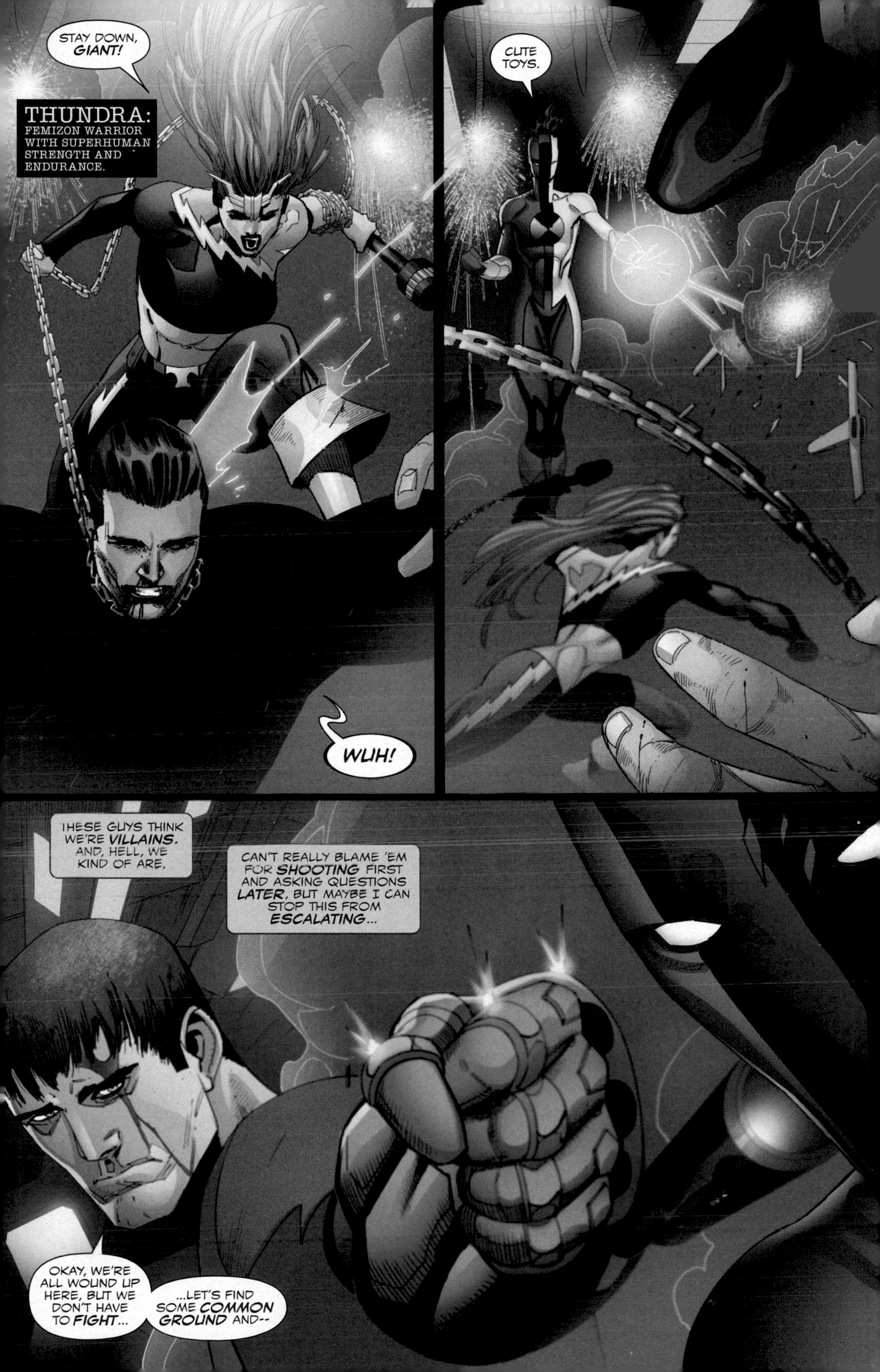
STAY DOWN, GIANT!
THUNDRA: FEMIZON WARRIOR WITH SUPERHUMAN STRENGTH AND ENDURANCE.
WUH!
CUTE TOYS.
THESE GUYS THINK WE'RE VILLAINS. AND, HELL, WE KIND OF ARE.
CAN'T REALLY BLAME 'EM FOR SHOOTING FIRST AND ASKING QUESTIONS LATER, BUT MAYBE I CAN STOP THIS FROM ESCALATING...
OKAY, WE'RE ALL WOUND UP HERE, BUT WE DON'T HAVE TO FIGHT...
...LET'S FIND SOME COMMON GROUND AND--

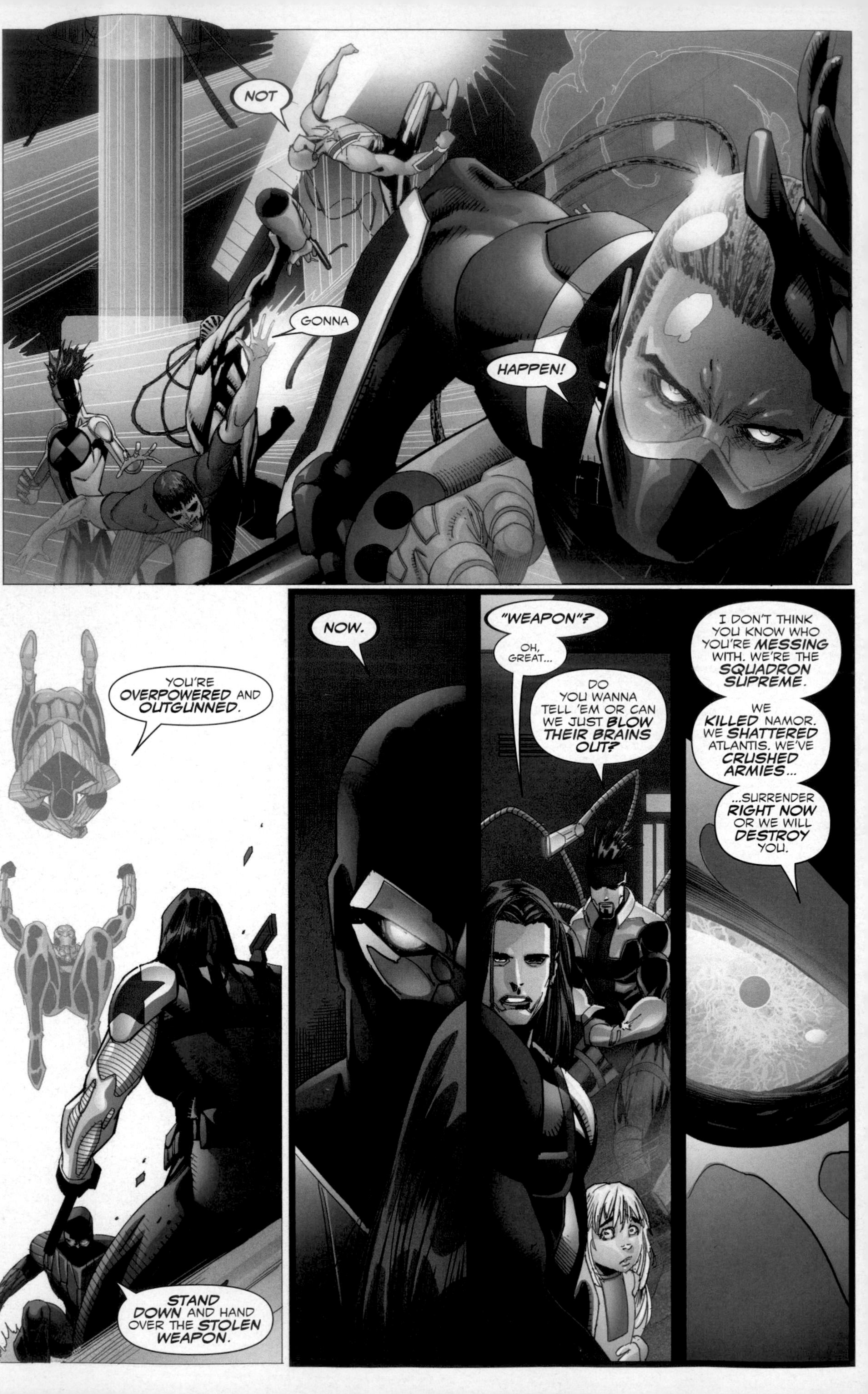
NOT
GONNA
HAPPEN!
YOU'RE OVERPOWERED AND OUTGUNNED.
STAND DOWN AND HAND OVER THE STOLEN WEAPON.
NOW.
"WEAPON"?
OH, GREAT...
DO YOU WANNA TELL 'EM OR CAN WE JUST BLOW THEIR BRAINS OUT?
I DON'T THINK YOU KNOW WHO YOU'RE MESSING WITH. WE'RE THE SQUADRON SUPREME.
WE KILLED NAMOR. WE SHATTERED ATLANTIS. WE'VE CRUSHED ARMIES...
...SURRENDER RIGHT NOW OR WE WILL DESTROY YOU.

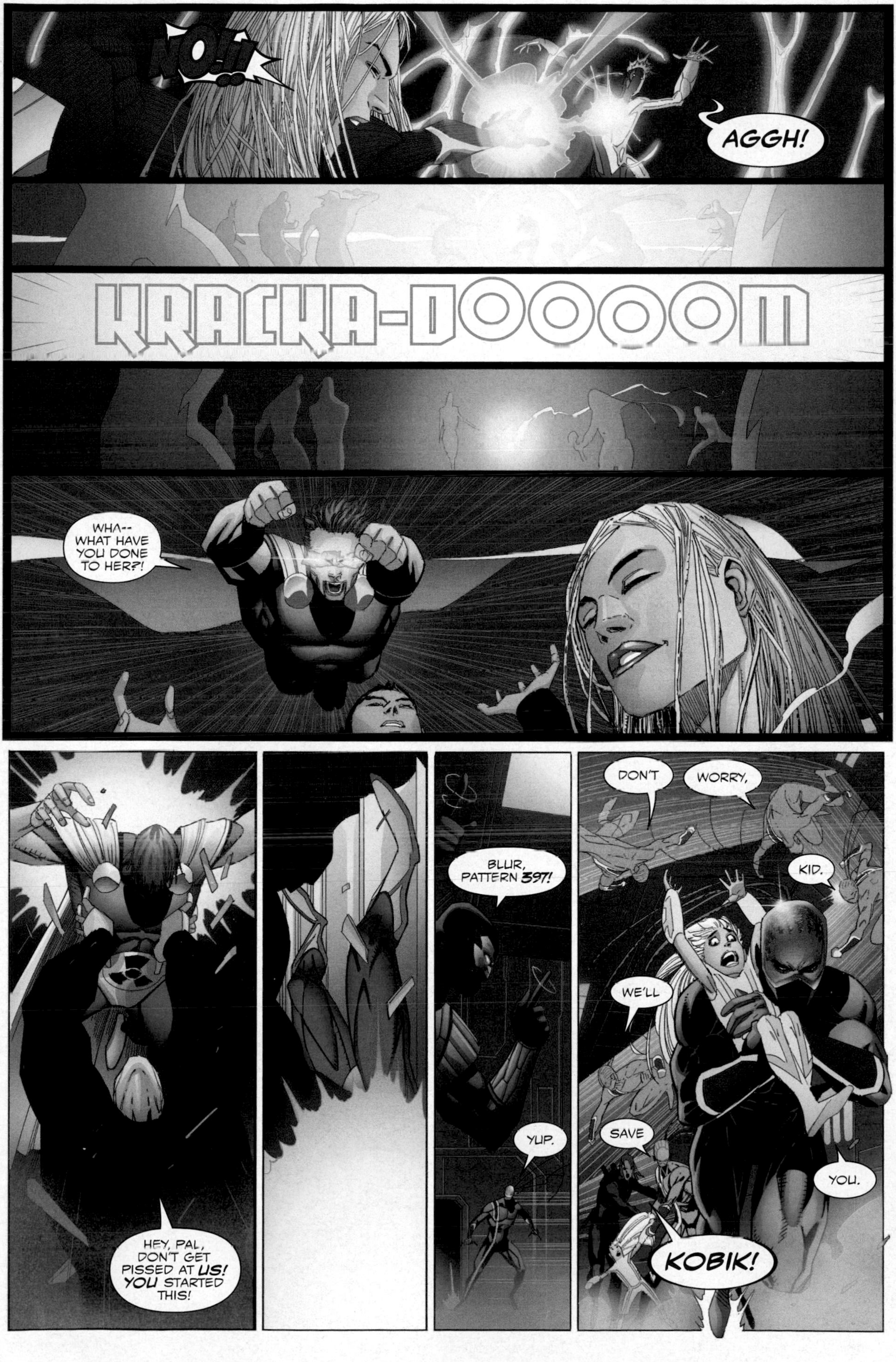
NO!!
AGGH!
KRACKA-DOOOOM
WHA-- WHAT HAVE YOU DONE TO HER?!
HEY, PAL, DON'T GET PISSED AT US! YOU STARTED THIS!
BLUR, PATTERN 397!
YUP.
DON'T
WORRY,
KID.
WE'LL
SAVE
YOU.
KOBIK!

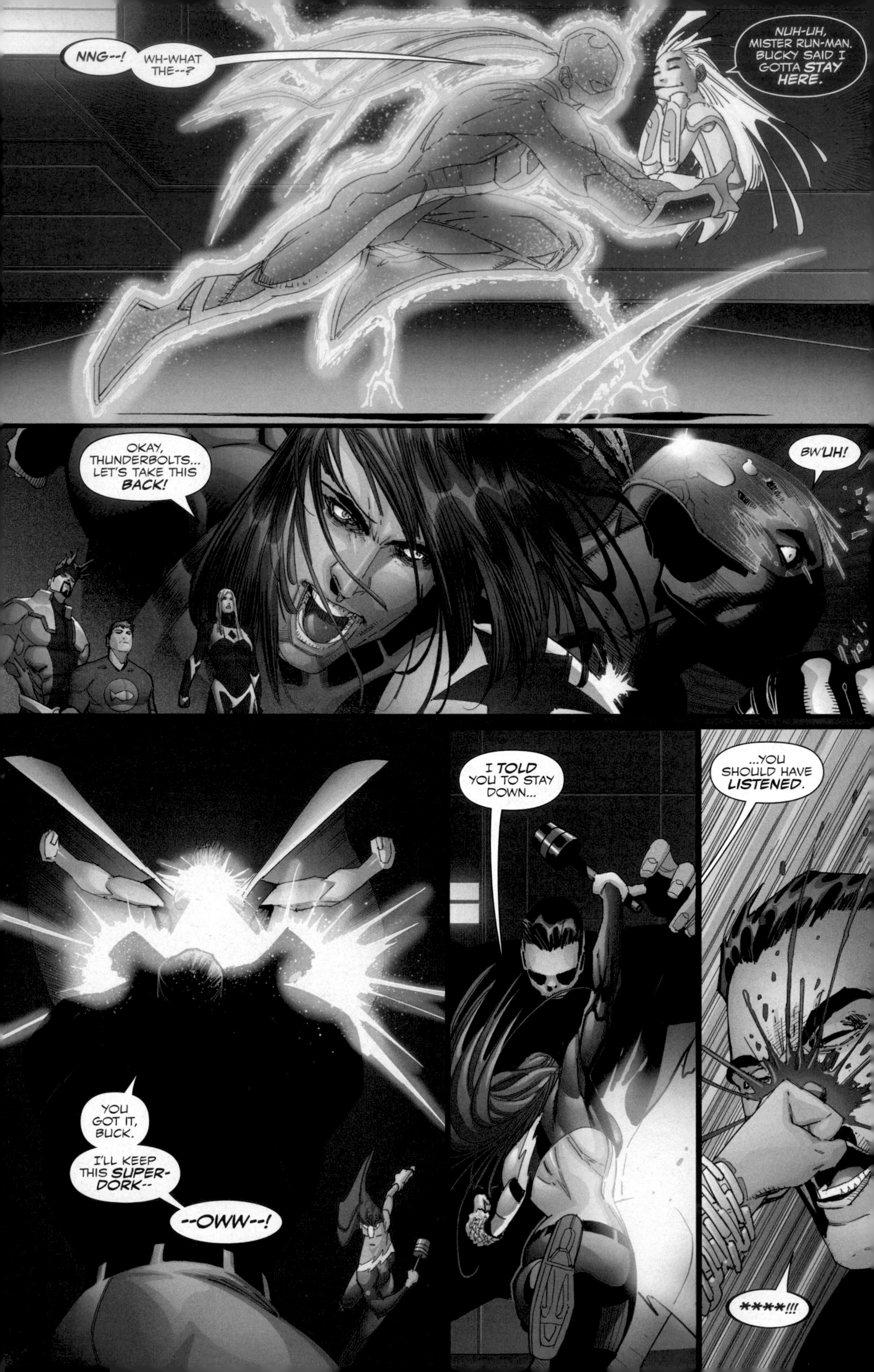

NNG--!
WH-WHAT THE--?
NUH-UH, MISTER RUN-MAN. BUCKY SAID I GOTTA STAY HERE.
OKAY, THUNDERBOLTS... LET'S TAKE THIS BACK!
BW'UH!
YOU GOT IT, BUCK.
I'LL KEEP THIS SUPER-DORK--
--OWW--!
I TOLD YOU TO STAY DOWN...
...YOU SHOULD HAVE LISTENED.
****!!!

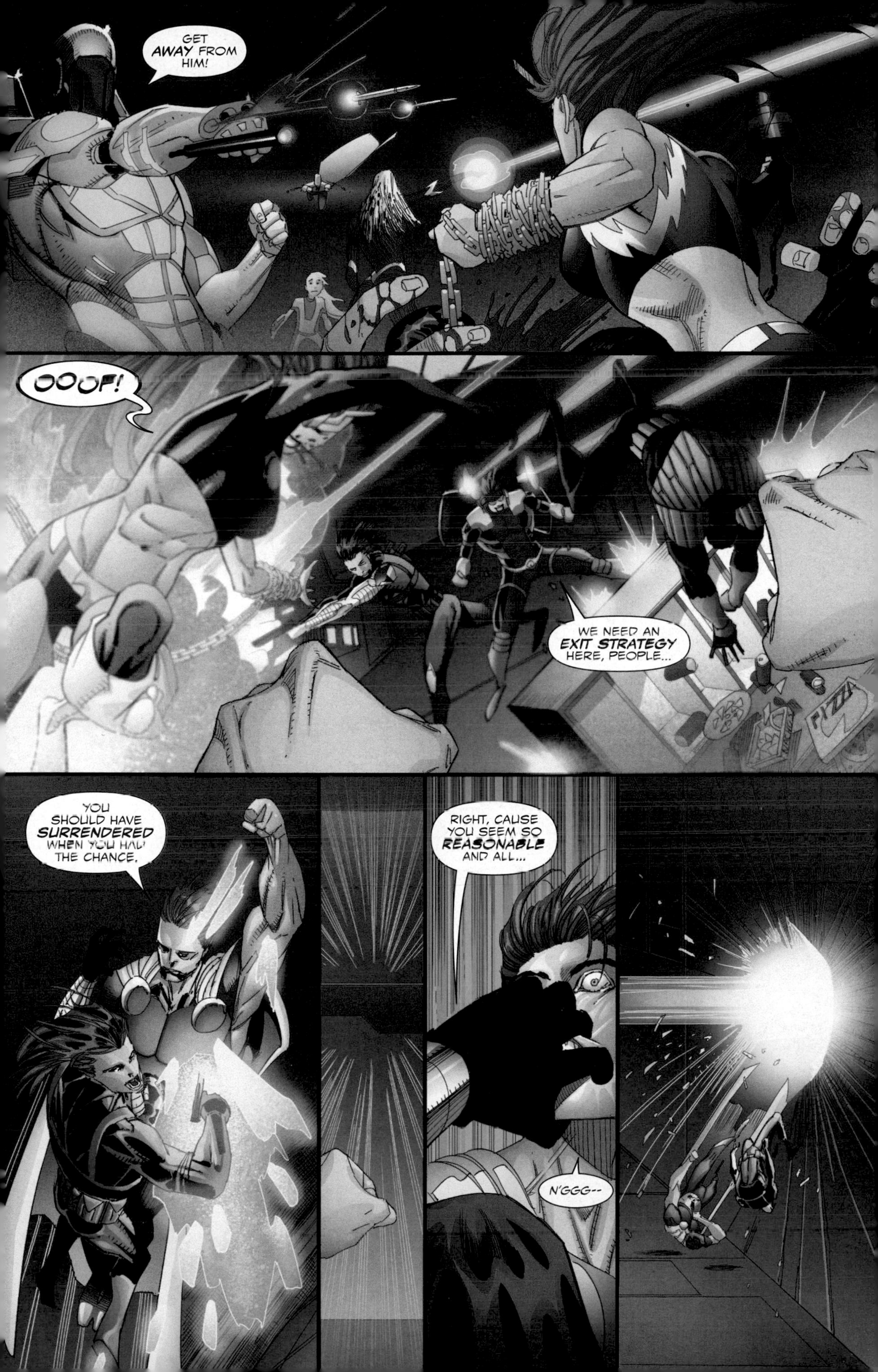
GET AWAY FROM HIM!
OOOF!
WE NEED AN EXIT STRATEGY HERE, PEOPLE...
YOU SHOULD HAVE SURRENDERED WHEN YOU HAD THE CHANCE.
RIGHT, CAUSE YOU SEEM SO REASONABLE AND ALL...
N'GGG--
PIZZA

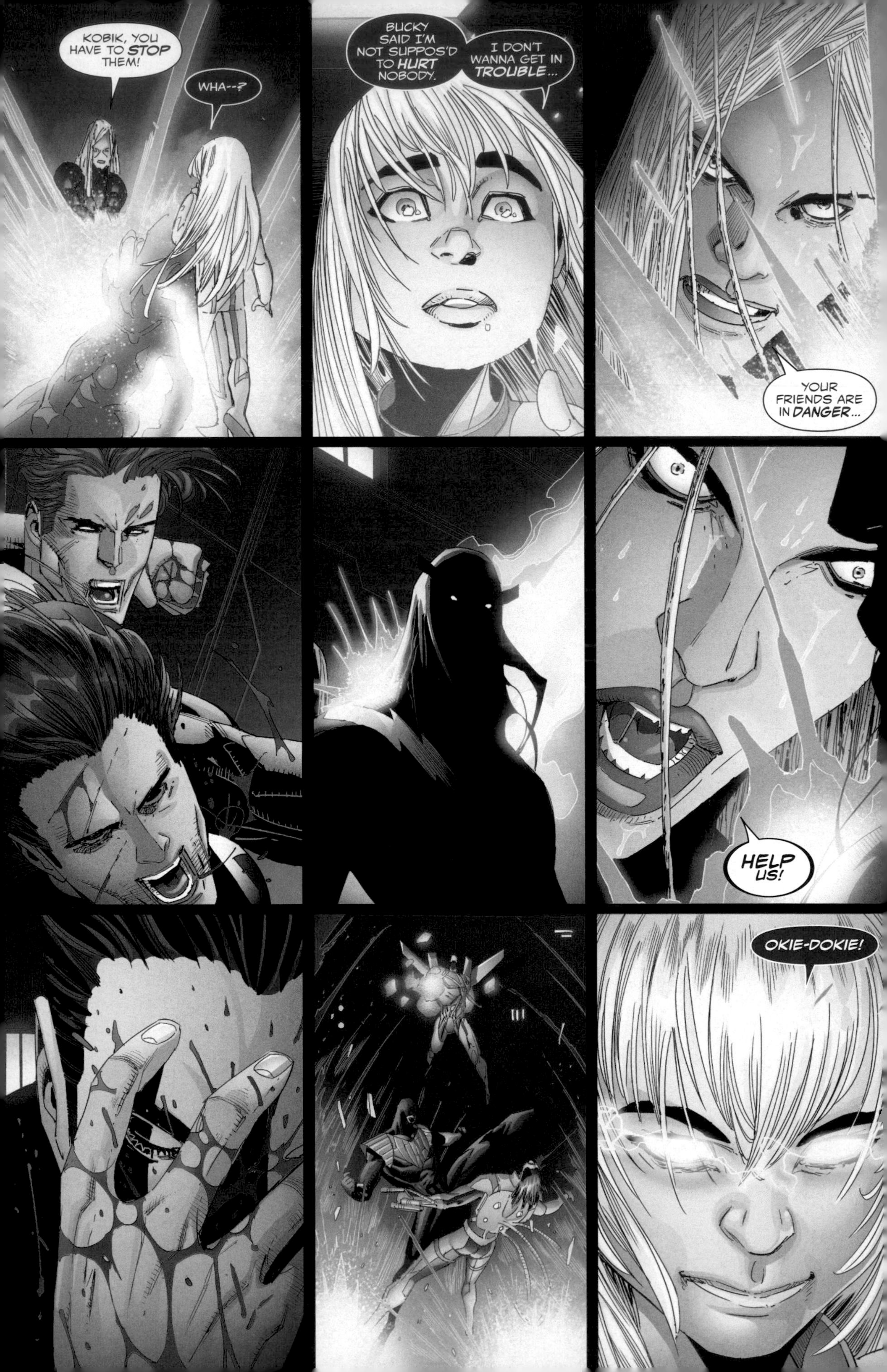
KOBIK, YOU HAVE TO STOP THEM!
WHA--?
BUCKY SAID I'M NOT SUPPOS'D TO HURT NOBODY.
I DON'T WANNA GET IN TROUBLE...
YOUR FRIENDS ARE IN DANGER...
HELP US!
OKIE-DOKIE!

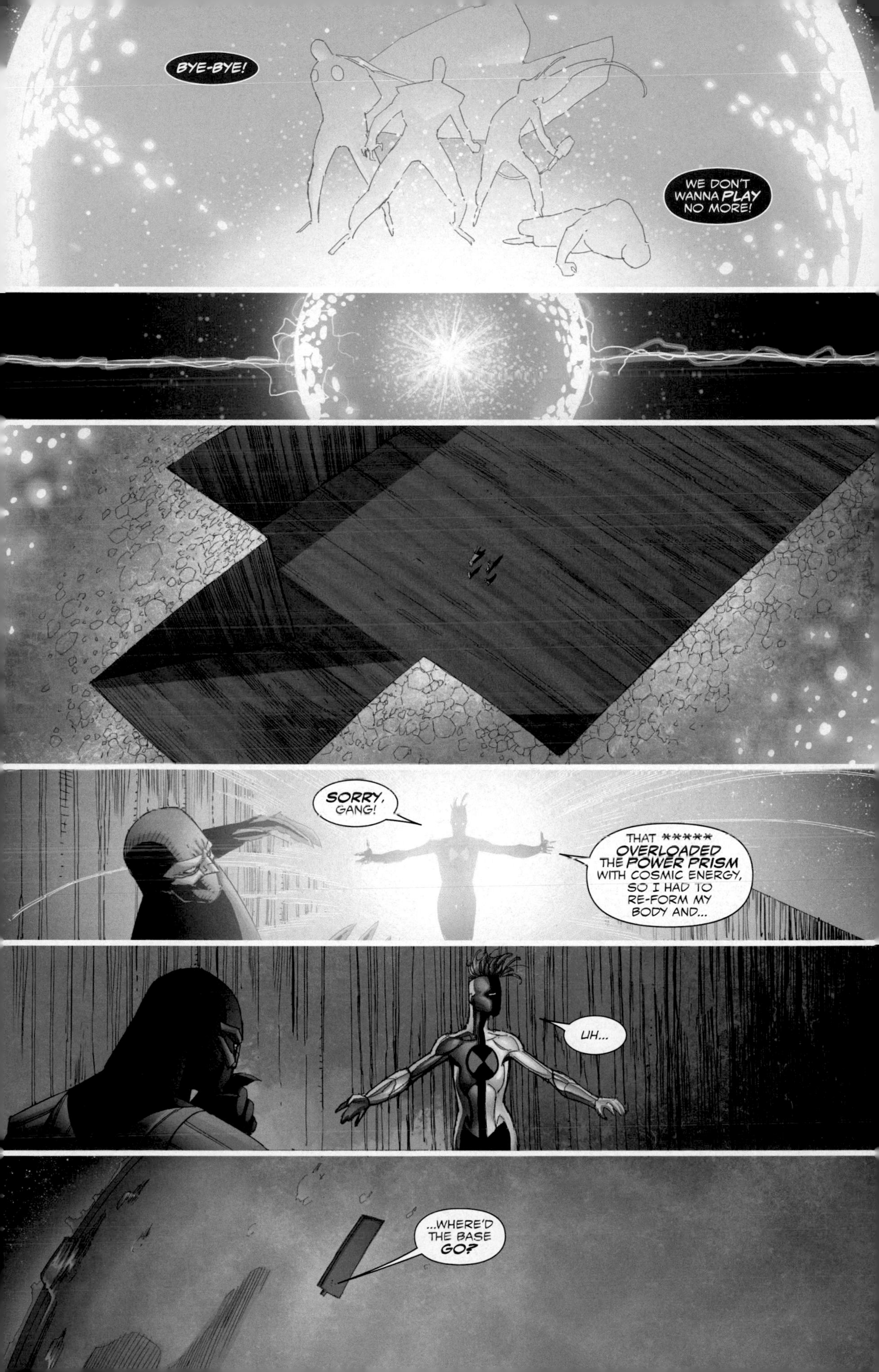
BYE-BYE!
WE DON'T WANNA PLAY NO MORE!
SORRY, GANG!
THAT ***** OVERLOADED THE POWER PRISM WITH COSMIC ENERGY, SO I HAD TO RE-FORM MY BODY AND...
UH...
...WHERE'D THE BASE GO?

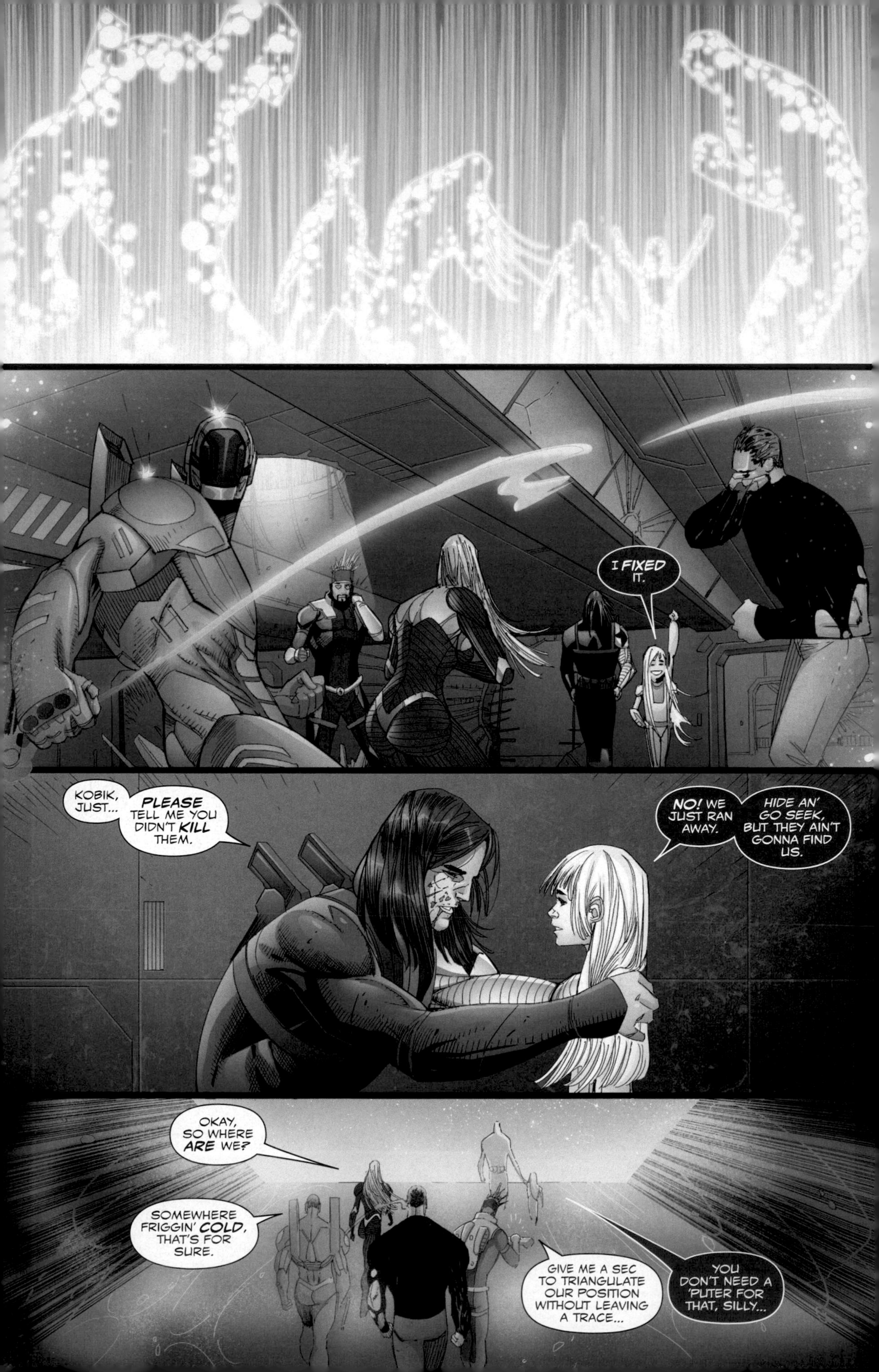
I FIXED IT.
KOBIK, JUST...
PLEASE TELL ME YOU DIDN'T KILL THEM.
NO! WE JUST RAN AWAY.
HIDE AN' GO SEEK, BUT THEY AIN'T GONNA FIND US.
OKAY, SO WHERE ARE WE?
SOMEWHERE FRIGGIN' COLD, THAT'S FOR SURE.
GIVE ME A SEC TO TRIANGULATE OUR POSITION WITHOUT LEAVING A TRACE...
YOU DON'T NEED A 'PUTER FOR THAT, SILLY...

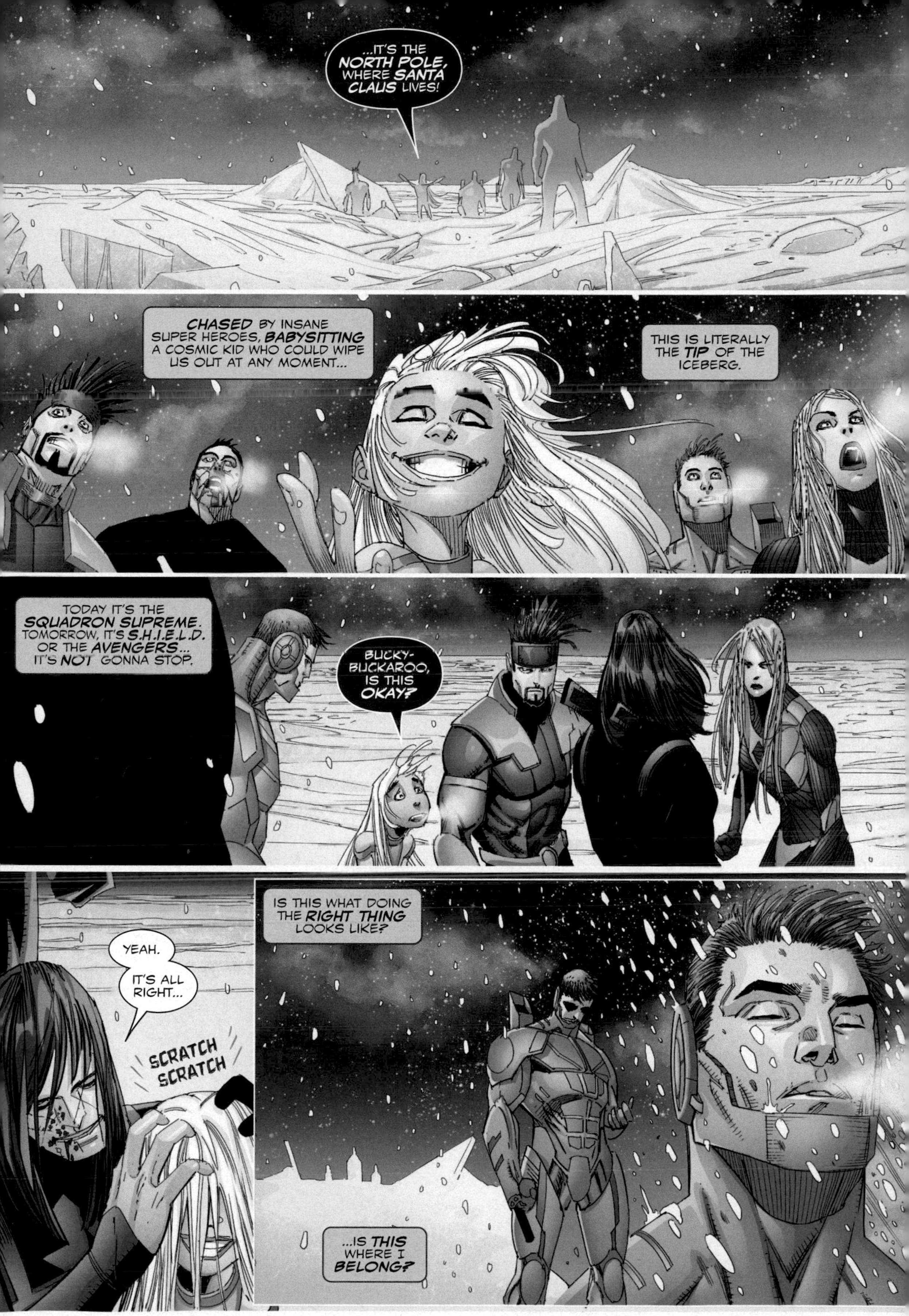
...IT'S THE NORTH POLE, WHERE SANTA CLAUS LIVES!
CHASED BY INSANE SUPER HEROES, BABYSITTING A COSMIC KID WHO COULD WIPE US OUT AT ANY MOMENT...
THIS IS LITERALLY THE TIP OF THE ICEBERG.
TODAY IT'S THE SQUADRON SUPREME. TOMORROW, IT'S S.H.I.E.L.D. OR THE AVENGERS... IT'S NOT GONNA STOP.
BUCKY-BUCKAROO, IS THIS OKAY?
YEAH.
IT'S ALL RIGHT...
SCRATCH SCRATCH
IS THIS WHAT DOING THE RIGHT THING LOOKS LIKE?
...IS THIS WHERE I BELONG?

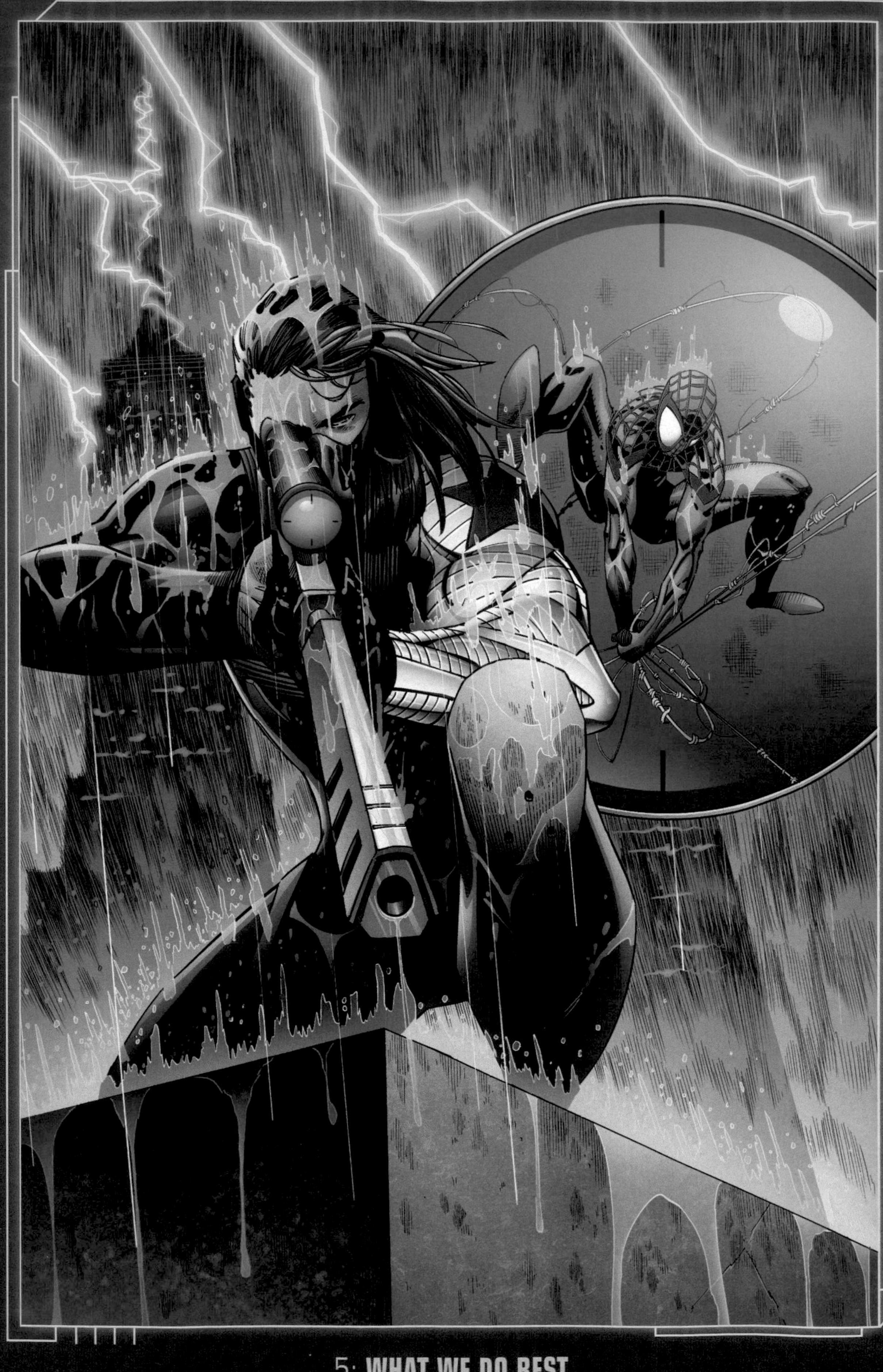

5: WHAT WE DO BEST

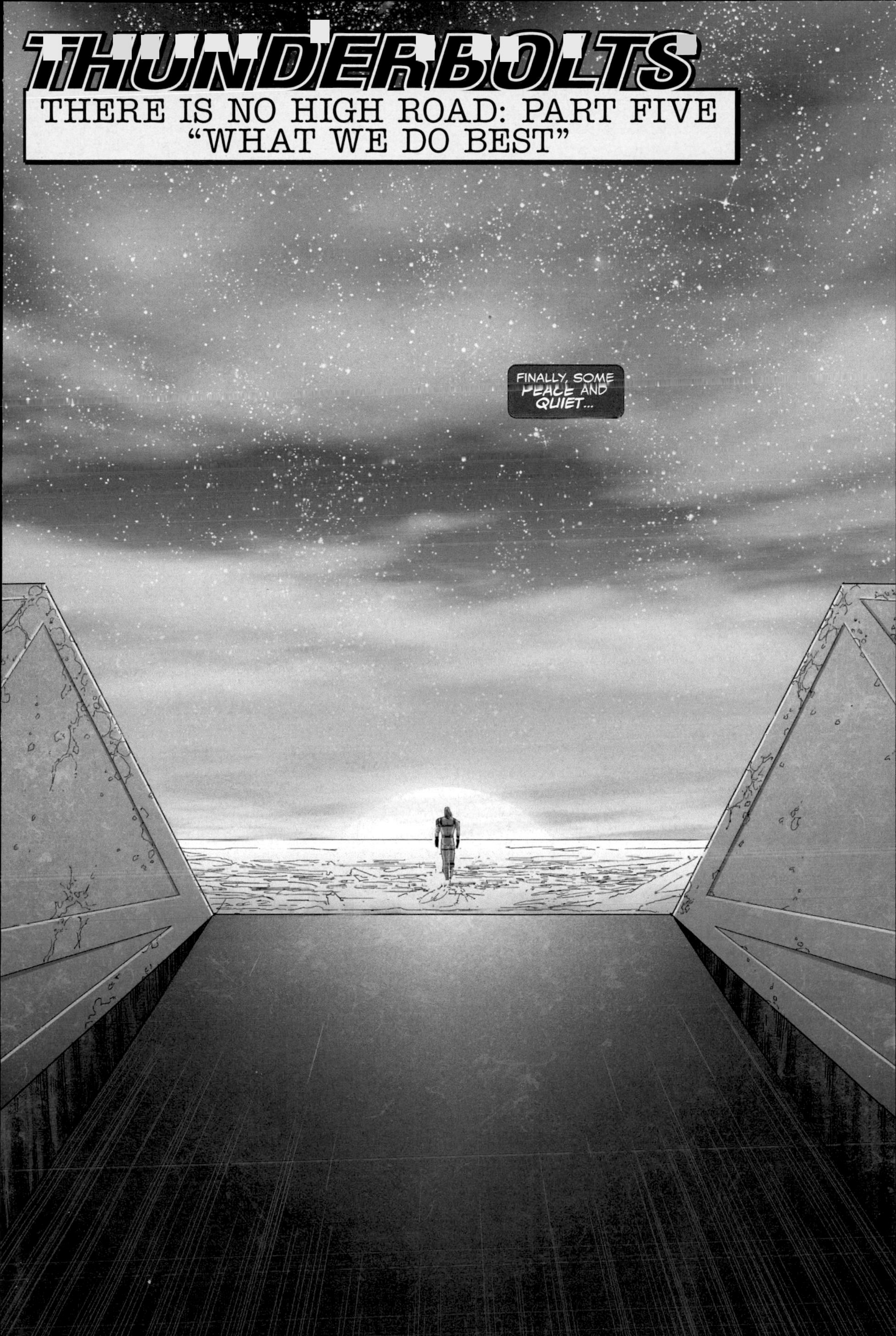
THUNDERBOLTS
THERE IS NO HIGH ROAD: PART FIVE
"WHAT WE DO BEST"
FINALLY, SOME PEACE AND QUIET...

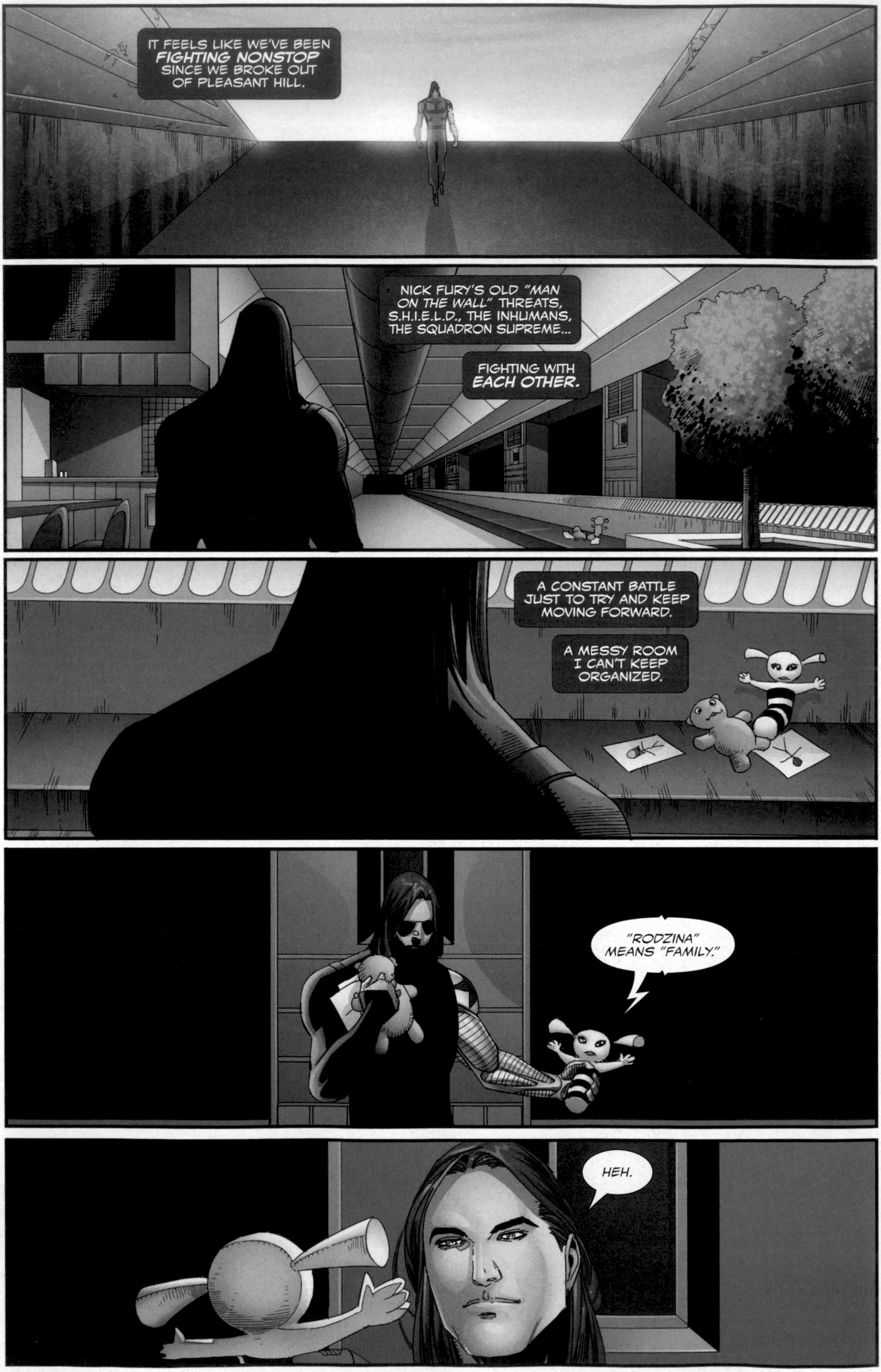
IT FEELS LIKE WE'VE BEEN FIGHTING NONSTOP SINCE WE BROKE OUT OF PLEASANT HILL.
NICK FURY'S OLD "MAN ON THE WALL" THREATS, S.H.I.E.L.D., THE INHUMANS, THE SQUADRON SUPREME...
FIGHTING WITH EACH OTHER.
A CONSTANT BATTLE JUST TO TRY AND KEEP MOVING FORWARD.
A MESSY ROOM I CAN'T KEEP ORGANIZED.
"RODZINA" MEANS "FAMILY."
HEH.

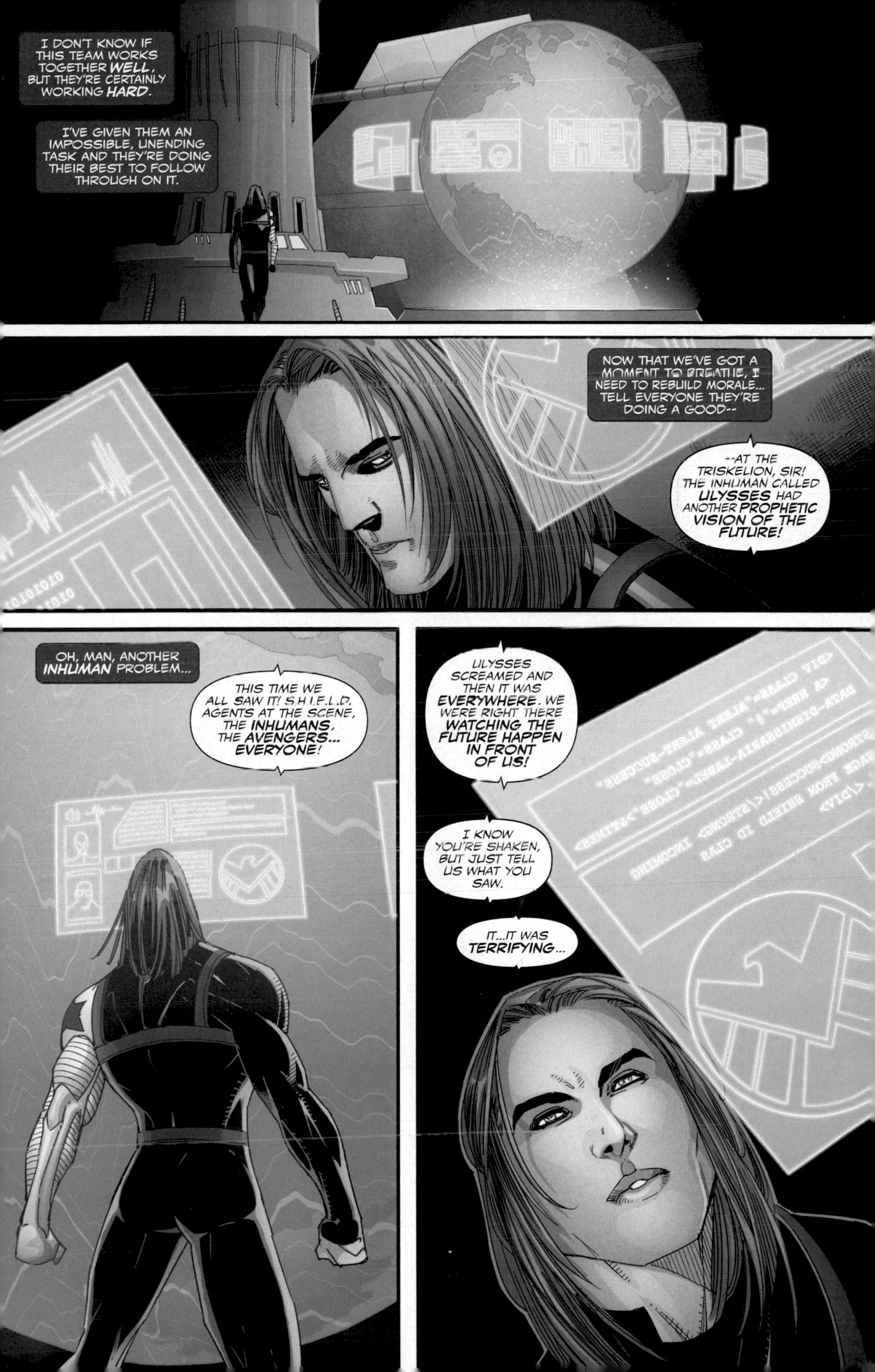
I DON'T KNOW IF THIS TEAM WORKS TOGETHER **WELL**, BUT THEY'RE CERTAINLY WORKING **HARD**.
I'VE GIVEN THEM AN IMPOSSIBLE, UNENDING TASK AND THEY'RE DOING THEIR BEST TO FOLLOW THROUGH ON IT.
NOW THAT WE'VE GOT A MOMENT TO BREATHE, I NEED TO REBUILD MORALE... TELL EVERYONE THEY'RE DOING A GOOD--
--AT THE TRISKELION, SIR! THE INHUMAN CALLED **ULYSSES** HAD ANOTHER **PROPHETIC VISION OF THE FUTURE!**
OH, MAN, ANOTHER **INHUMAN** PROBLEM...
THIS TIME WE ALL SAW IT! S.H.I.E.L.D. AGENTS AT THE SCENE, THE **INHUMANS**, THE **AVENGERS... EVERYONE**!
ULYSSES SCREAMED AND THEN IT WAS **EVERYWHERE**. WE WERE RIGHT THERE **WATCHING THE FUTURE HAPPEN IN FRONT OF US!**
I KNOW YOU'RE SHAKEN, BUT JUST TELL US WHAT YOU SAW.
IT...IT WAS **TERRIFYING**...

...SPIDER-MAN **MURDERED STEVE ROGERS!**

WHAT?!

THE NEW **SPIDER-MAN,** HE KILLED CAPTAIN AMERICA!

I KNOW IT WASN'T **REAL**... I MEAN, IT HASN'T **HAPPENED** YET...

...BUT I **SAW** IT, WE ALL DID!

IT **LOOKED** REAL, BUT THAT DOESN'T MEAN IT **WILL** HAPPEN THAT WAY...

CAPTAIN MARVEL SAID ULYSSES HAS BEEN **COMPLETELY ACCURATE!**

HIS VISIONS ARE **OUR FUTURE!**

HAS SPIDER-MAN BEEN **APPREHENDED?**

NO.

THEY...WELL, THEY **ARGUED** ABOUT IT BUT, IN THE END, THE AVENGERS **LET** HIM LEAVE.

THEY DID **WHAT?!**

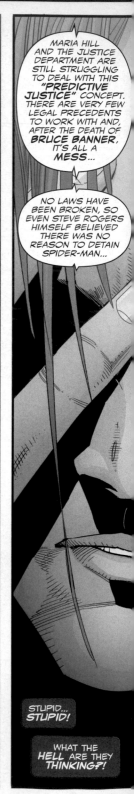

MARIA HILL AND THE JUSTICE DEPARTMENT ARE STILL STRUGGLING TO DEAL WITH THIS **"PREDICTIVE JUSTICE"** CONCEPT. THERE ARE VERY FEW LEGAL PRECEDENTS TO WORK WITH AND, AFTER THE DEATH OF **BRUCE BANNER,** IT'S ALL A **MESS**...

NO LAWS HAVE BEEN BROKEN, SO EVEN STEVE ROGERS HIMSELF BELIEVED THERE WAS NO REASON TO DETAIN SPIDER-MAN...

STUPID... **STUPID!**

WHAT THE **HELL** ARE THEY **THINKING?!**

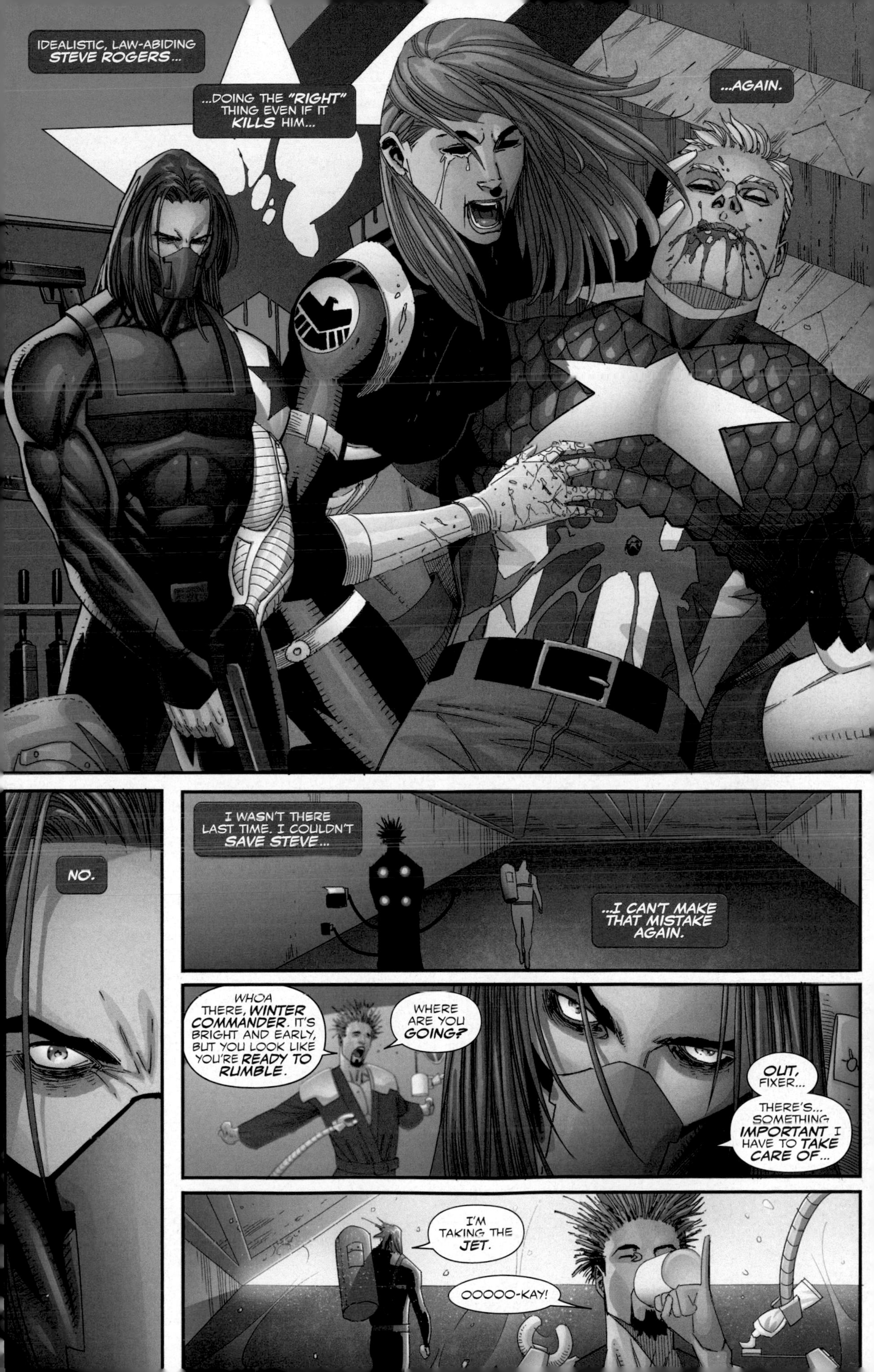
IDEALISTIC, LAW-ABIDING STEVE ROGERS...
...DOING THE "RIGHT" THING EVEN IF IT KILLS HIM...
...AGAIN.
NO.
I WASN'T THERE LAST TIME. I COULDN'T SAVE STEVE...
...I CAN'T MAKE THAT MISTAKE AGAIN.
WHOA THERE, WINTER COMMANDER. IT'S BRIGHT AND EARLY, BUT YOU LOOK LIKE YOU'RE READY TO RUMBLE.
WHERE ARE YOU GOING?
OUT, FIXER...
THERE'S... SOMETHING IMPORTANT I HAVE TO TAKE CARE OF...
I'M TAKING THE JET.
OOOOO-KAY!

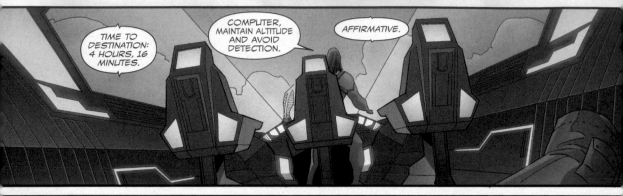

I SHOULDN'T DO THIS...

...BUT NO ONE ELSE WILL.

TIME TO DESTINATION: 4 HOURS, 16 MINUTES.

COMPUTER, MAINTAIN ALTITUDE AND AVOID DETECTION.

AFFIRMATIVE.

BACK IN THE SADDLE...

...BACK ON THE *HUNT*.

ZVEZDA MOYA...*

⟨I LOVE WATCHING YOU GET READY FOR *WORK*.⟩

*RUSSIAN FOR "MY STAR."

DON'T THINK ABOUT *NAT*.

JUST...

...*DON'T*.

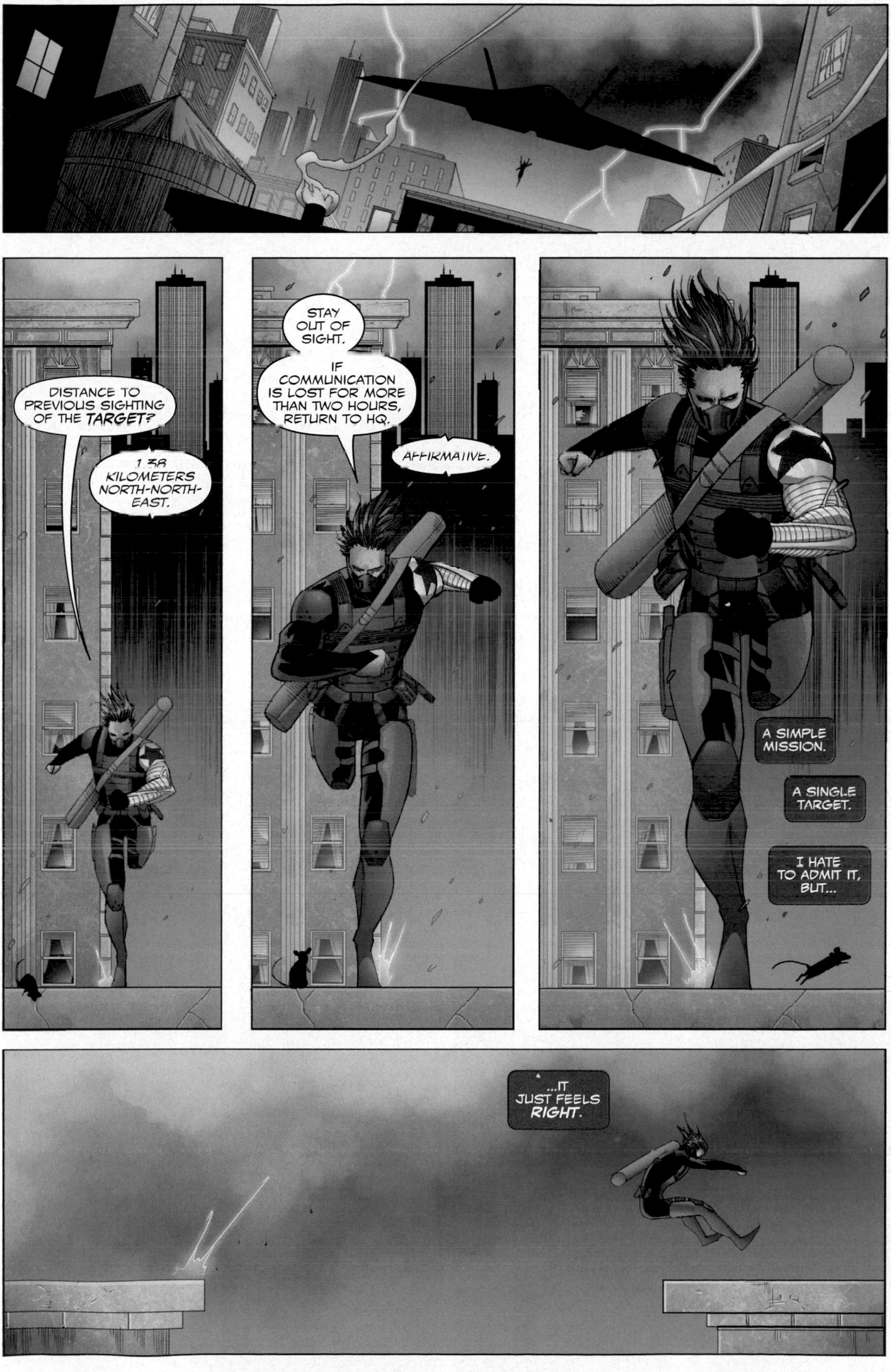

DISTANCE TO PREVIOUS SIGHTING OF THE TARGET?
1.38 KILOMETERS NORTH-NORTH-EAST.
STAY OUT OF SIGHT.
IF COMMUNICATION IS LOST FOR MORE THAN TWO HOURS, RETURN TO HQ.
AFFIRMATIVE.
A SIMPLE MISSION.
A SINGLE TARGET.
I HATE TO ADMIT IT, BUT...
...IT JUST FEELS RIGHT.

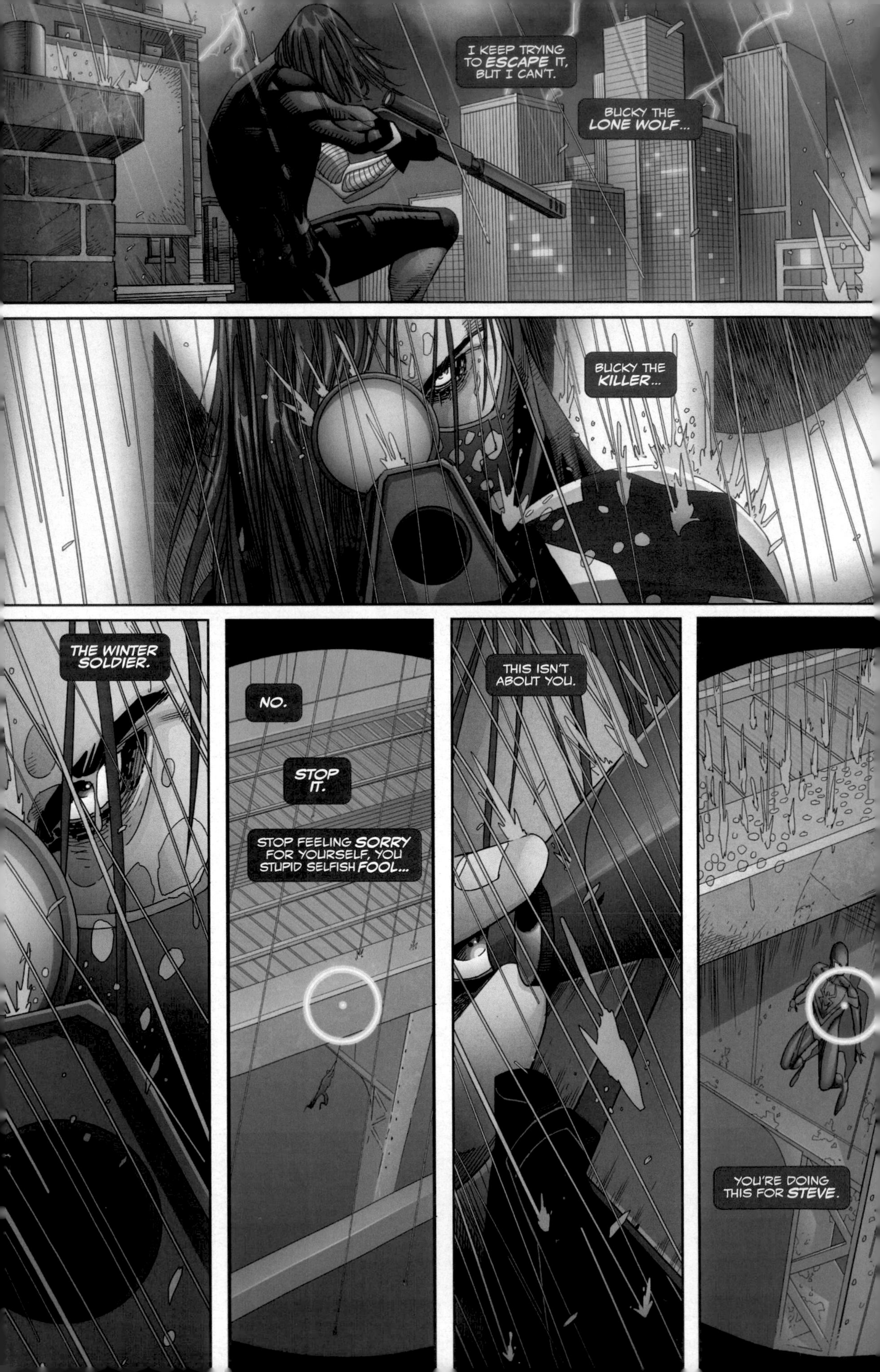
I KEEP TRYING TO ESCAPE IT, BUT I CAN'T.
BUCKY THE LONE WOLF...
BUCKY THE KILLER...
THE WINTER SOLDIER.
NO.
STOP IT.
STOP FEELING SORRY FOR YOURSELF, YOU STUPID SELFISH FOOL...
THIS ISN'T ABOUT YOU.
YOU'RE DOING THIS FOR STEVE.

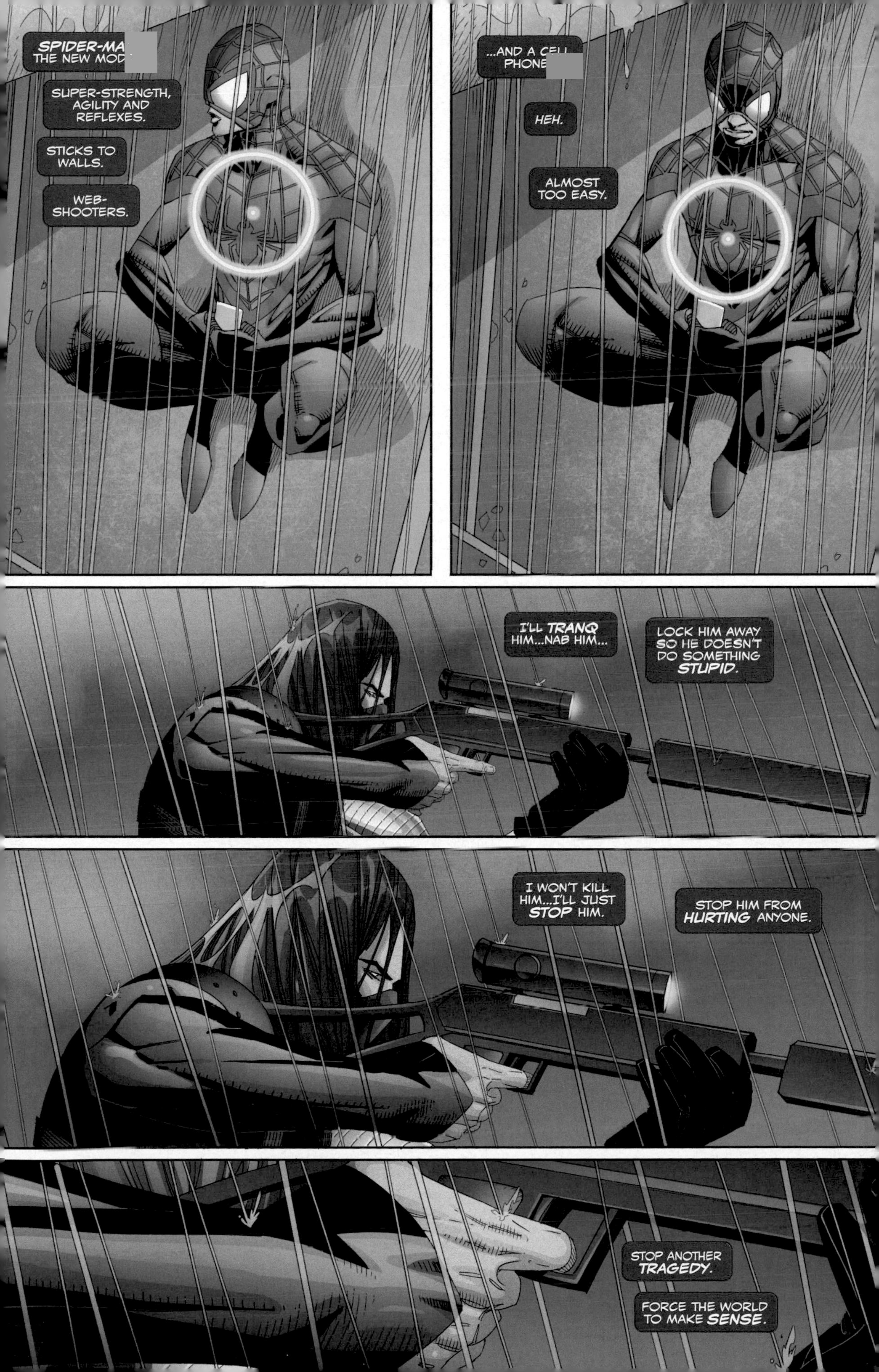
SPIDER-MA
THE NEW MOD
SUPER-STRENGTH, AGILITY AND REFLEXES.
STICKS TO WALLS.
WEB-SHOOTERS.
...AND A CEL
PHONE
HEH.
ALMOST TOO EASY.
I'LL TRANQ HIM...NAB HIM...
LOCK HIM AWAY SO HE DOESN'T DO SOMETHING STUPID.
I WON'T KILL HIM...I'LL JUST STOP HIM.
STOP HIM FROM HURTING ANYONE.
STOP ANOTHER TRAGEDY.
FORCE THE WORLD TO MAKE SENSE.

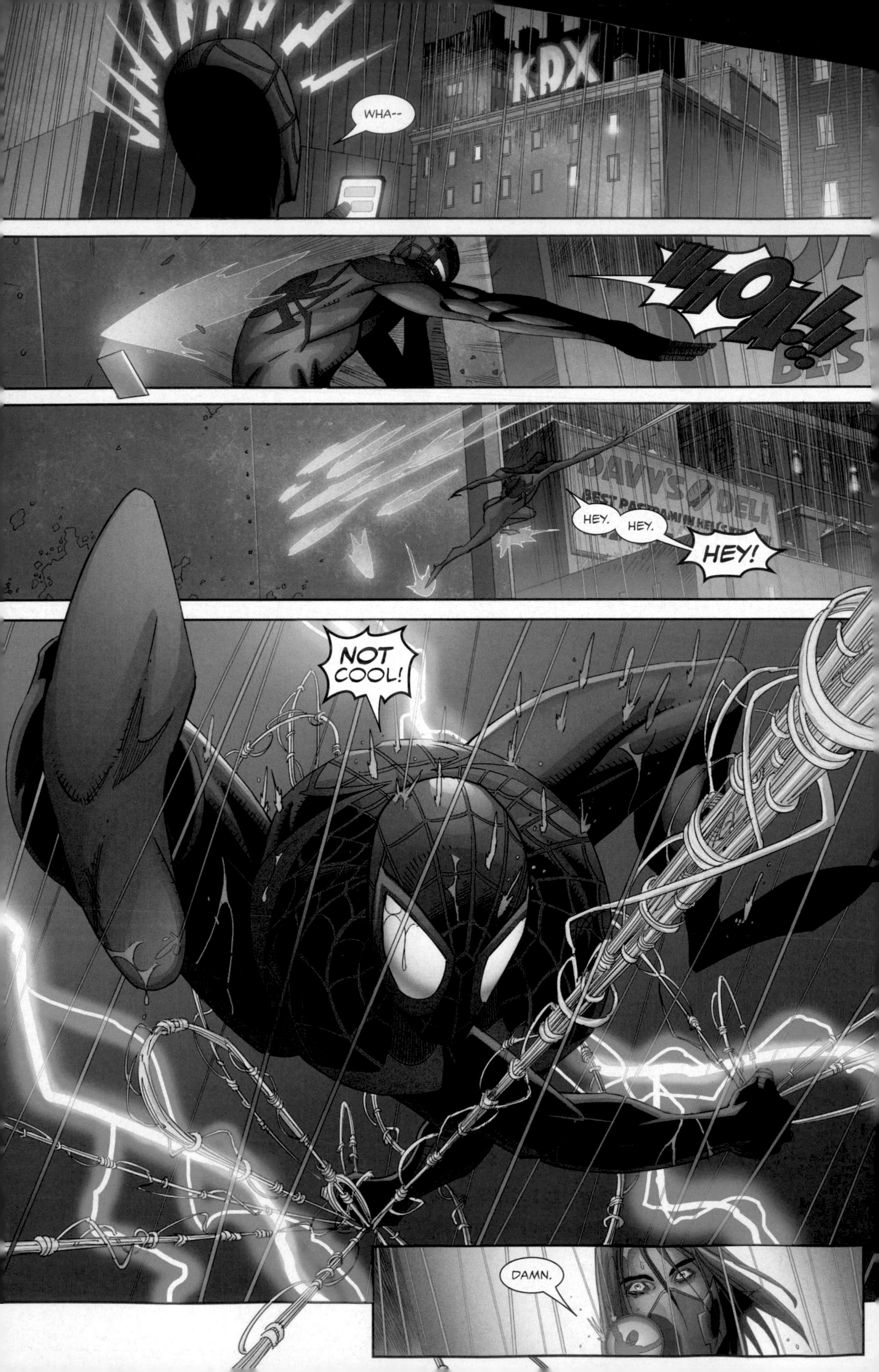
WHA--
WHOA!!!
HEY.
HEY.
HEY!
NOT COOL!
DAMN.

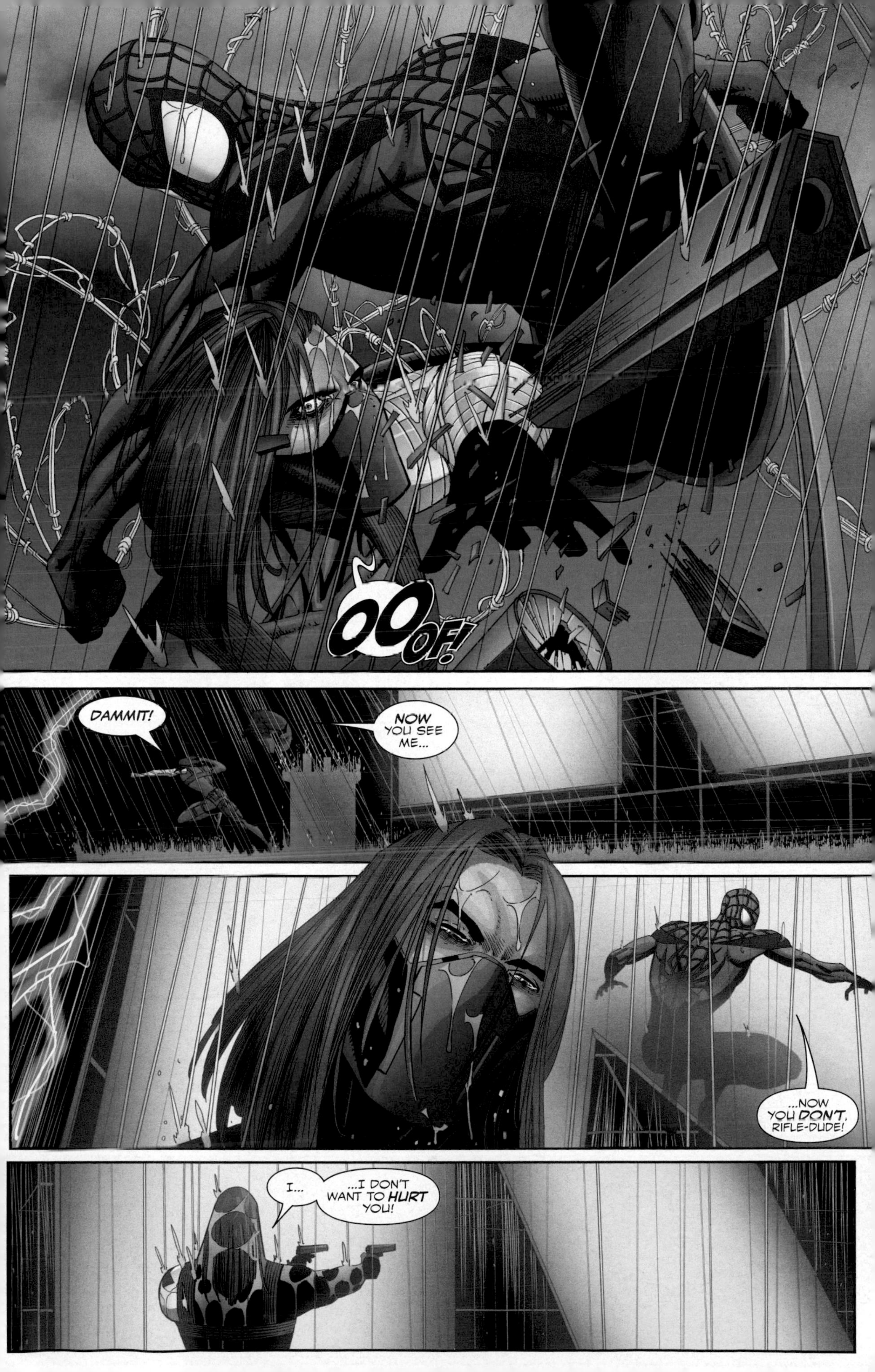
OOOF!
DAMMIT!
NOW YOU SEE ME...
...NOW YOU DON'T, RIFLE-DUDE!
I...
...I DON'T WANT TO HURT YOU!

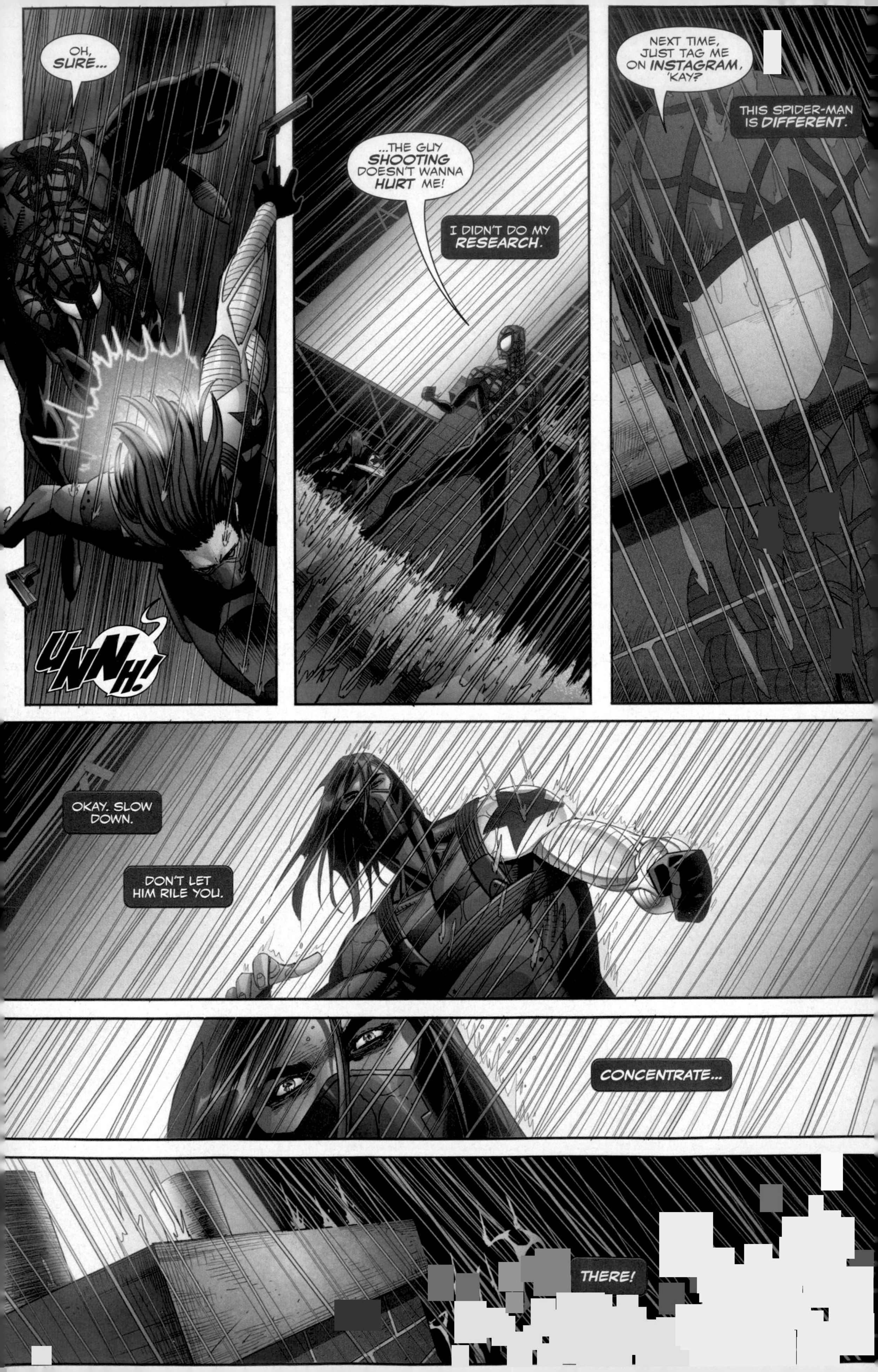
OH, SURE...
UNNH!
...THE GUY SHOOTING DOESN'T WANNA HURT ME!
I DIDN'T DO MY RESEARCH.
NEXT TIME, JUST TAG ME ON INSTAGRAM, 'KAY?
THIS SPIDER-MAN IS DIFFERENT.
OKAY. SLOW DOWN.
DON'T LET HIM RILE YOU.
CONCENTRATE...
THERE!

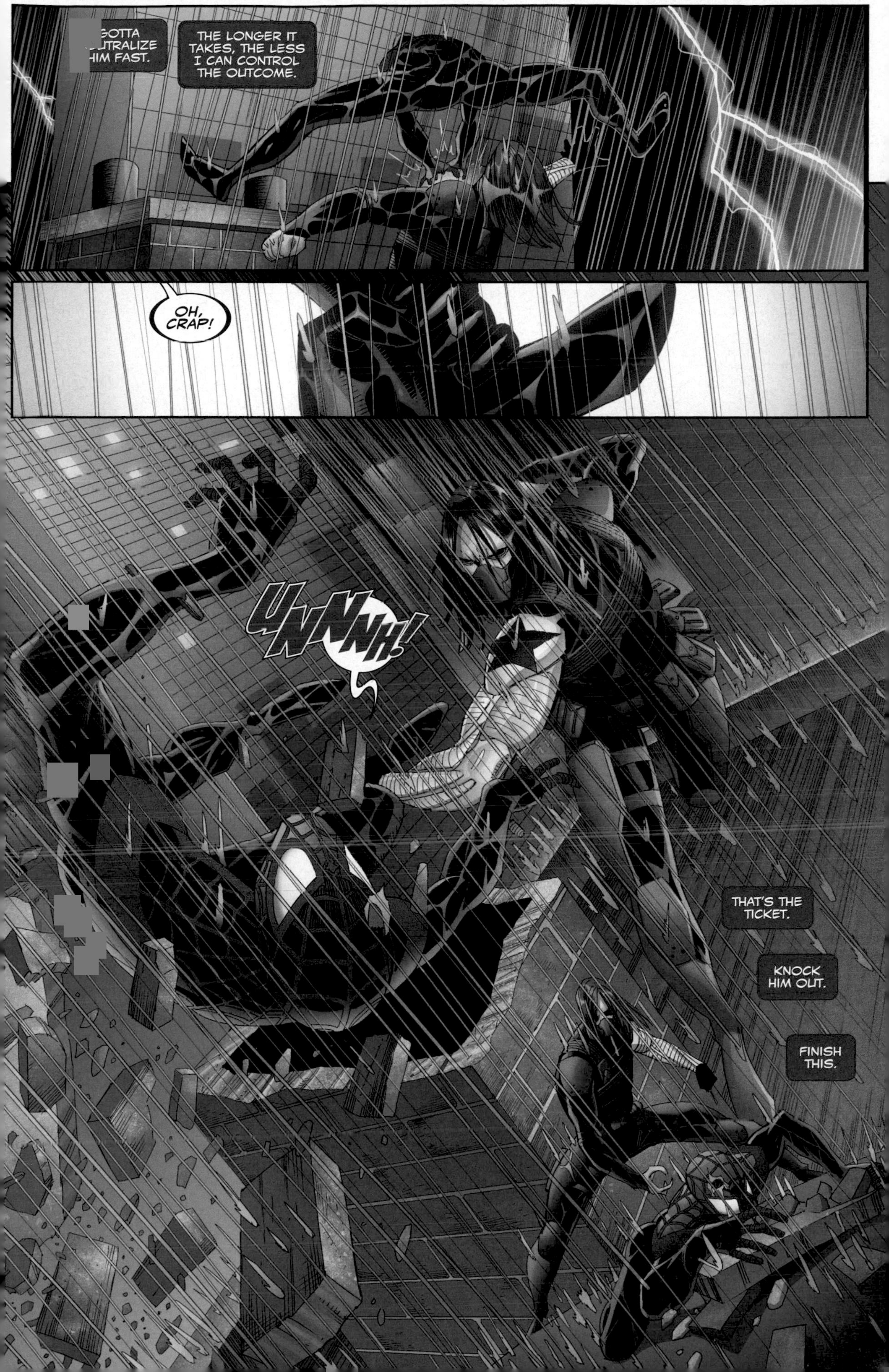

GOTTA UTRALIZE HIM FAST.
THE LONGER IT TAKES, THE LESS I CAN CONTROL THE OUTCOME.
OH, CRAP!
UNNNH!
THAT'S THE TICKET.
KNOCK HIM OUT.
FINISH THIS.

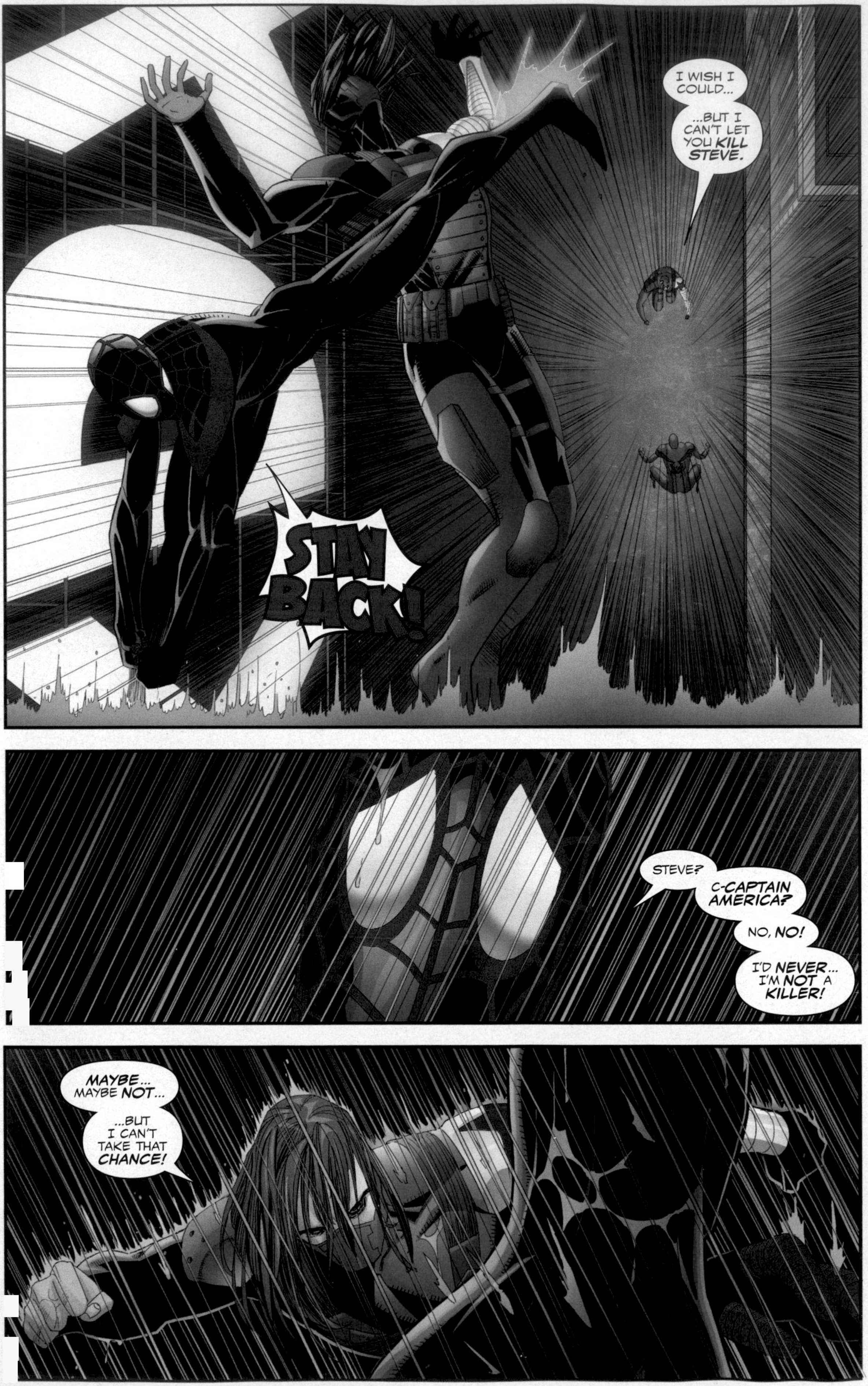
I WISH I COULD...
...BUT I CAN'T LET YOU KILL STEVE.
STAY BACK!
STEVE?
C-CAPTAIN AMERICA?
NO, NO!
I'D NEVER... I'M NOT A KILLER!
MAYBE... MAYBE NOT...
...BUT I CAN'T TAKE THAT CHANCE!

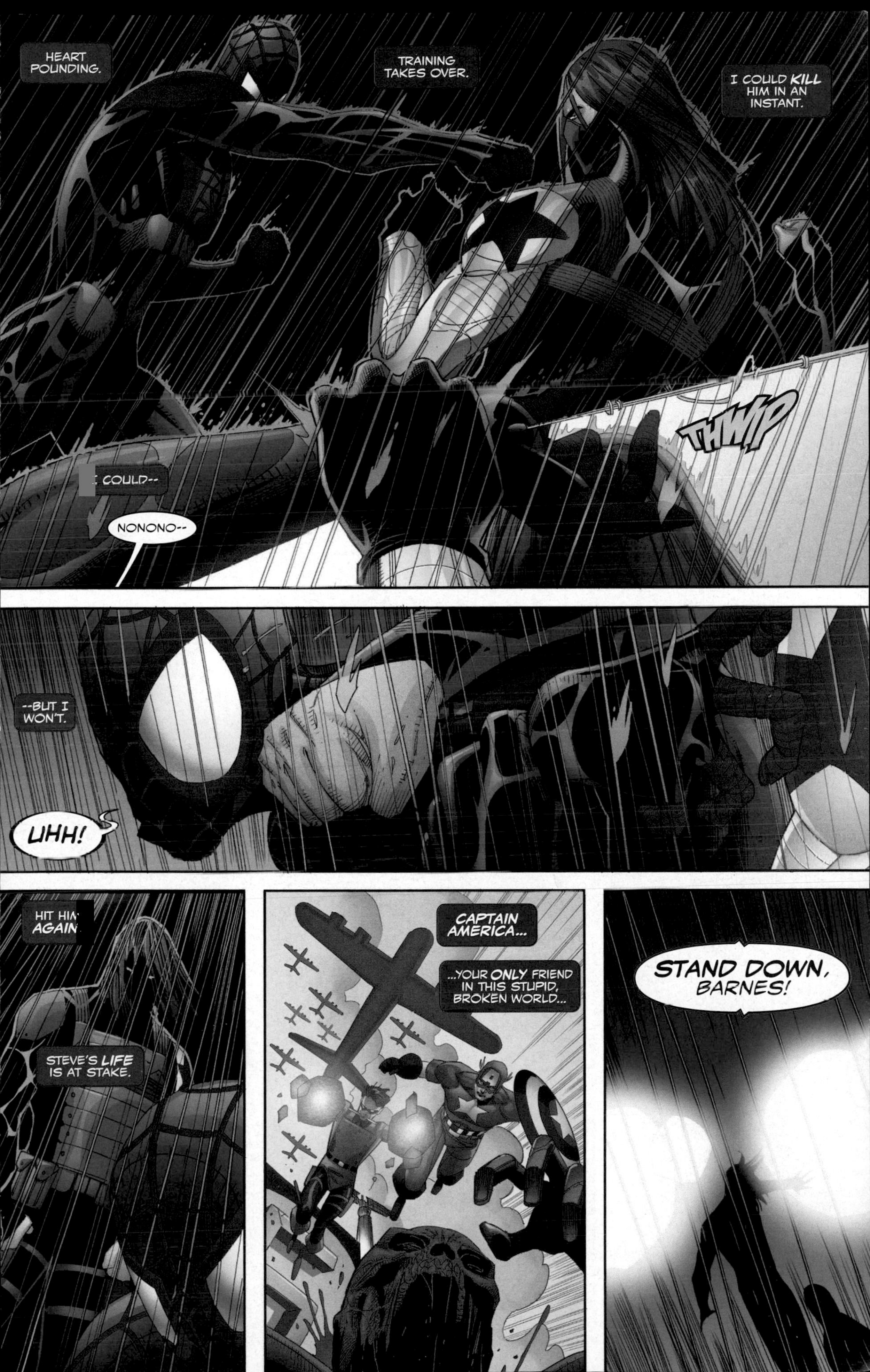
HEART POUNDING.
TRAINING TAKES OVER.
I COULD KILL HIM IN AN INSTANT.
THWIP
[redacted] COULD--
NONONO--
--BUT I WON'T.
UHH!
HIT HI[redacted]
AGAIN[redacted]
STEVE'S LIFE IS AT STAKE.
CAPTAIN AMERICA...
...YOUR ONLY FRIEND IN THIS STUPID, BROKEN WORLD...
STAND DOWN, BARNES!

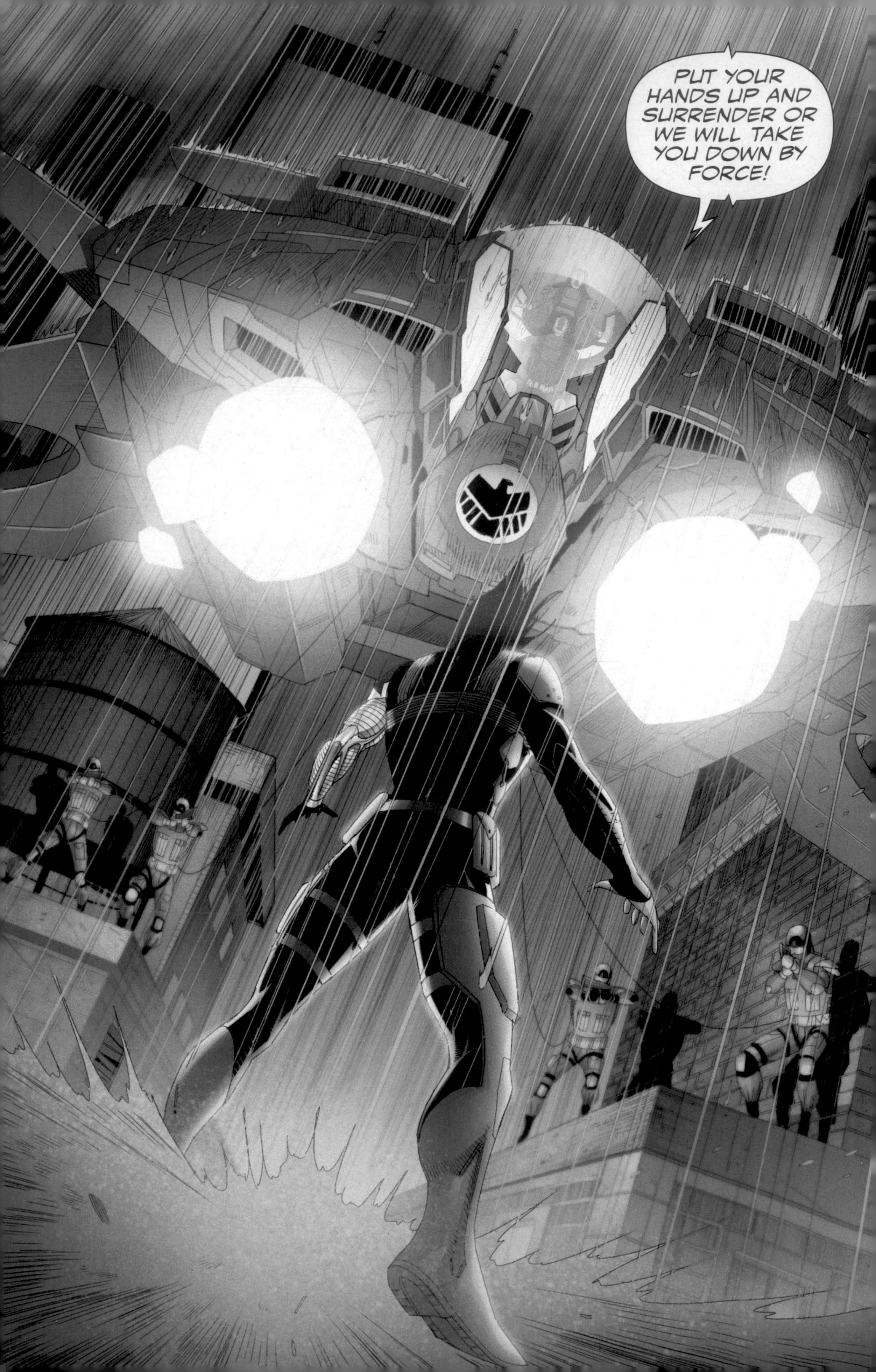
PUT YOUR HANDS UP AND SURRENDER OR WE WILL TAKE YOU DOWN BY FORCE!

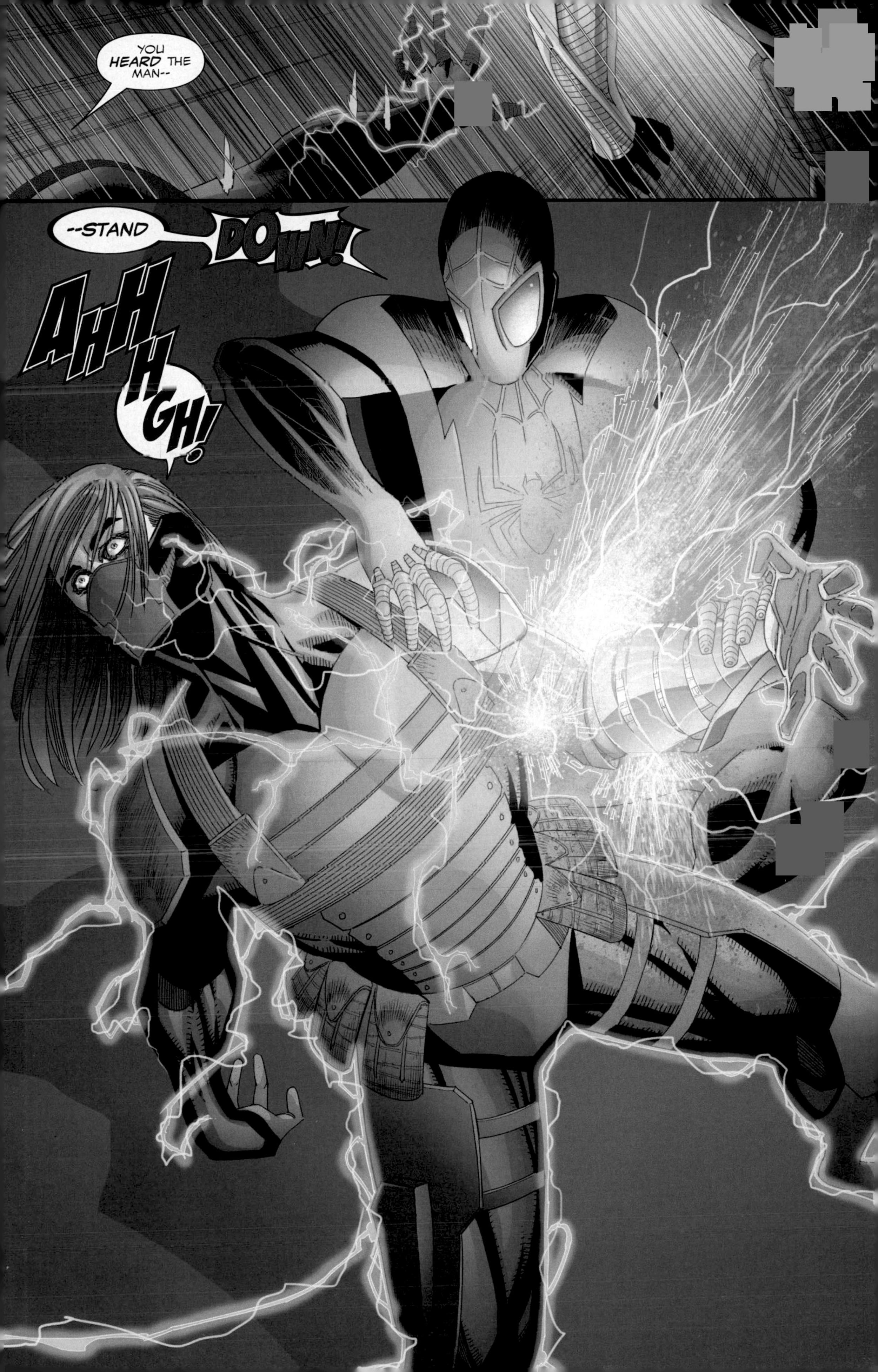
YOU HEARD THE MAN--
--STAND DOWN!
AHHHGH!

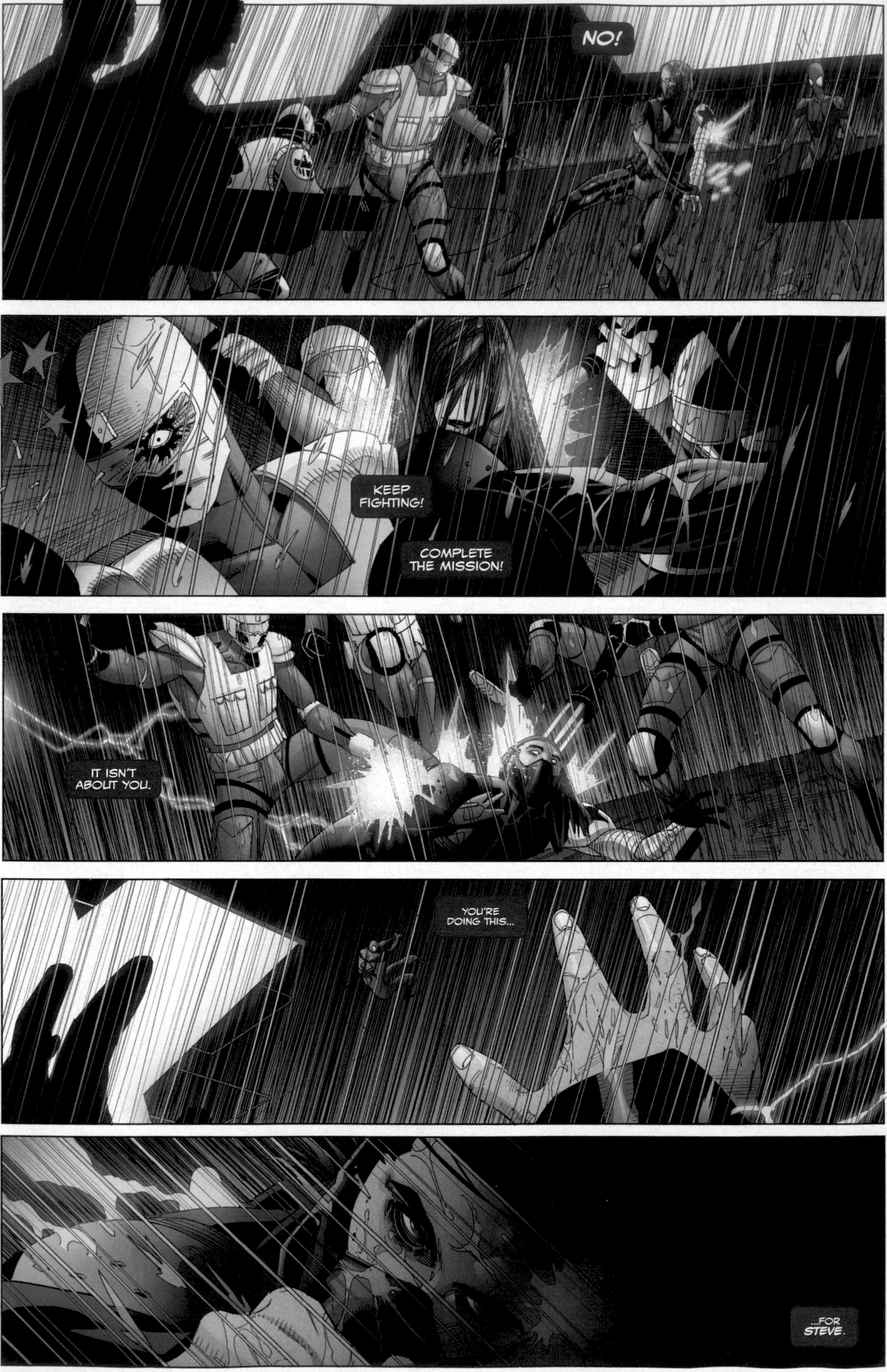
NO!
KEEP FIGHTING!
COMPLETE THE MISSION!
IT ISN'T ABOUT YOU.
YOU'RE DOING THIS...
...FOR STEVE.

TARGET CAPTURED AT 0900 HOURS.

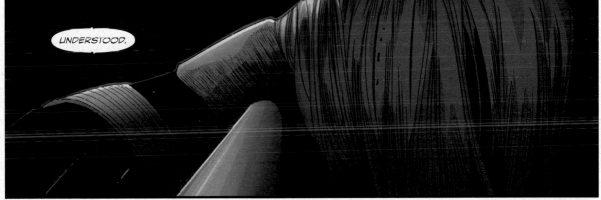

SEVERAL AGENTS ARE INJURED AND RECEIVING TREATMENT, BUT NO CASUALTIES HAVE BEEN REPORTED.

UNDERSTOOD.

DIRECTOR HILL HAS BEEN NOTIFIED AND IS EN ROUTE.

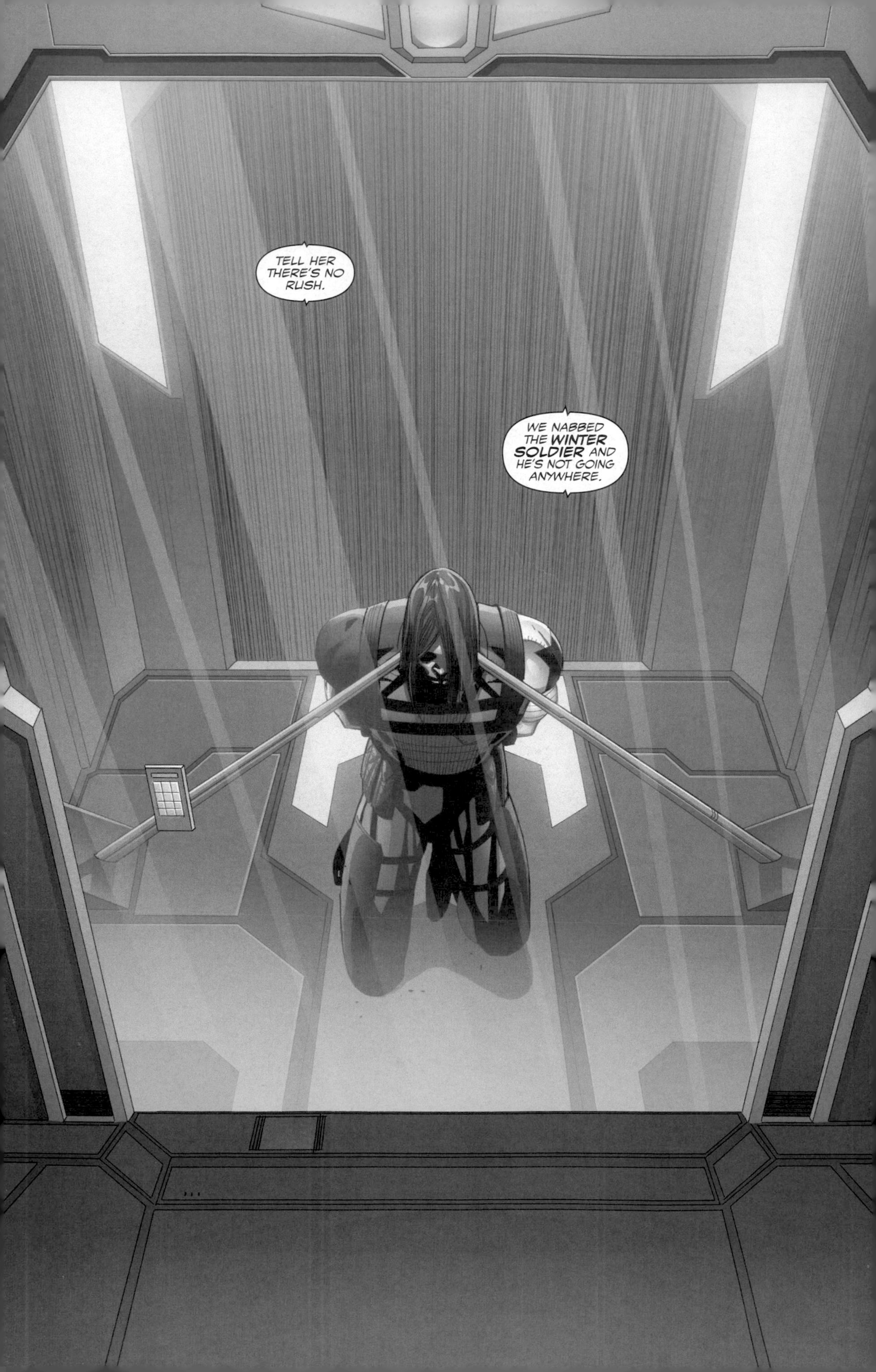
TELL HER THERE'S NO RUSH.
WE NABBED THE WINTER SOLDIER AND HE'S NOT GOING ANYWHERE.

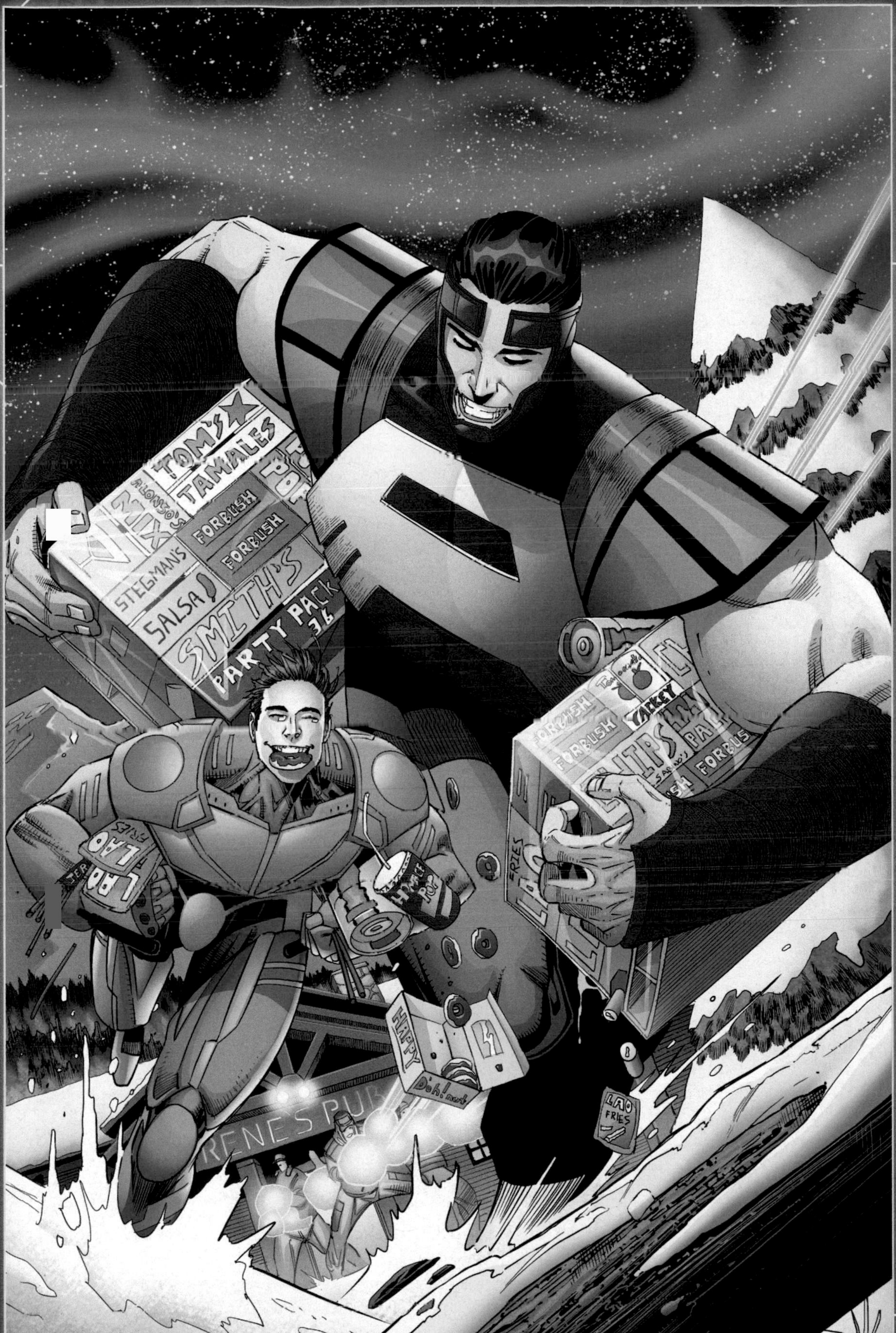
TOM'S
TAMALES
ALONSO'S
MIX
STEGMAN'S
SALSA
FORBUSH
FORBUSH
SMITH'S
PARTY PACK
36
LAO
FRIES
HAPPY
RENE'S PUB

6: THE BEER RUN

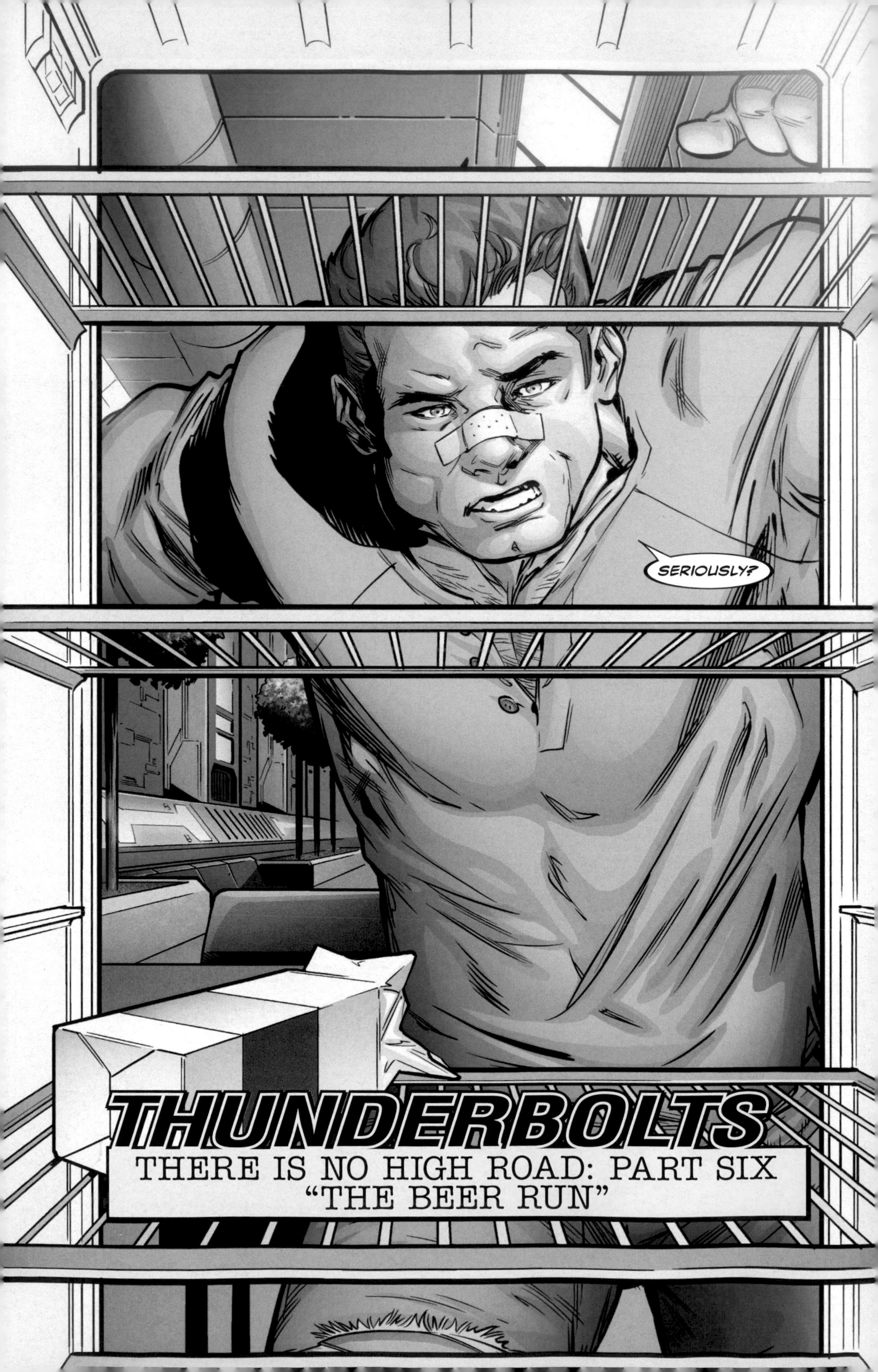

SERIOUSLY?
THUNDERBOLTS
THERE IS NO HIGH ROAD: PART SIX
"THE BEER RUN"

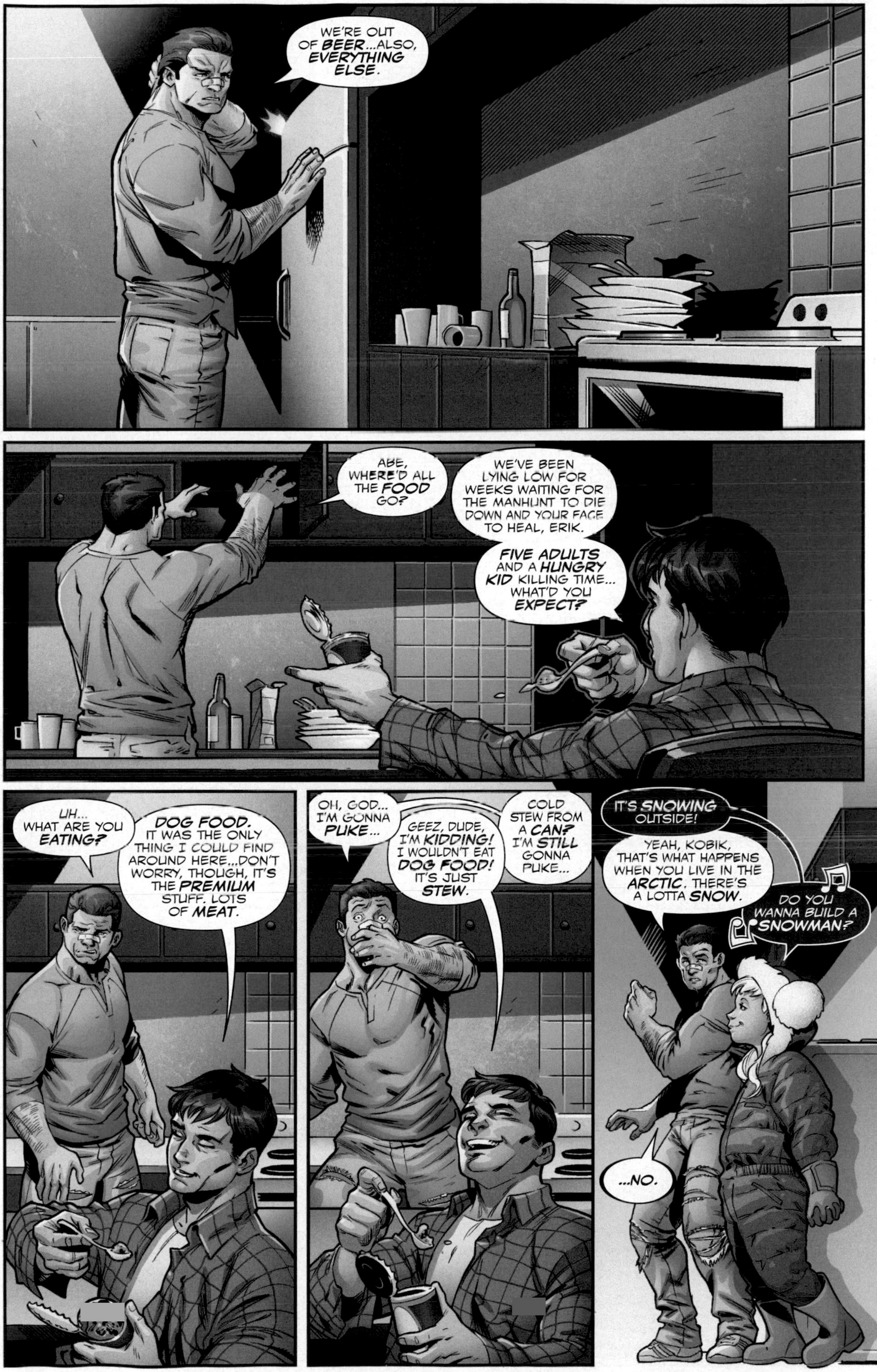
WE'RE OUT OF BEER...ALSO, EVERYTHING ELSE.
ABE, WHERE'D ALL THE FOOD GO?
WE'VE BEEN LYING LOW FOR WEEKS WAITING FOR THE MANHUNT TO DIE DOWN AND YOUR FACE TO HEAL, ERIK.
FIVE ADULTS AND A HUNGRY KID KILLING TIME... WHAT'D YOU EXPECT?
UH... WHAT ARE YOU EATING?
DOG FOOD. IT WAS THE ONLY THING I COULD FIND AROUND HERE...DON'T WORRY, THOUGH, IT'S THE PREMIUM STUFF. LOTS OF MEAT.
OH, GOD... I'M GONNA PUKE...
GEEZ, DUDE, I'M KIDDING! I WOULDN'T EAT DOG FOOD! IT'S JUST STEW.
COLD STEW FROM A CAN? I'M STILL GONNA PUKE...
IT'S SNOWING OUTSIDE!
YEAH, KOBIK, THAT'S WHAT HAPPENS WHEN YOU LIVE IN THE ARCTIC. THERE'S A LOTTA SNOW.
DO YOU WANNA BUILD A SNOWMAN?
...NO.

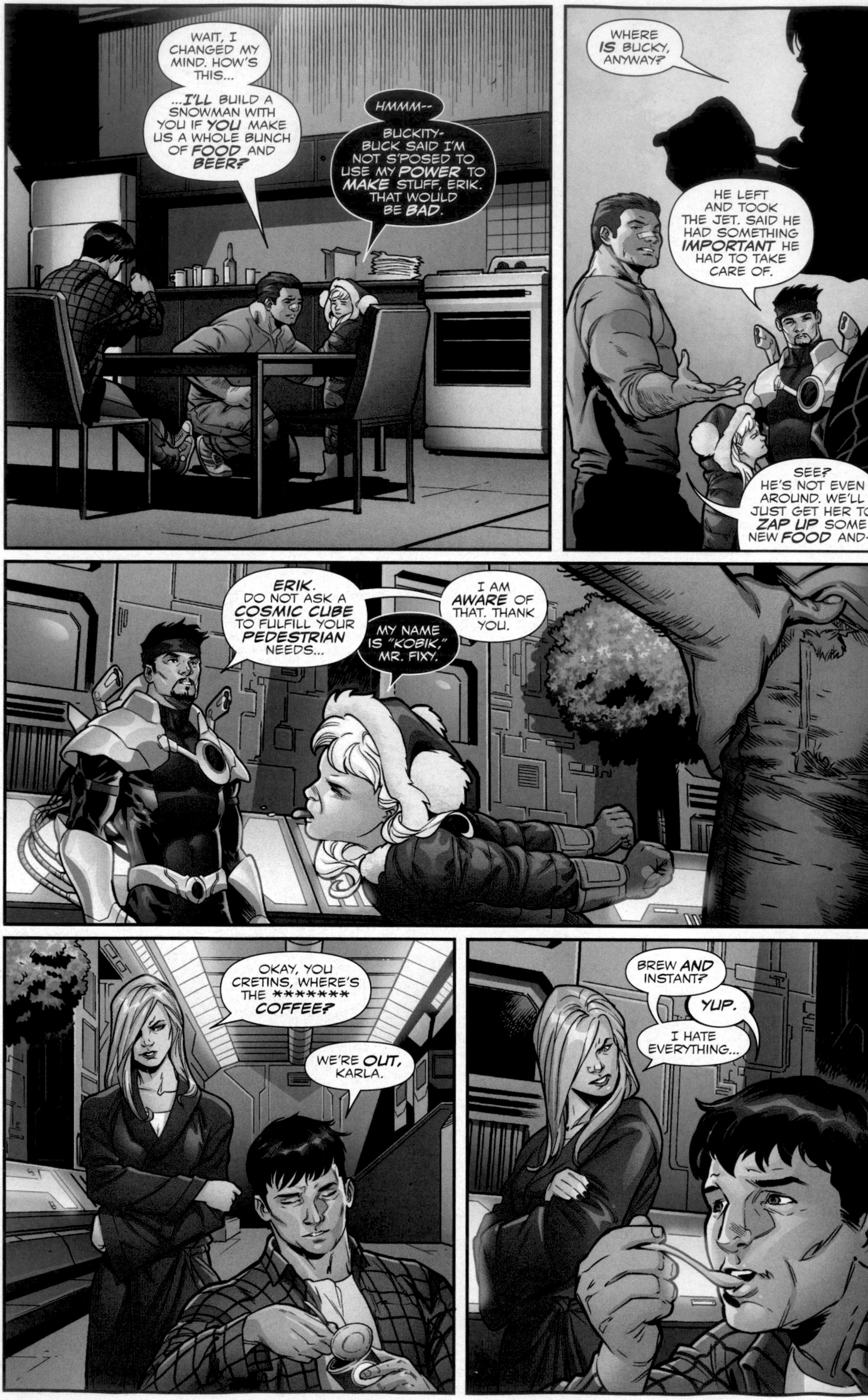
WAIT, I CHANGED MY MIND. HOW'S THIS...
...I'LL BUILD A SNOWMAN WITH YOU IF YOU MAKE US A WHOLE BUNCH OF FOOD AND BEER?
HMMM--
BUCKITY-BUCK SAID I'M NOT S'POSED TO USE MY POWER TO MAKE STUFF, ERIK. THAT WOULD BE BAD.
WHERE IS BUCKY, ANYWAY?
HE LEFT AND TOOK THE JET. SAID HE HAD SOMETHING IMPORTANT HE HAD TO TAKE CARE OF.
SEE? HE'S NOT EVEN AROUND. WE'LL JUST GET HER TO ZAP UP SOME NEW FOOD AND--
ERIK. DO NOT ASK A COSMIC CUBE TO FULFILL YOUR PEDESTRIAN NEEDS...
I AM AWARE OF THAT. THANK YOU.
MY NAME IS "KOBIK," MR. FIXY.
OKAY, YOU CRETINS, WHERE'S THE ******* COFFEE?
WE'RE OUT, KARLA.
BREW AND INSTANT?
YUP.
I HATE EVERYTHING...

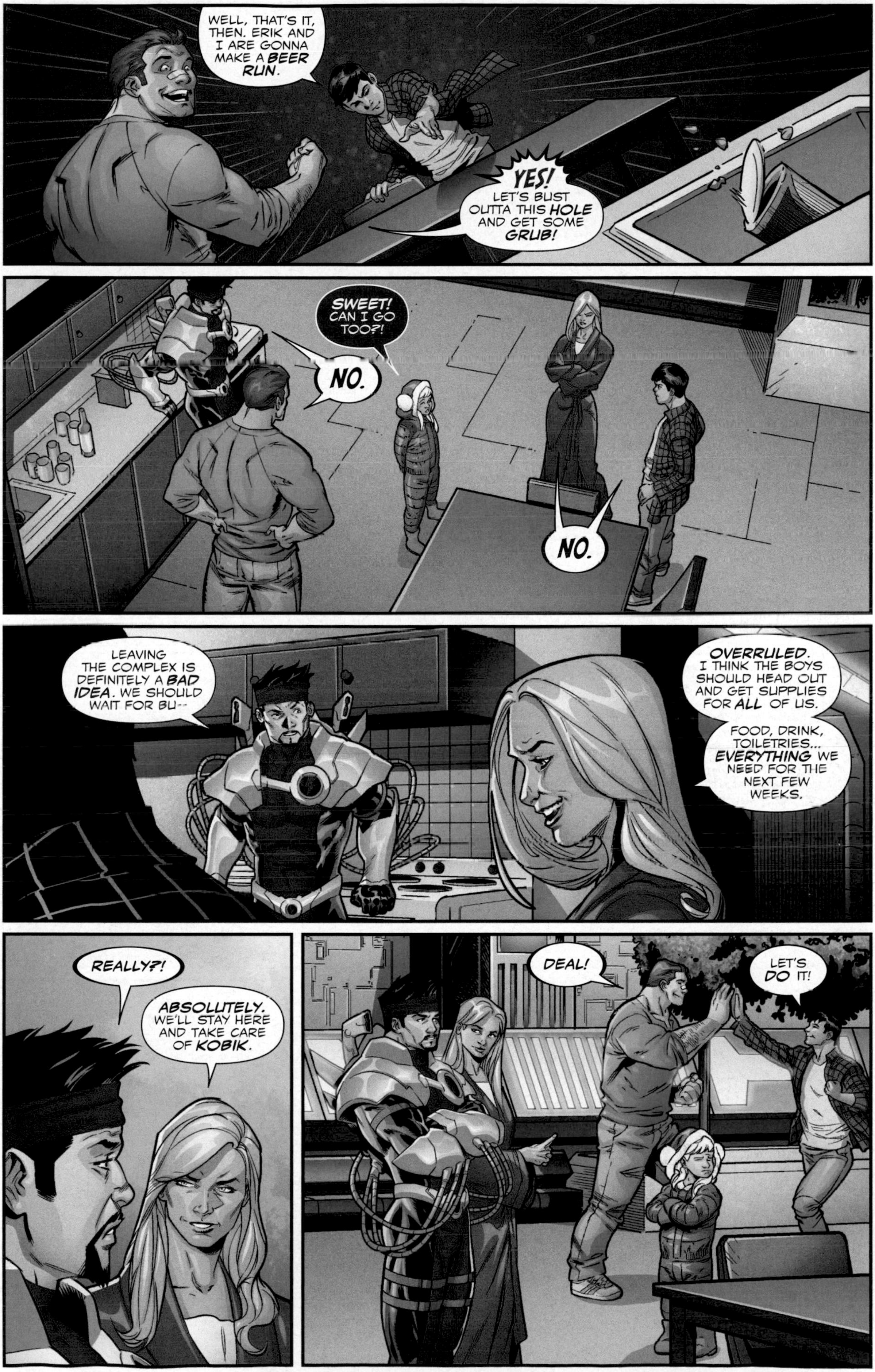
WELL, THAT'S IT, THEN. ERIK AND I ARE GONNA MAKE A BEER RUN.
YES! LET'S BUST OUTTA THIS HOLE AND GET SOME GRUB!
SWEET! CAN I GO TOO?!
NO.
NO.
LEAVING THE COMPLEX IS DEFINITELY A BAD IDEA. WE SHOULD WAIT FOR BU--
OVERRULED. I THINK THE BOYS SHOULD HEAD OUT AND GET SUPPLIES FOR ALL OF US.
FOOD, DRINK, TOILETRIES... EVERYTHING WE NEED FOR THE NEXT FEW WEEKS.
REALLY?!
ABSOLUTELY. WE'LL STAY HERE AND TAKE CARE OF KOBIK.
DEAL!
LET'S DO IT!

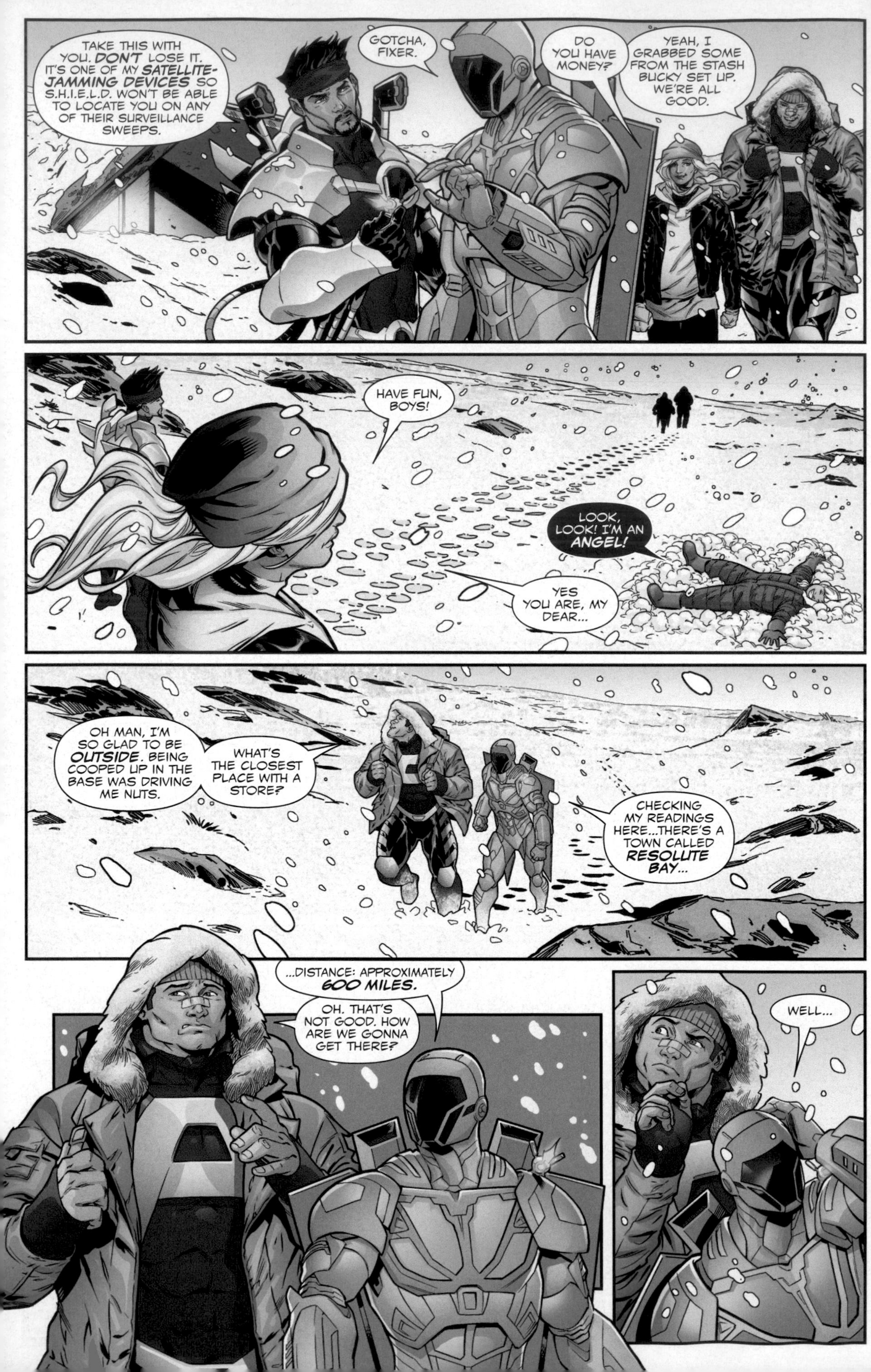
TAKE THIS WITH YOU. DON'T LOSE IT. IT'S ONE OF MY SATELLITE-JAMMING DEVICES SO S.H.I.E.L.D. WON'T BE ABLE TO LOCATE YOU ON ANY OF THEIR SURVEILLANCE SWEEPS.
GOTCHA, FIXER.
DO YOU HAVE MONEY?
YEAH, I GRABBED SOME FROM THE STASH BUCKY SET UP. WE'RE ALL GOOD.
HAVE FUN, BOYS!
LOOK, LOOK! I'M AN ANGEL!
YES YOU ARE, MY DEAR...
OH MAN, I'M SO GLAD TO BE OUTSIDE. BEING COOPED UP IN THE BASE WAS DRIVING ME NUTS.
WHAT'S THE CLOSEST PLACE WITH A STORE?
CHECKING MY READINGS HERE...THERE'S A TOWN CALLED RESOLUTE BAY...
...DISTANCE: APPROXIMATELY 600 MILES.
OH. THAT'S NOT GOOD. HOW ARE WE GONNA GET THERE?
WELL...

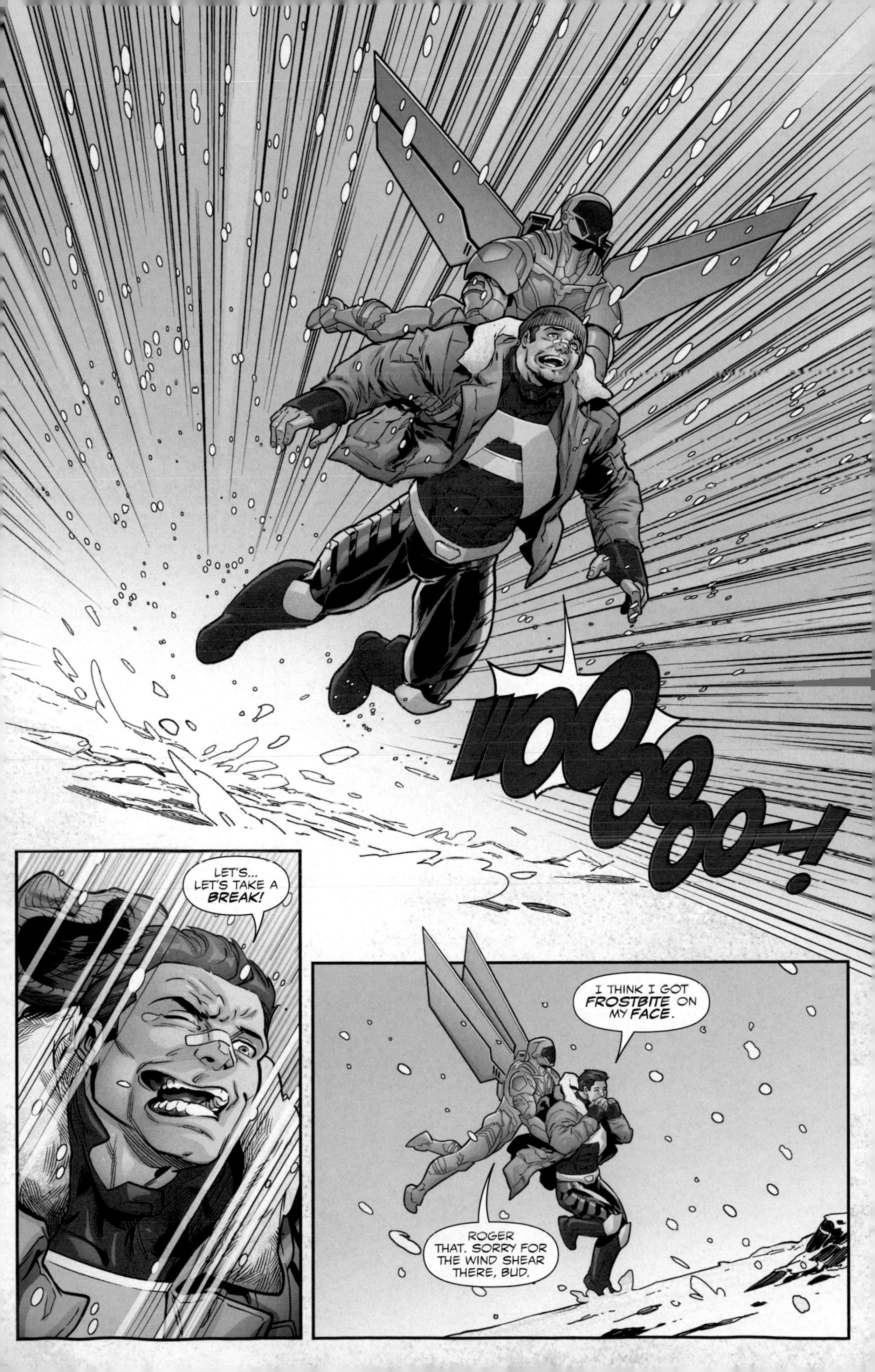
WOOOOOOOOO--!
LET'S... LET'S TAKE A BREAK!
I THINK I GOT FROSTBITE ON MY FACE.
ROGER THAT. SORRY FOR THE WIND SHEAR THERE, BUD.

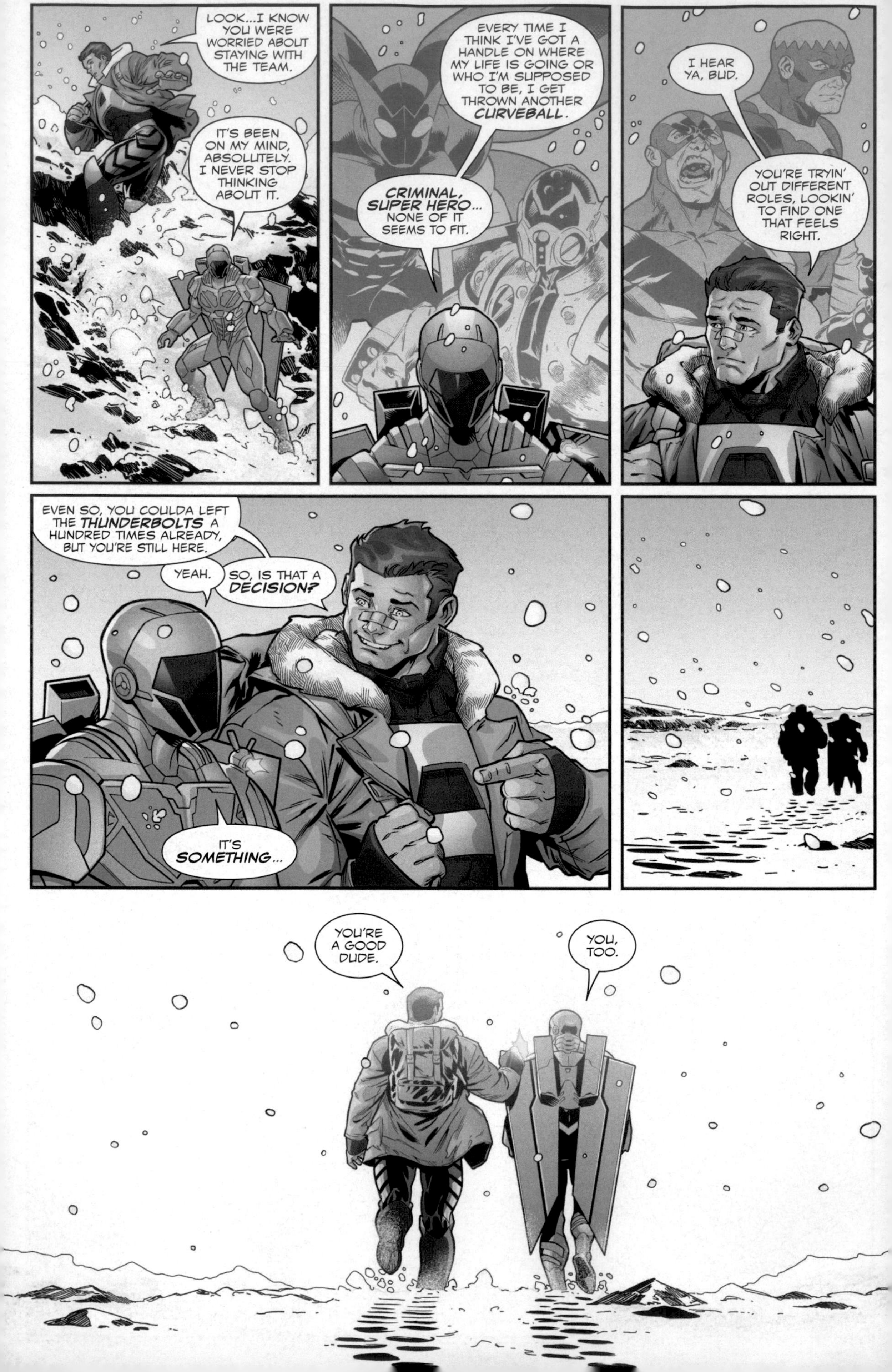
LOOK...I KNOW YOU WERE WORRIED ABOUT STAYING WITH THE TEAM.
IT'S BEEN ON MY MIND, ABSOLUTELY. I NEVER STOP THINKING ABOUT IT.
EVERY TIME I THINK I'VE GOT A HANDLE ON WHERE MY LIFE IS GOING OR WHO I'M SUPPOSED TO BE, I GET THROWN ANOTHER CURVEBALL.
CRIMINAL, SUPER HERO... NONE OF IT SEEMS TO FIT.
I HEAR YA, BUD.
YOU'RE TRYIN' OUT DIFFERENT ROLES, LOOKIN' TO FIND ONE THAT FEELS RIGHT.
EVEN SO, YOU COULDA LEFT THE THUNDERBOLTS A HUNDRED TIMES ALREADY, BUT YOU'RE STILL HERE.
YEAH.
SO, IS THAT A DECISION?
IT'S SOMETHING...
YOU'RE A GOOD DUDE.
YOU, TOO.

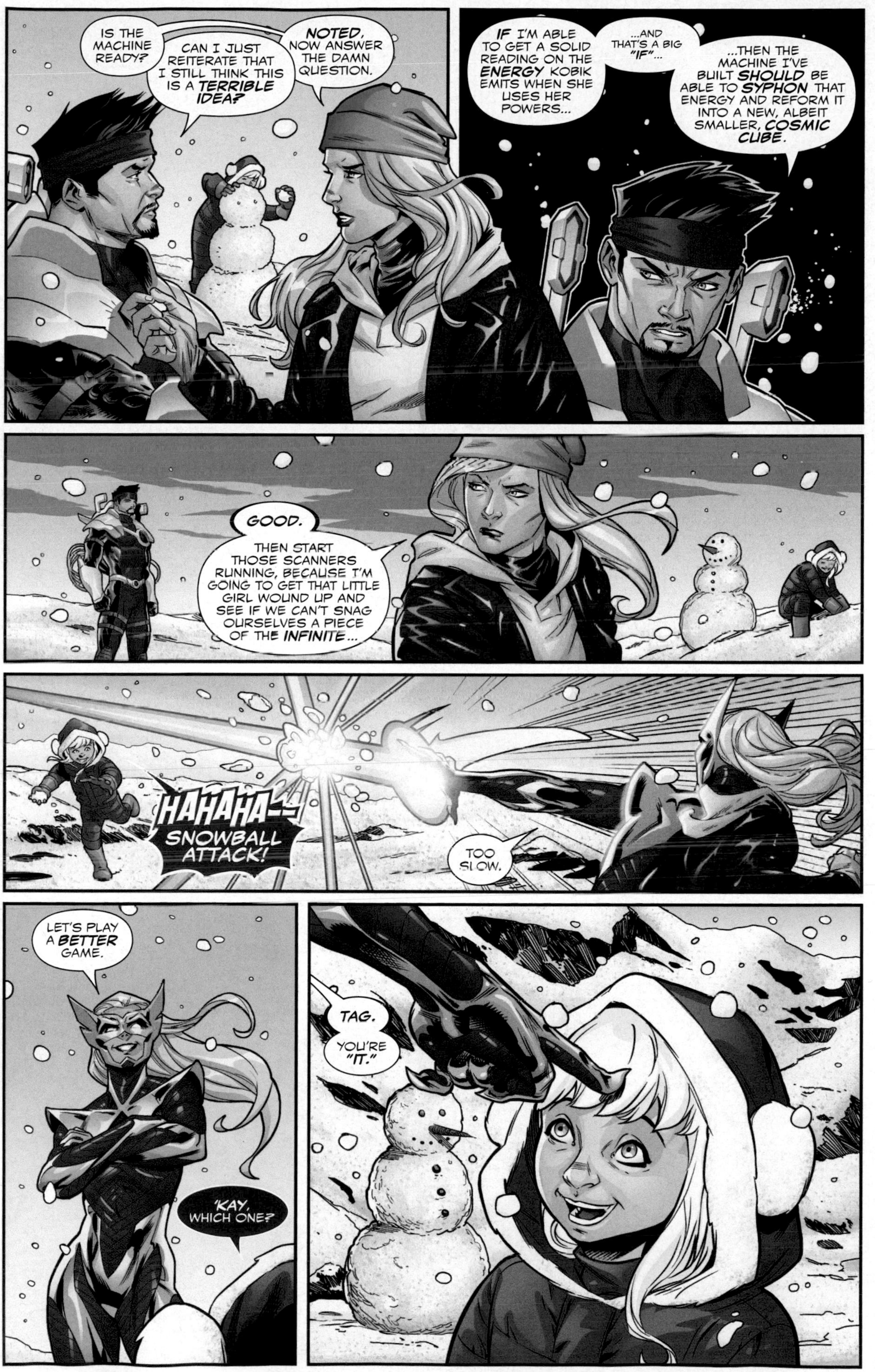
IS THE MACHINE READY?
CAN I JUST REITERATE THAT I STILL THINK THIS IS A TERRIBLE IDEA?
NOTED, NOW ANSWER THE DAMN QUESTION.
IF I'M ABLE TO GET A SOLID READING ON THE ENERGY KOBIK EMITS WHEN SHE USES HER POWERS...
...AND THAT'S A BIG "IF"...
...THEN THE MACHINE I'VE BUILT SHOULD BE ABLE TO SYPHON THAT ENERGY AND REFORM IT INTO A NEW, ALBEIT SMALLER, COSMIC CUBE.
GOOD.
THEN START THOSE SCANNERS RUNNING, BECAUSE I'M GOING TO GET THAT LITTLE GIRL WOUND UP AND SEE IF WE CAN'T SNAG OURSELVES A PIECE OF THE INFINITE...
HAHAHA--
SNOWBALL ATTACK!
TOO SLOW.
LET'S PLAY A BETTER GAME.
'KAY, WHICH ONE?
TAG.
YOU'RE "IT."

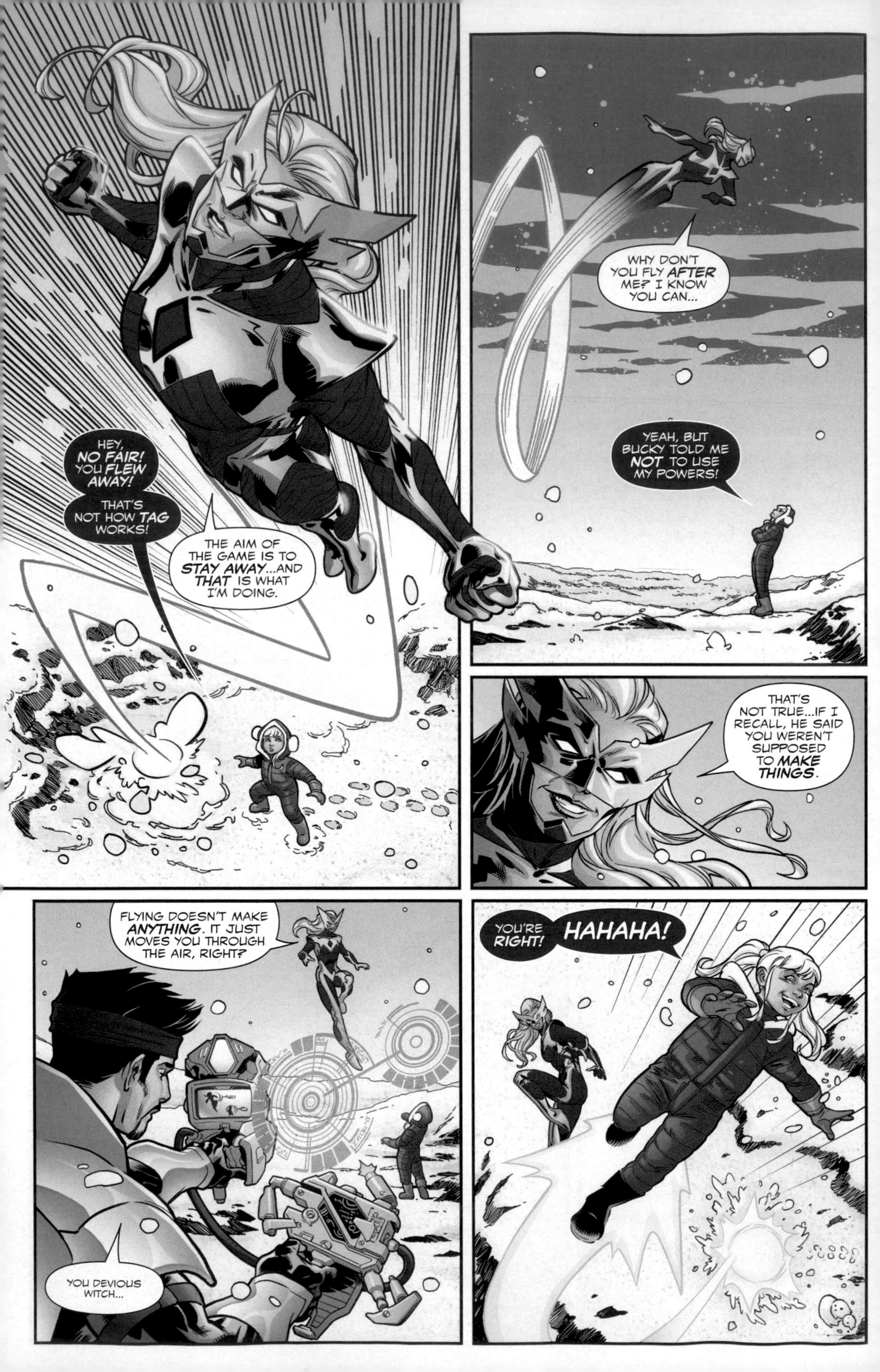
HEY, NO FAIR! YOU FLEW AWAY!
THAT'S NOT HOW TAG WORKS!
THE AIM OF THE GAME IS TO STAY AWAY...AND THAT IS WHAT I'M DOING.
WHY DON'T YOU FLY AFTER ME? I KNOW YOU CAN...
YEAH, BUT BUCKY TOLD ME NOT TO USE MY POWERS!
THAT'S NOT TRUE...IF I RECALL, HE SAID YOU WEREN'T SUPPOSED TO MAKE THINGS.
FLYING DOESN'T MAKE ANYTHING. IT JUST MOVES YOU THROUGH THE AIR, RIGHT?
YOU DEVIOUS WITCH...
YOU'RE RIGHT!
HAHAHA!

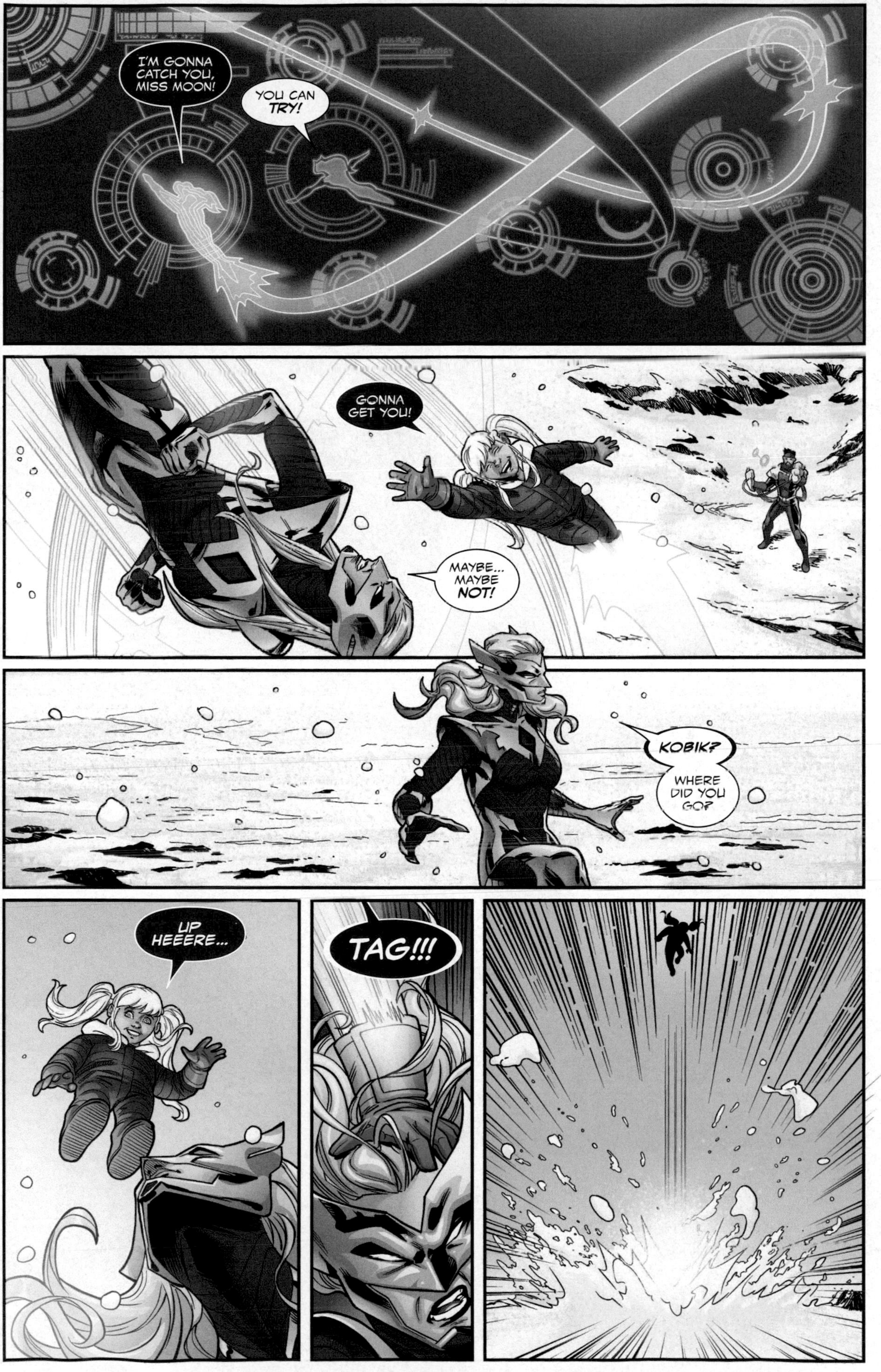

I'M GONNA CATCH YOU, MISS MOON!
YOU CAN TRY!
GONNA GET YOU!
MAYBE... MAYBE NOT!
KOBIK?
WHERE DID YOU GO?
UP HEEERE...
TAG!!!

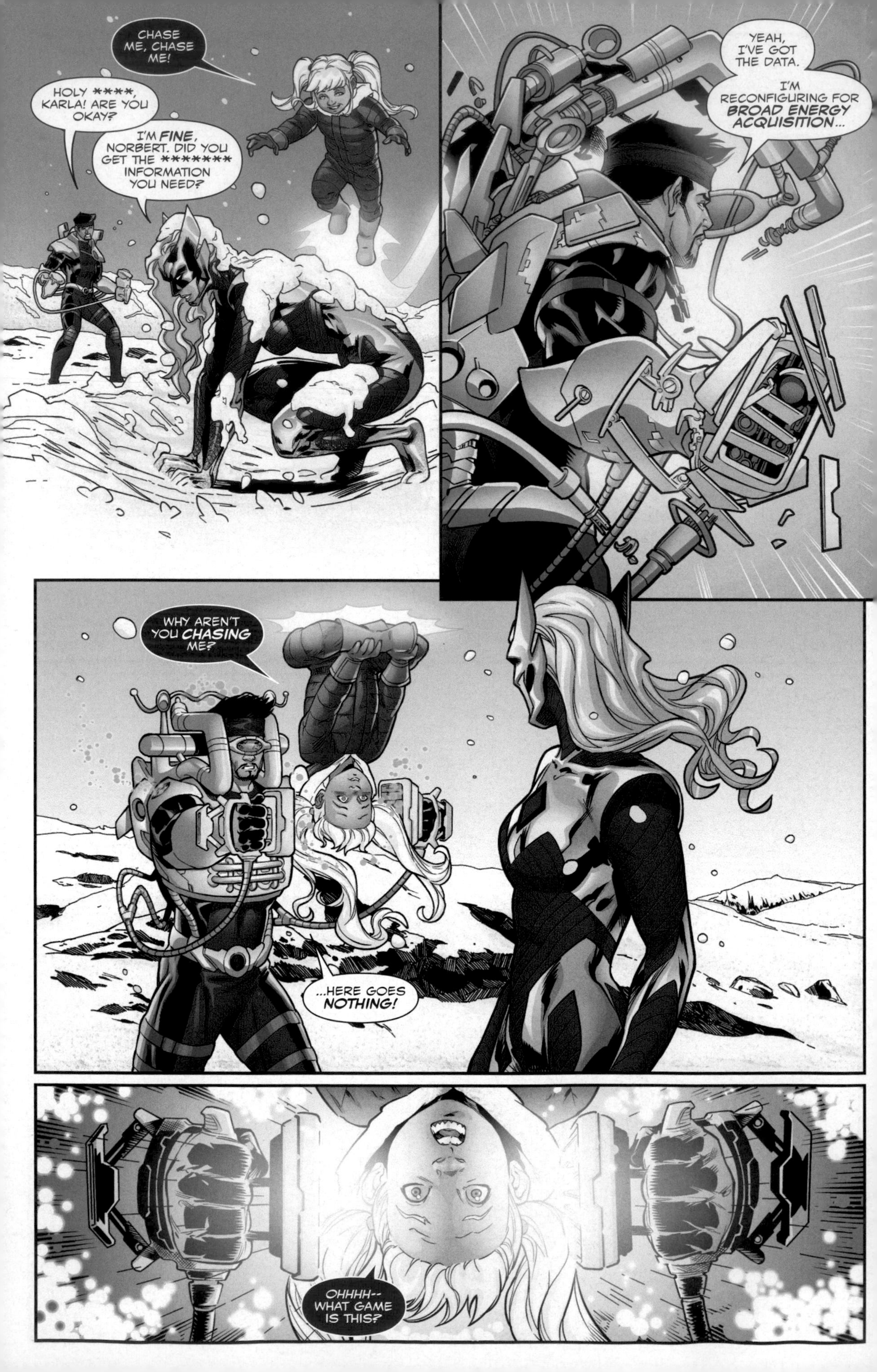

CHASE ME, CHASE ME!
HOLY ****, KARLA! ARE YOU OKAY?
I'M FINE, NORBERT. DID YOU GET THE ******* INFORMATION YOU NEED?
YEAH, I'VE GOT THE DATA.
I'M RECONFIGURING FOR BROAD ENERGY ACQUISITION...
WHY AREN'T YOU CHASING ME?
...HERE GOES NOTHING!
OHHHH-- WHAT GAME IS THIS?

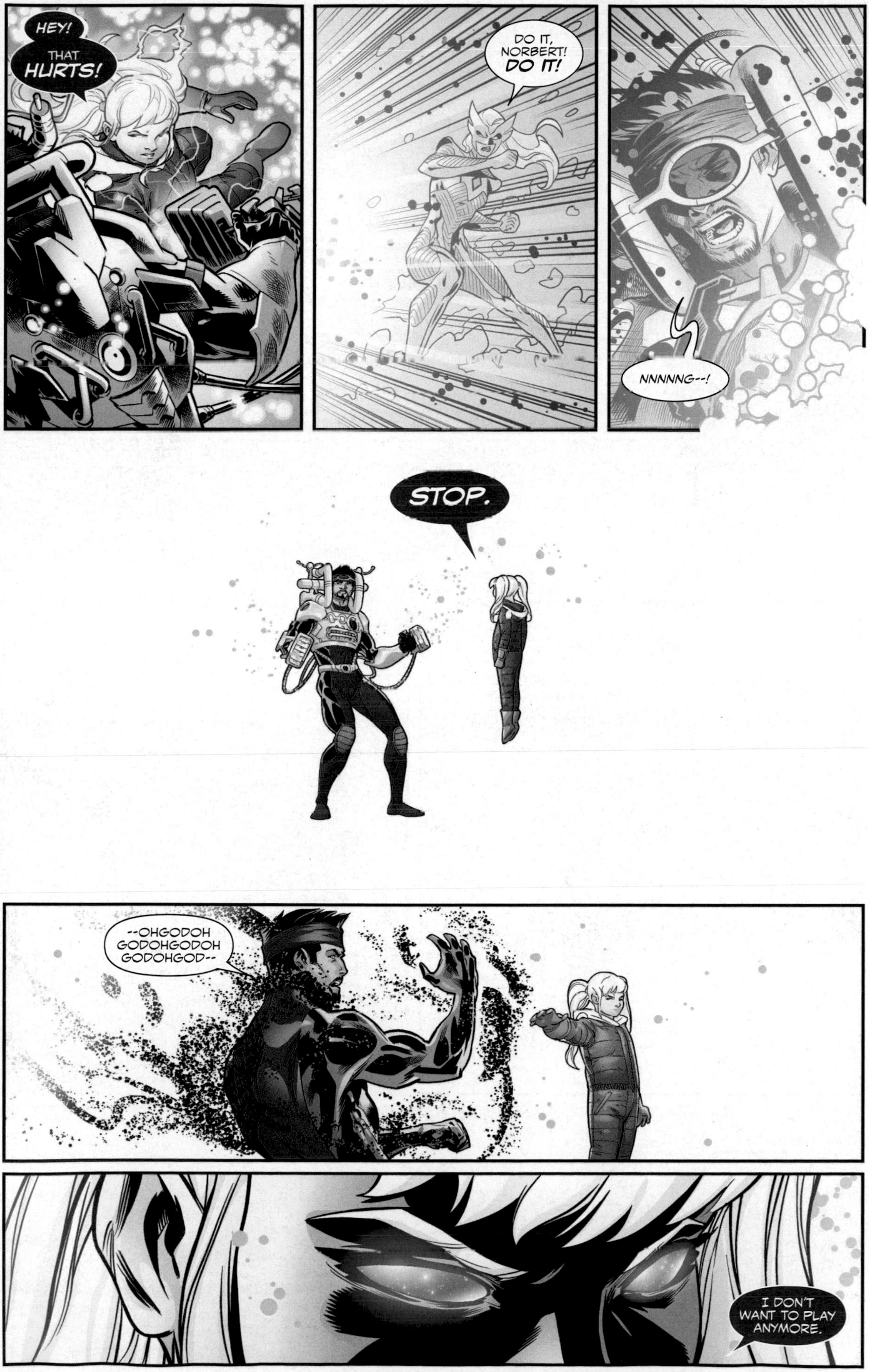
HEY!
THAT HURTS!
DO IT, NORBERT! DO IT!
NNNNNG--!
STOP.
--OHGODOH GODOHGODOH GODOHGOD--
I DON'T WANT TO PLAY ANYMORE.

RESOLUTE BAY, NUNAVUT.

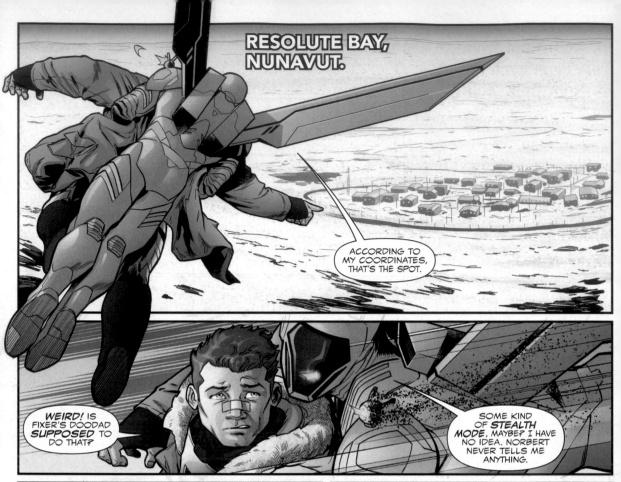

ACCORDING TO MY COORDINATES, THAT'S THE SPOT.

WEIRD! IS FIXER'S DOODAD *SUPPOSED* TO DO THAT?

SOME KIND OF *STEALTH MODE*, MAYBE? I HAVE NO IDEA. NORBERT NEVER TELLS ME ANYTHING.

LET'S MAKE IT FAST. GRAB SUPPLIES AND GET BACK TO BASE.

YUP, YUP.

IF NO ONE LOOKS TOO CLOSE, THIS SHOULD PASS FOR A *SNOWSUIT*...

YEAH. JUST TWO DUDES GRABBIN' *BEER*.

IF ANYONE ASKS, YOU'RE *"BOB"* AND I'M *"DOUG."*

HEH.

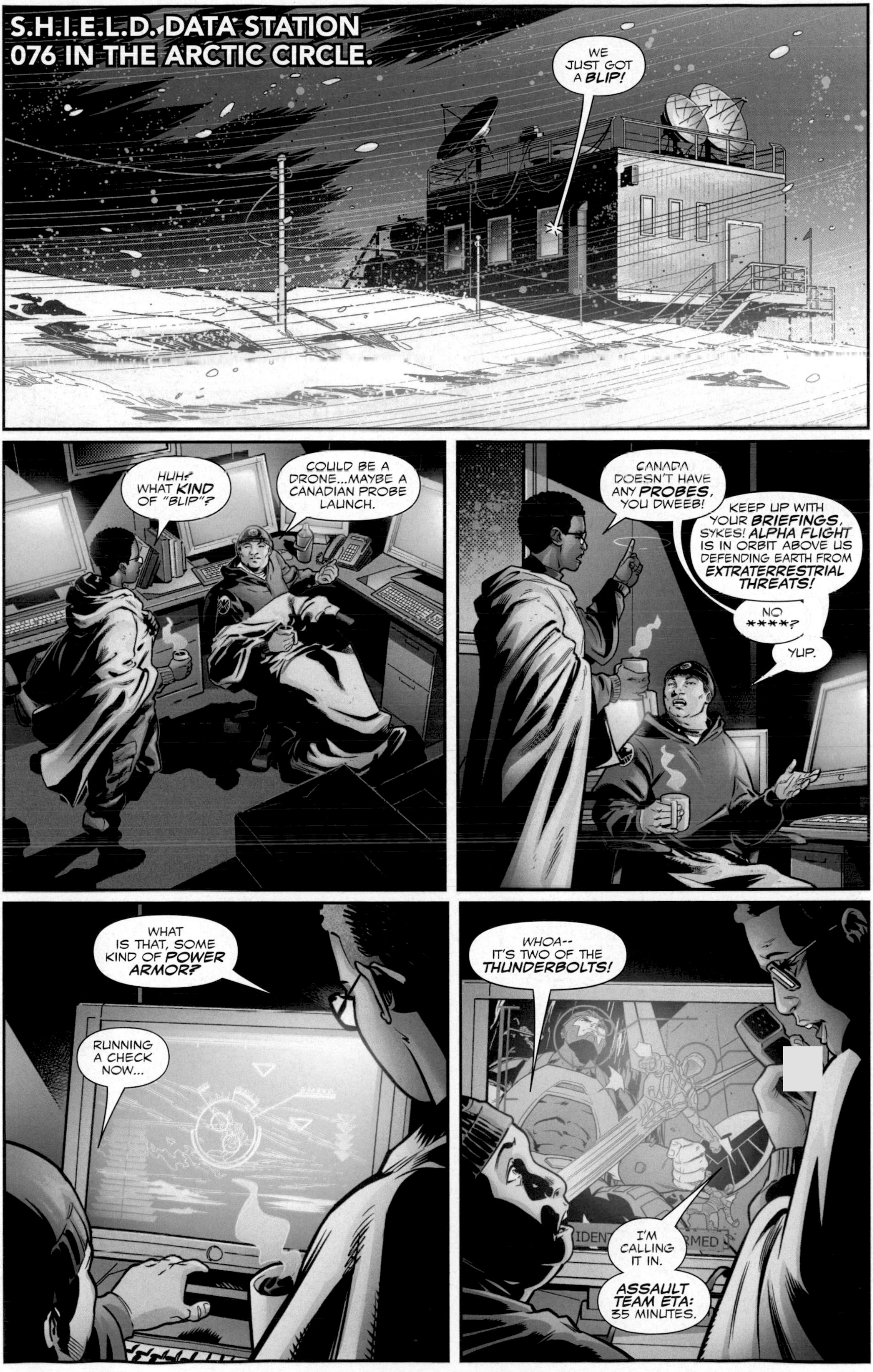
S.H.I.E.L.D. DATA STATION 076 IN THE ARCTIC CIRCLE.
WE JUST GOT A BLIP!
HUH? WHAT KIND OF "BLIP"?
COULD BE A DRONE...MAYBE A CANADIAN PROBE LAUNCH.
CANADA DOESN'T HAVE ANY PROBES, YOU DWEEB!
KEEP UP WITH YOUR BRIEFINGS, SYKES! ALPHA FLIGHT IS IN ORBIT ABOVE US DEFENDING EARTH FROM EXTRATERRESTRIAL THREATS!
NO ****?
YUP.
WHAT IS THAT, SOME KIND OF POWER ARMOR?
RUNNING A CHECK NOW...
WHOA-- IT'S TWO OF THE THUNDERBOLTS!
I'M CALLING IT IN.
ASSAULT TEAM ETA: 35 MINUTES.

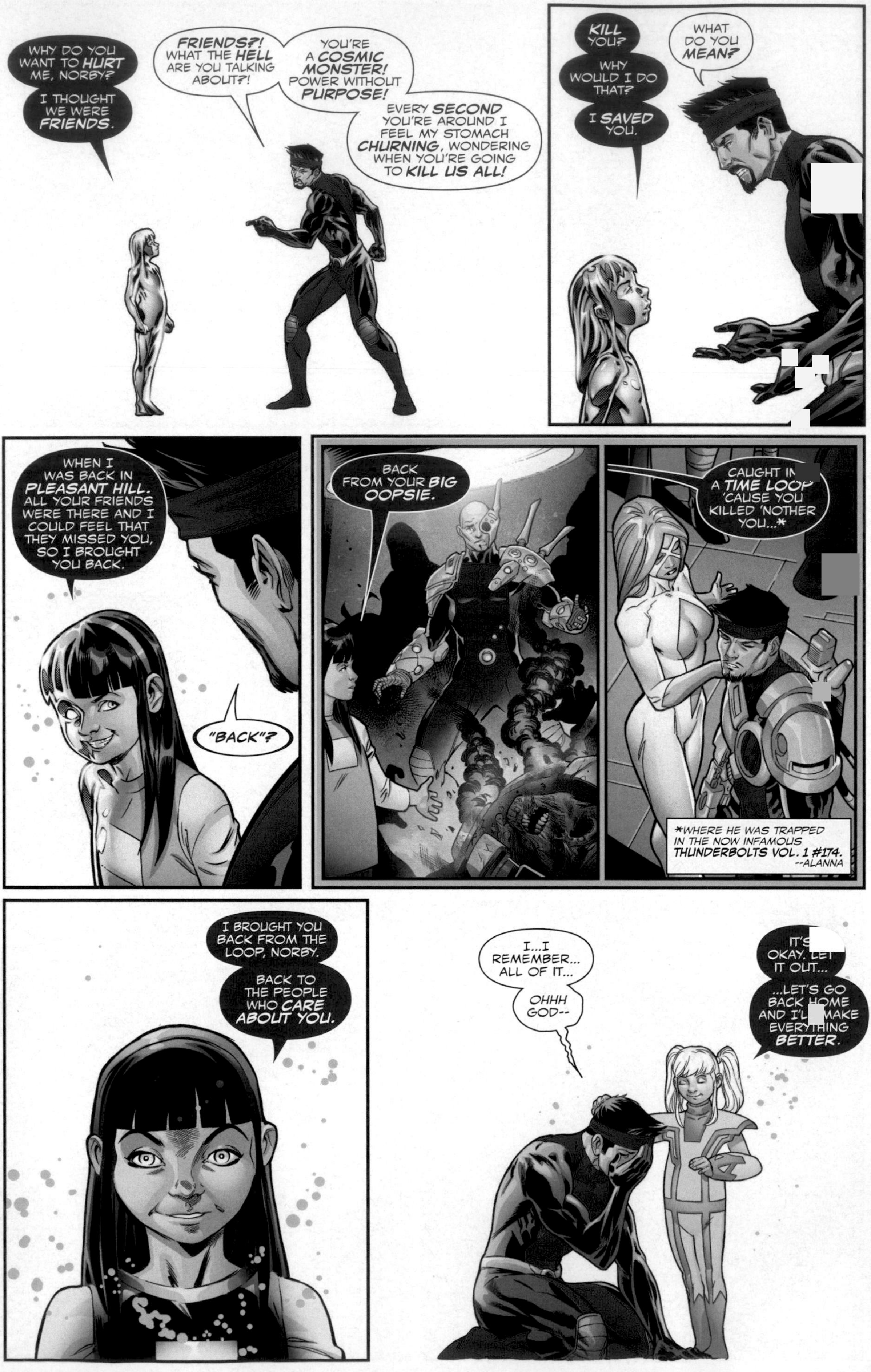
WHY DO YOU WANT TO HURT ME, NORBY?
I THOUGHT WE WERE FRIENDS.
FRIENDS?! WHAT THE HELL ARE YOU TALKING ABOUT?!
YOU'RE A COSMIC MONSTER! POWER WITHOUT PURPOSE!
EVERY SECOND YOU'RE AROUND I FEEL MY STOMACH CHURNING, WONDERING WHEN YOU'RE GOING TO KILL US ALL!
KILL YOU?
WHY WOULD I DO THAT?
I SAVED YOU.
WHAT DO YOU MEAN?
WHEN I WAS BACK IN PLEASANT HILL, ALL YOUR FRIENDS WERE THERE AND I COULD FEEL THAT THEY MISSED YOU, SO I BROUGHT YOU BACK.
"BACK"?
BACK FROM YOUR BIG OOPSIE.
CAUGHT IN A TIME LOOP 'CAUSE YOU KILLED 'NOTHER YOU...*
*WHERE HE WAS TRAPPED IN THE NOW INFAMOUS THUNDERBOLTS VOL. 1 #174. --ALANNA
I BROUGHT YOU BACK FROM THE LOOP, NORBY.
BACK TO THE PEOPLE WHO CARE ABOUT YOU.
I...I REMEMBER... ALL OF IT...
OHHH GOD--
IT'S OKAY. LET IT OUT...
...LET'S GO BACK HOME AND I'LL MAKE EVERYTHING BETTER.

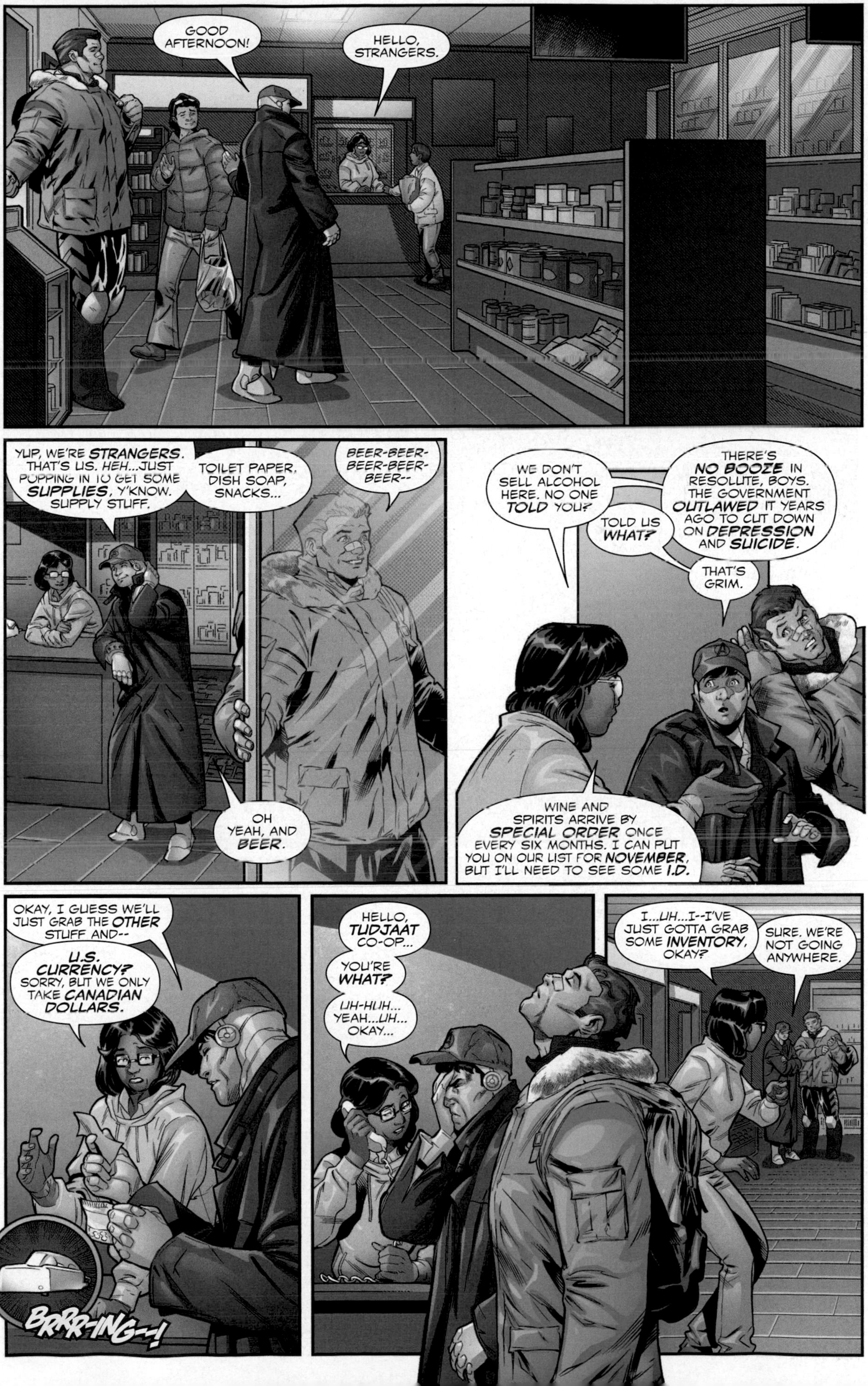
GOOD AFTERNOON!
HELLO, STRANGERS.
YUP, WE'RE STRANGERS. THAT'S US. HEH...JUST POPPING IN TO GET SOME SUPPLIES, Y'KNOW. SUPPLY STUFF.
TOILET PAPER, DISH SOAP, SNACKS...
BEER-BEER-BEER-BEER-BEER--
OH YEAH, AND BEER.
WE DON'T SELL ALCOHOL HERE. NO ONE TOLD YOU?
THERE'S NO BOOZE IN RESOLUTE, BOYS. THE GOVERNMENT OUTLAWED IT YEARS AGO TO CUT DOWN ON DEPRESSION AND SUICIDE.
TOLD US WHAT?
THAT'S GRIM.
WINE AND SPIRITS ARRIVE BY SPECIAL ORDER ONCE EVERY SIX MONTHS. I CAN PUT YOU ON OUR LIST FOR NOVEMBER, BUT I'LL NEED TO SEE SOME I.D.
OKAY, I GUESS WE'LL JUST GRAB THE OTHER STUFF AND--
U.S. CURRENCY? SORRY, BUT WE ONLY TAKE CANADIAN DOLLARS.
BRRR-ING--!
HELLO, TUDJAAT CO-OP...
YOU'RE WHAT?
UH-HUH... YEAH...UH... OKAY...
I...UH...I--I'VE JUST GOTTA GRAB SOME INVENTORY, OKAY?
SURE. WE'RE NOT GOING ANYWHERE.

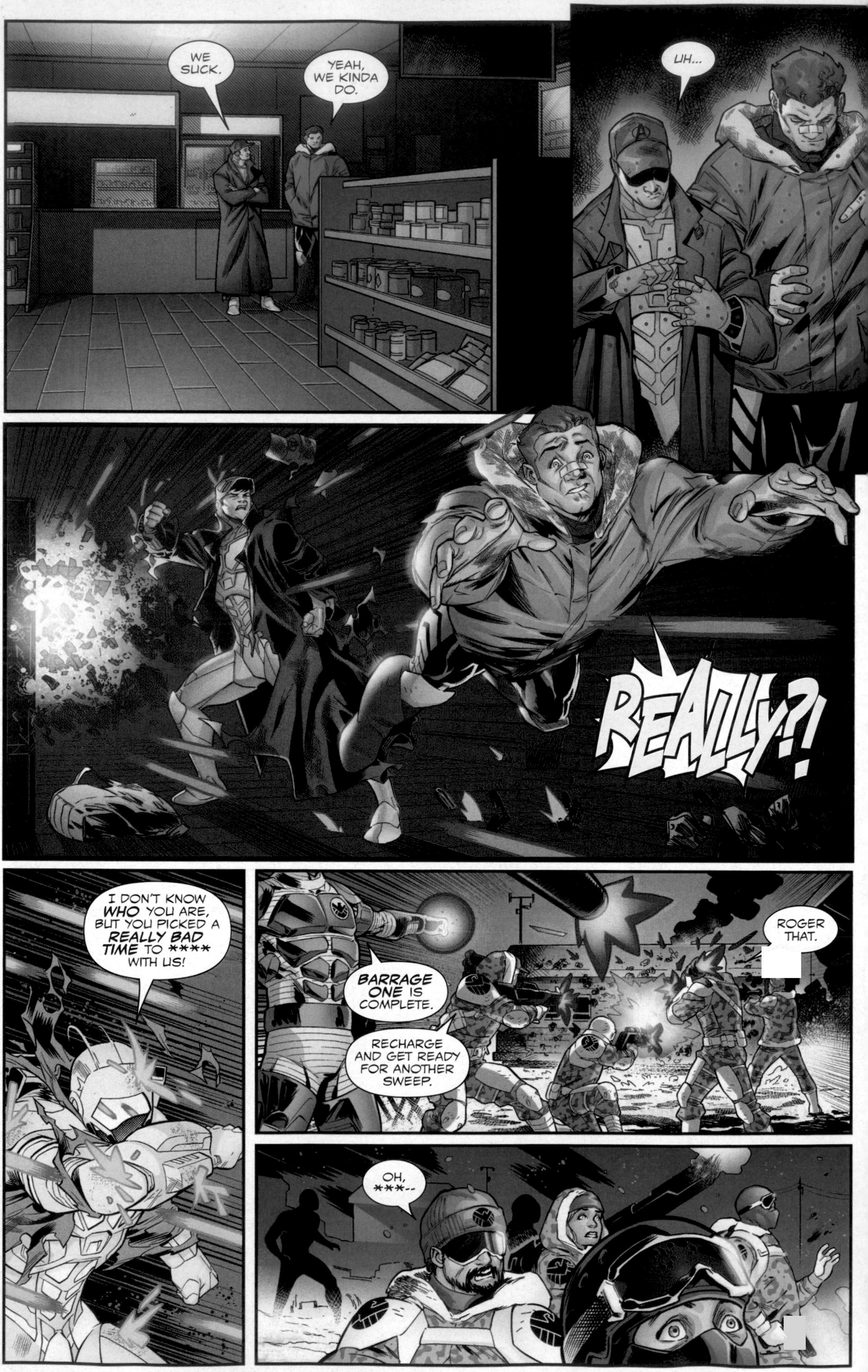
WE SUCK.
YEAH, WE KINDA DO.
UH...
REALLY?!
I DON'T KNOW WHO YOU ARE, BUT YOU PICKED A REALLY BAD TIME TO **** WITH US!
BARRAGE ONE IS COMPLETE.
RECHARGE AND GET READY FOR ANOTHER SWEEP.
ROGER THAT.
OH, ***--

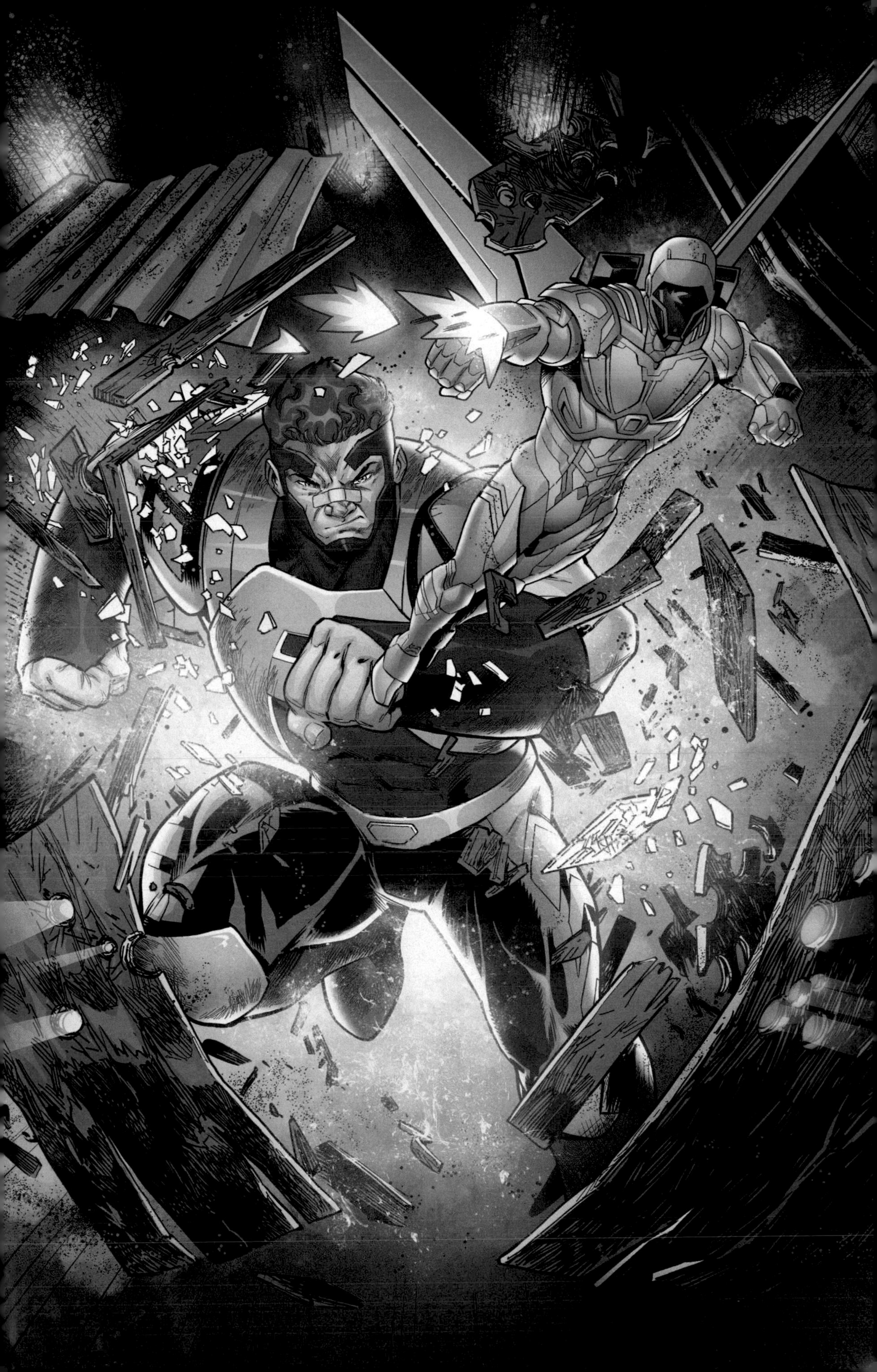

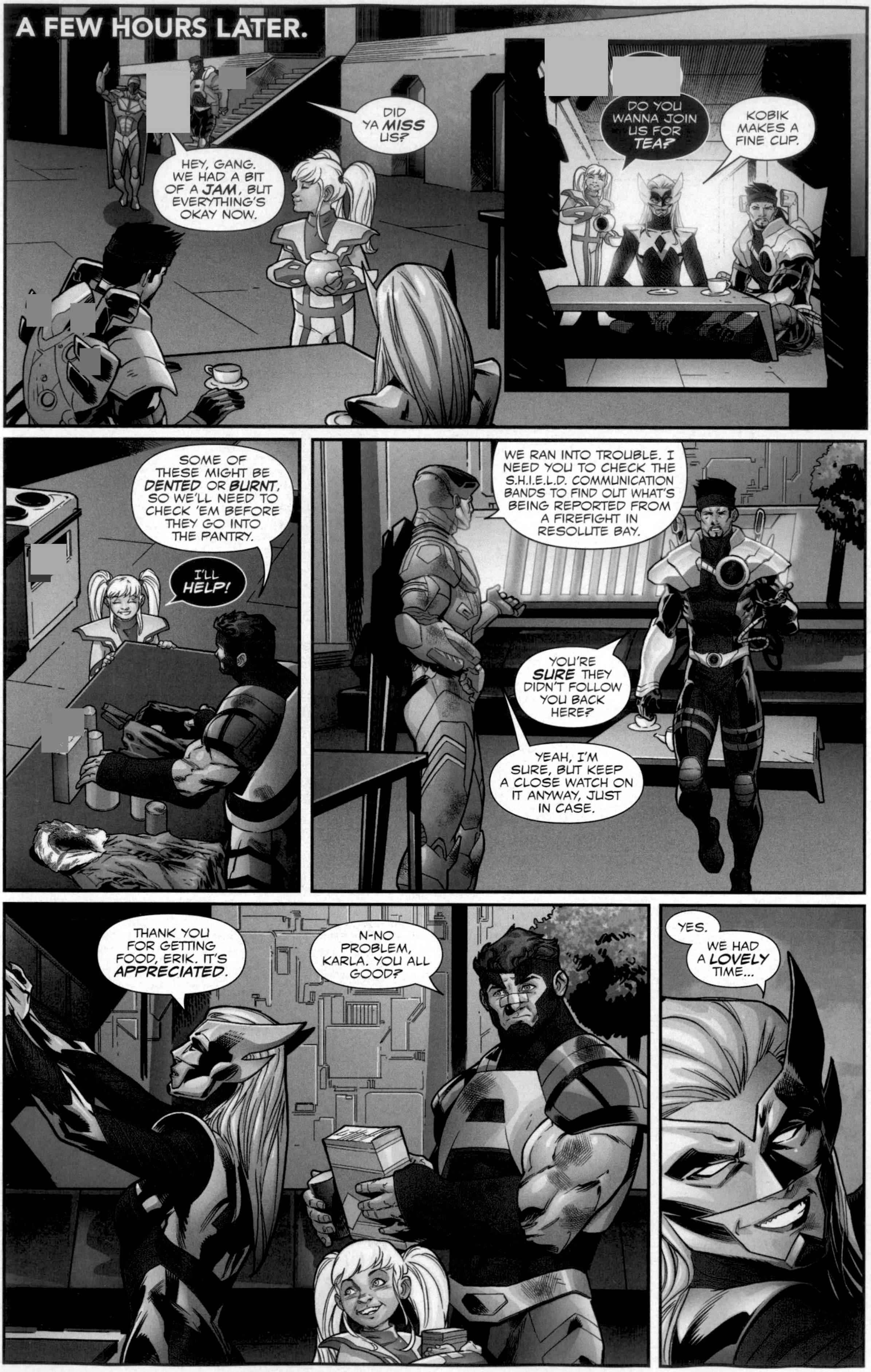
A FEW HOURS LATER.
HEY, GANG. WE HAD A BIT OF A JAM, BUT EVERYTHING'S OKAY NOW.
DID YA MISS US?
DO YOU WANNA JOIN US FOR TEA?
KOBIK MAKES A FINE CUP.
SOME OF THESE MIGHT BE DENTED OR BURNT, SO WE'LL NEED TO CHECK 'EM BEFORE THEY GO INTO THE PANTRY.
I'LL HELP!
WE RAN INTO TROUBLE. I NEED YOU TO CHECK THE S.H.I.E.L.D. COMMUNICATION BANDS TO FIND OUT WHAT'S BEING REPORTED FROM A FIREFIGHT IN RESOLUTE BAY.
YOU'RE SURE THEY DIDN'T FOLLOW YOU BACK HERE?
YEAH, I'M SURE, BUT KEEP A CLOSE WATCH ON IT ANYWAY, JUST IN CASE.
THANK YOU FOR GETTING FOOD, ERIK. IT'S APPRECIATED.
N-NO PROBLEM, KARLA. YOU ALL GOOD?
YES.
WE HAD A LOVELY TIME...

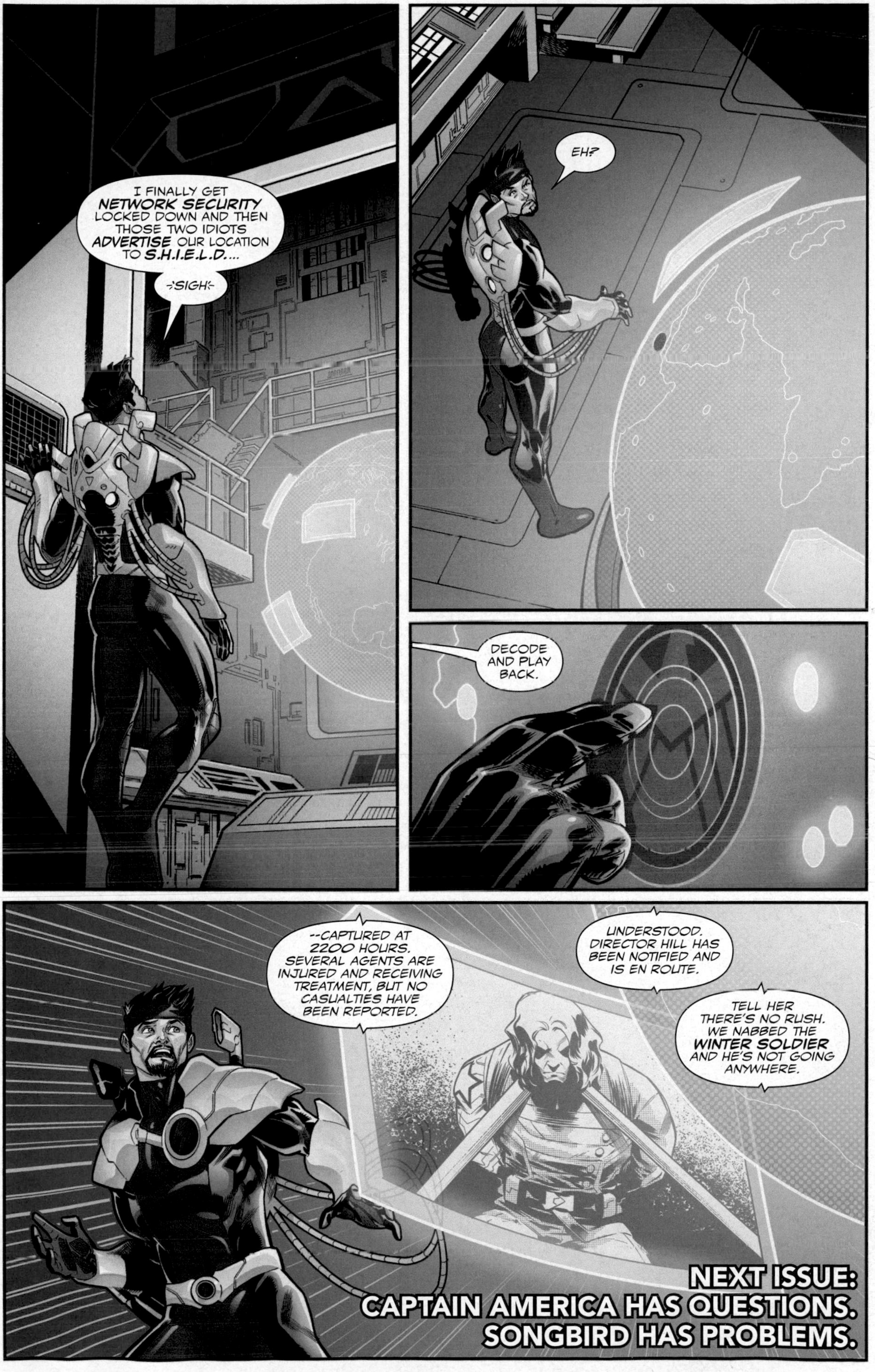
I FINALLY GET NETWORK SECURITY LOCKED DOWN AND THEN THOSE TWO IDIOTS ADVERTISE OUR LOCATION TO S.H.I.E.L.D....
-SIGH-
EH?
DECODE AND PLAY BACK.
--CAPTURED AT 2200 HOURS. SEVERAL AGENTS ARE INJURED AND RECEIVING TREATMENT, BUT NO CASUALTIES HAVE BEEN REPORTED.
UNDERSTOOD. DIRECTOR HILL HAS BEEN NOTIFIED AND IS EN ROUTE.
TELL HER THERE'S NO RUSH. WE NABBED THE WINTER SOLDIER AND HE'S NOT GOING ANYWHERE.
NEXT ISSUE:
CAPTAIN AMERICA HAS QUESTIONS.
SONGBIRD HAS PROBLEMS.

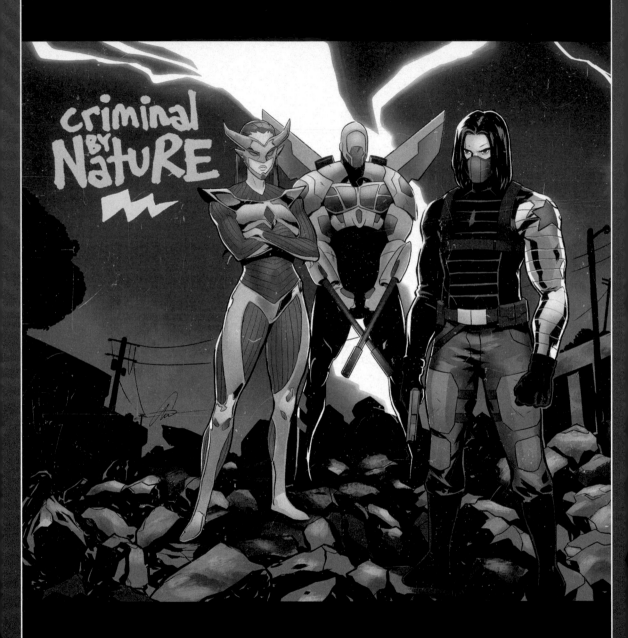

criminal BY NATURE

ANTHONY PIPER
1 Hip-Hop variant

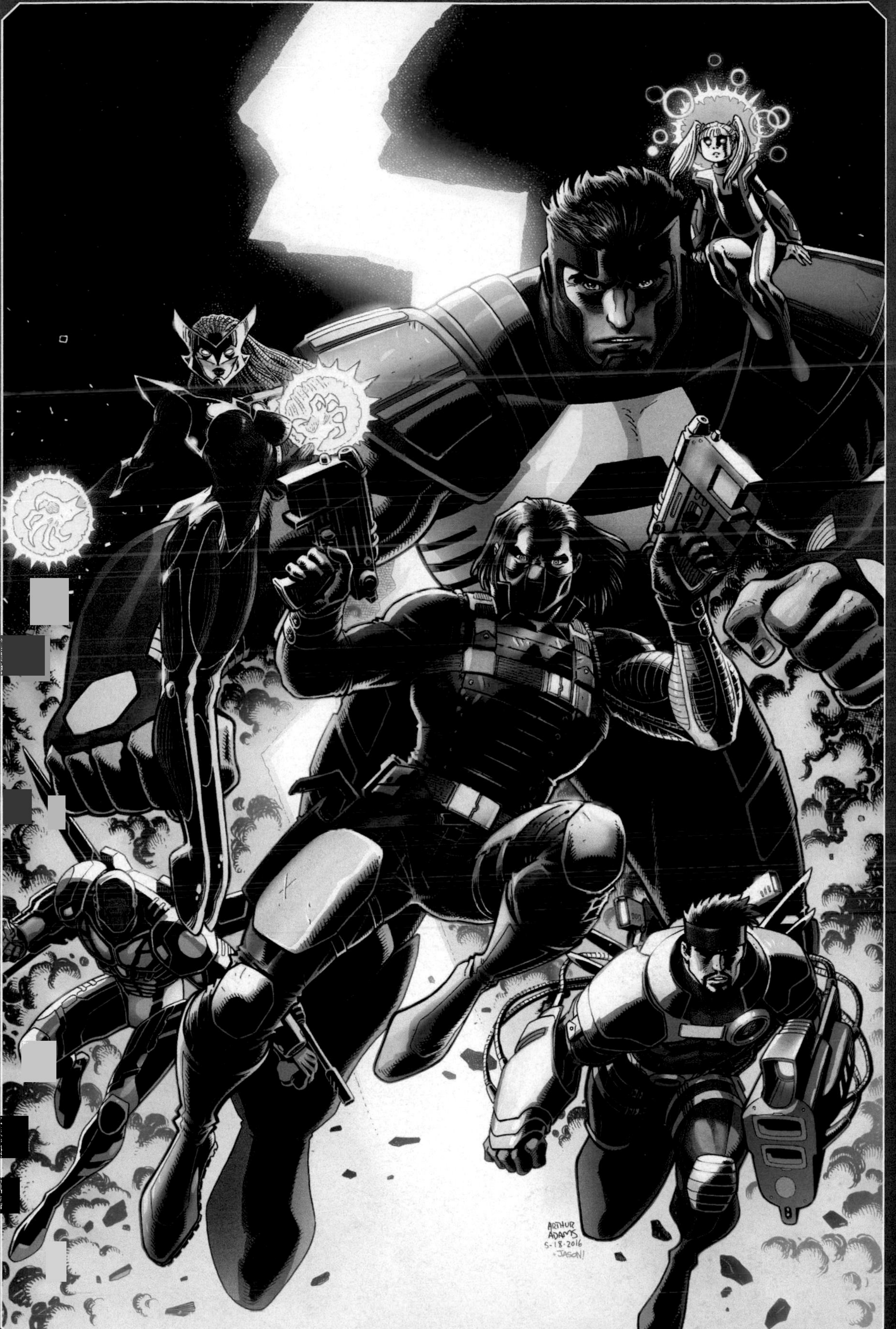
ARTHUR
ADAMS
5-18-2016
+JASON!

ART ADAMS & JASON KEITH

3 variant

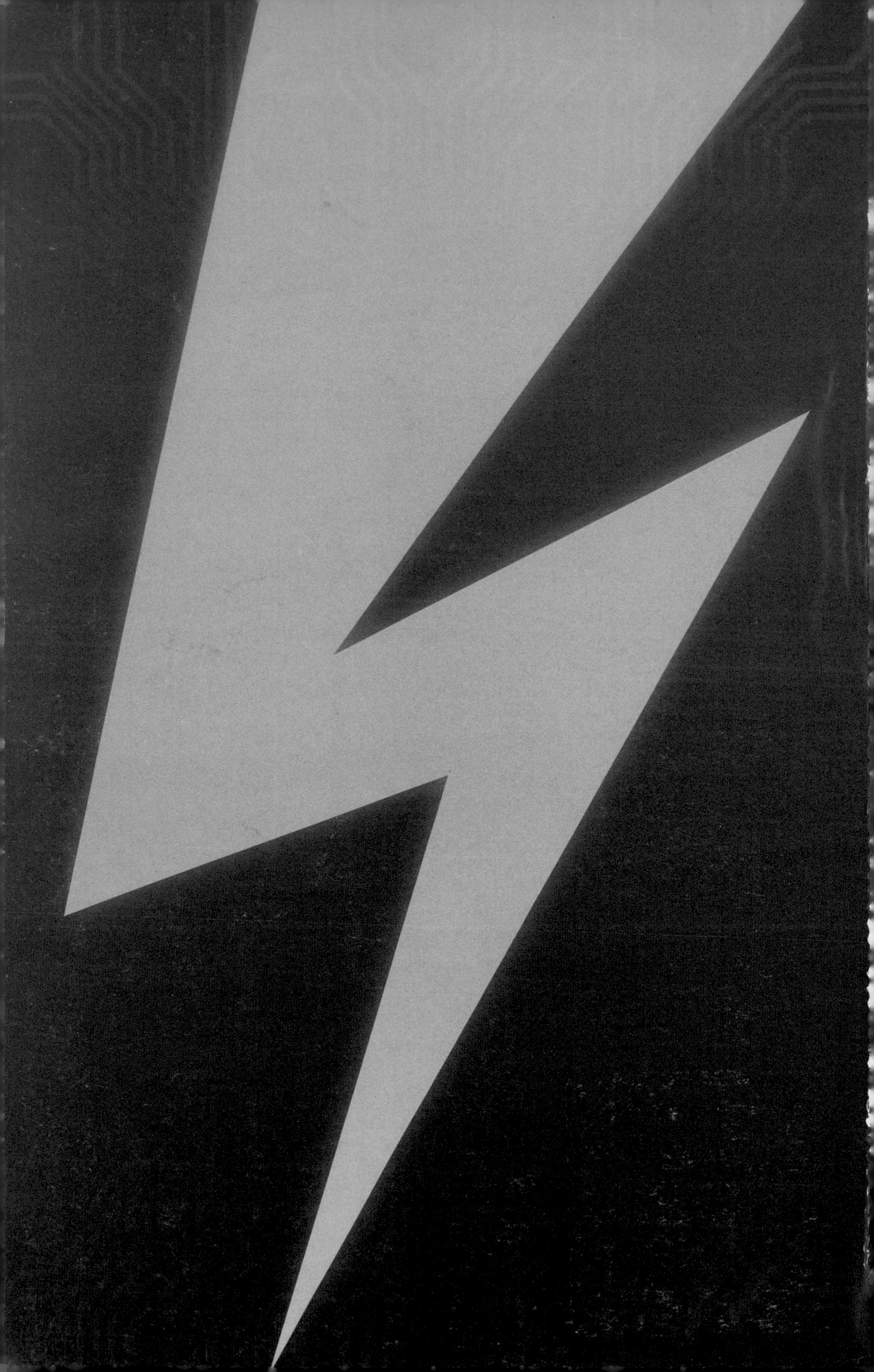

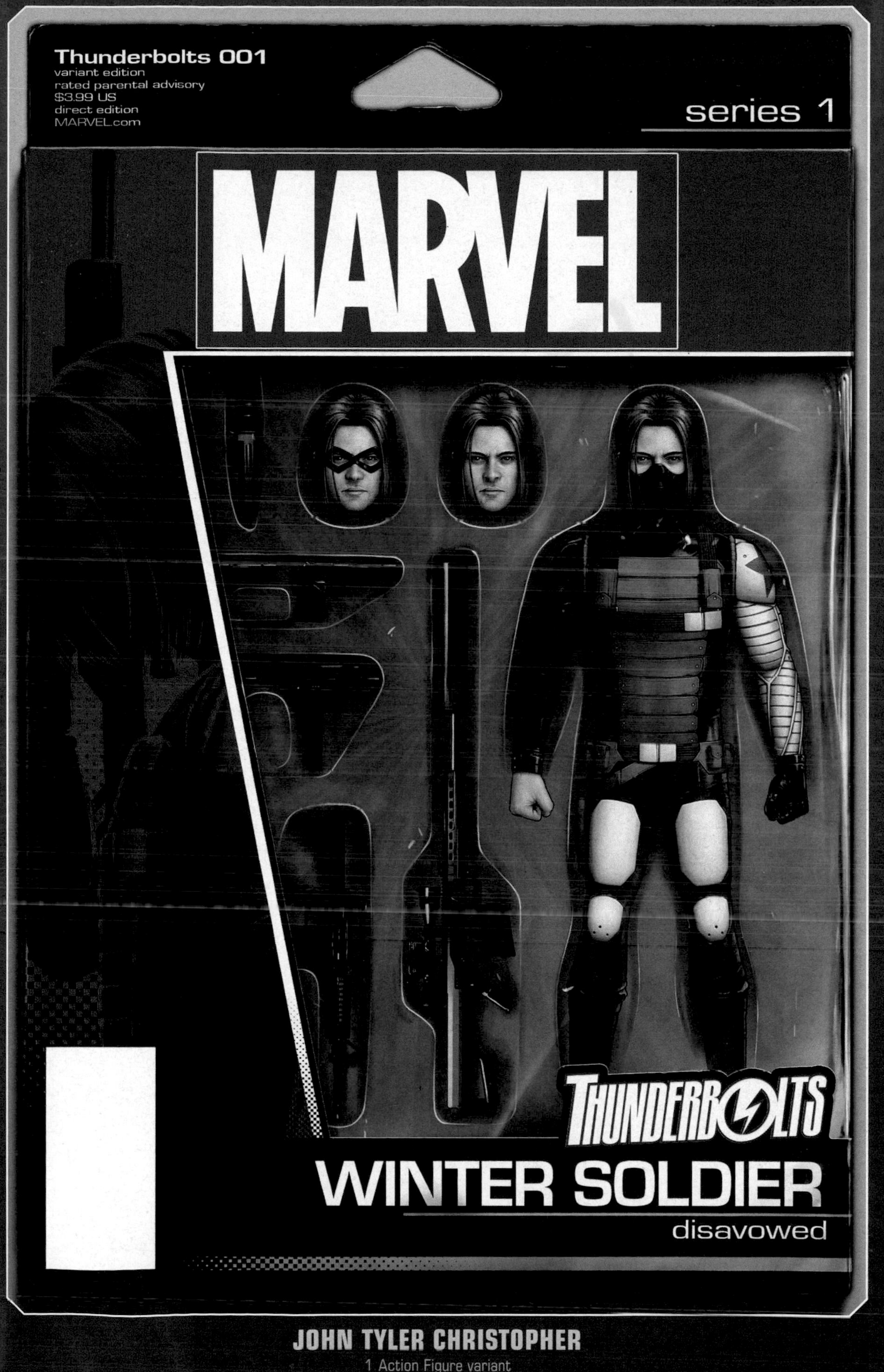

Thunderbolts 001
variant edition
rated parental advisory
$3.99 US
direct edition
MARVEL.com
series 1
MARVEL
THUNDERBOLTS
WINTER SOLDIER
disavowed

JOHN TYLER CHRISTOPHER
1 Action Figure variant

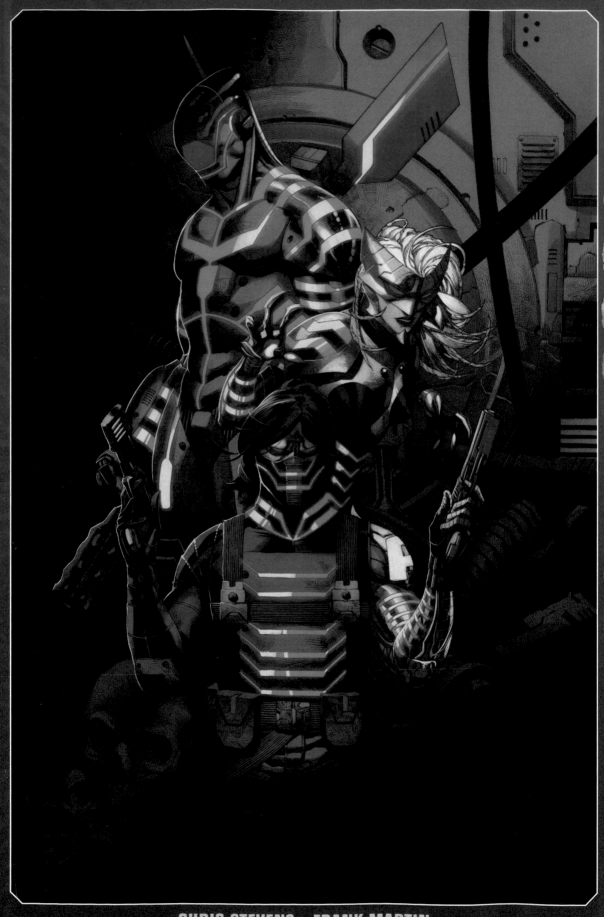

CHRIS STEVENS & **FRANK MARTIN**
1 Age of Apocalypse variant

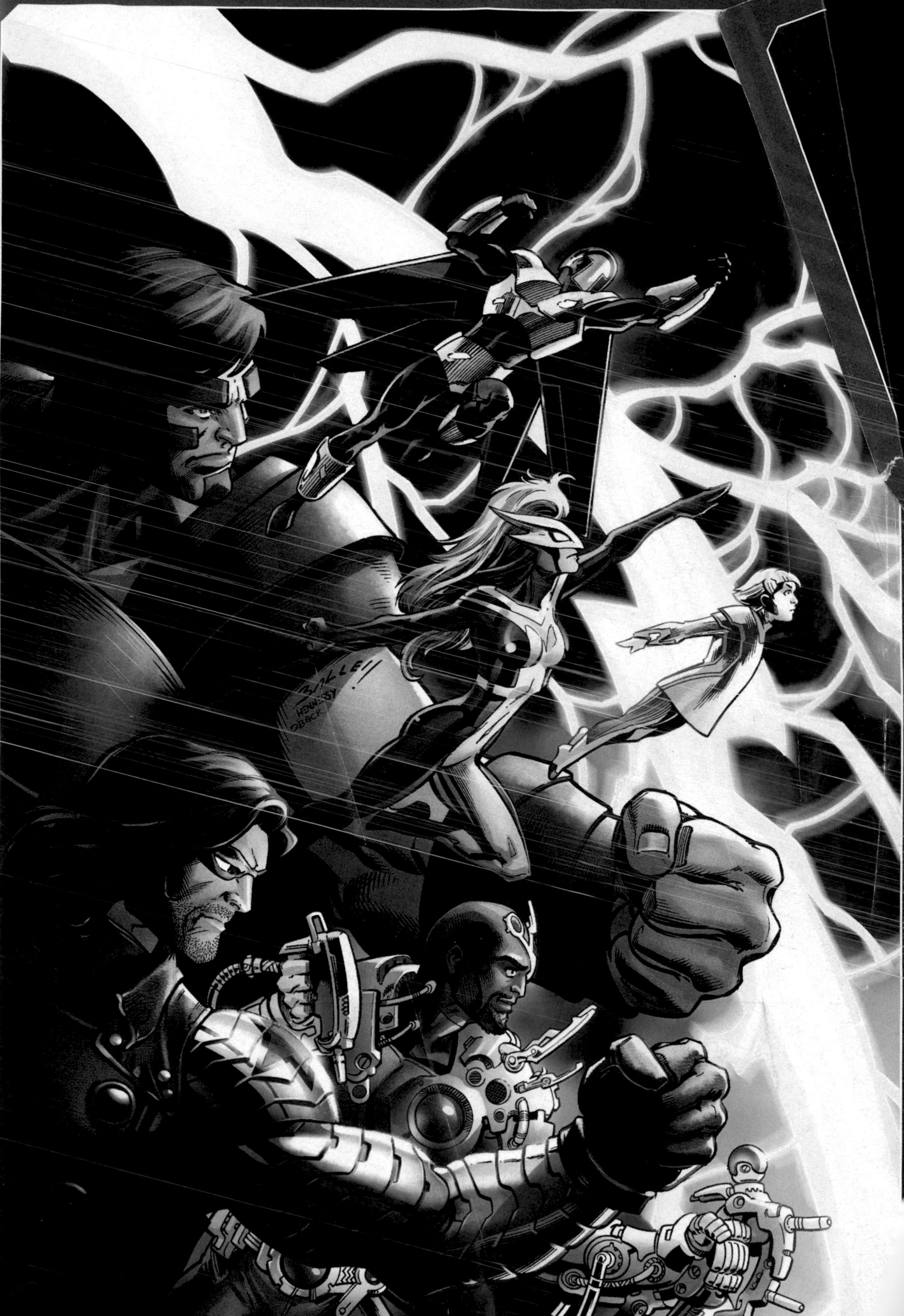

MARK BAGLEY & SONIA OBACK

1 variant

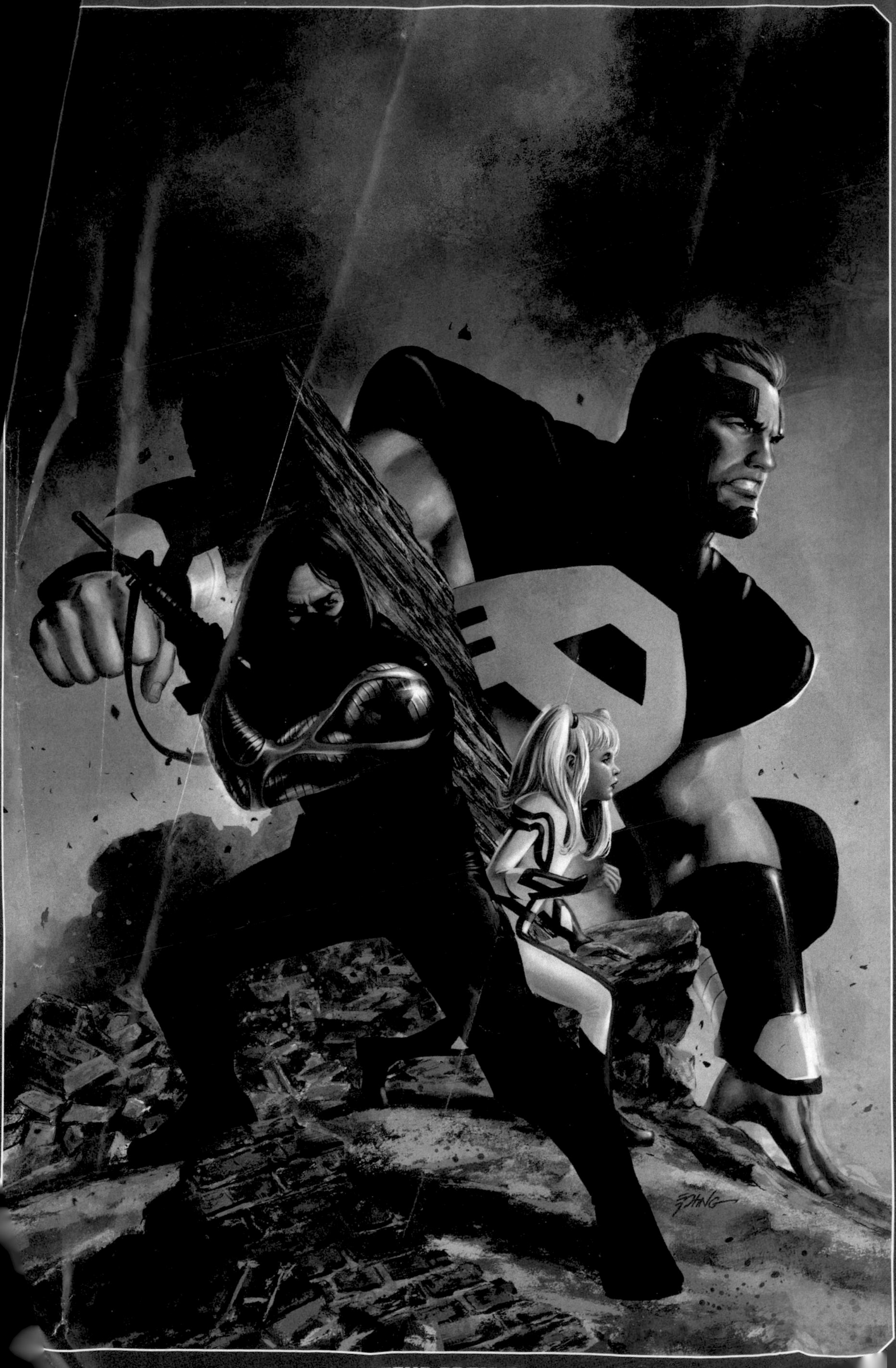

STEVE EPTING

2 variant